WAR AND THE MARXISTS

WAR AND THE MARXISTS

Socialist Theory and Practice in Capitalist Wars
Volume 1
1848-1918

S. F. KISSIN

Westview Press
BOULDER, SAN FRANCISCO, & LONDON

First published in 1988 by André Deutsch Limited, 105–106 Great Russell Street, London WC1B 3LJ

Published in 1989 in the United States of America by Westview Press, Inc., 5500 Central Avenue, Boulder, Colorado 80301

Library of Congress Cataloging-in-Publication Data
Kissin, S.F.
  War and the Marxists : socialist theory and practice in capitalist
wars / by S.F. Kissin.
    p. cm.
  Bibliography: p.
  Includes index.
  ISBN 0-8133-0953-0
  1. War and socialism—History. I. Title.
HX545.K54 1989
335.4′11—dc20   89-33747
                                                                     CIP

Printed and bound in the United States of America

The paper used in this publication meets the requirements of the American National Standard for Permanence of Paper for Printed Library Materials Z39.48-1984.

10   9   8   7   6   5   4   3   2   1

7-20-92

CONTENTS

Contents

A Personal Preface

This study concerns the attitudes of socialists towards war in general, and towards the major wars of the nineteenth and twentieth centuries.

Ever since the inception of modern socialism, well over a hundred years ago, its adherents have been debating issues relating to war: how to prevent it, how to respond to it, and what opportunities there were for advancing the socialist cause in wars between capitalist powers. These questions have been a major concern of mine for nearly half a century.

On the eve of the Second World War, I was a radical socialist and convinced Marxist. World war seemed inevitable; to people of my persuasion the question of how to react was not just an academic problem of Marxist theory: it had immediate practical and personal significance. As revolutionary socialists, should we be neutral in a war between 'imperialist' powers, or should we support the less reactionary side, for example, the Western democracies in conflict with fascist Italy and nazi Germany? If so, what form should our support take? The probable involvement of the Soviet Union, which most of us considered a socialist country, created additional problems of principle.

At the time I was a political exile from Hitler's Germany, a militant of the Trotskyist International Communist League (Bolshevik-Leninist), which became the Fourth International in 1938. For several months in 1937 I belonged to the Paris executive of the German section (International Communists of Germany – IKD), but when war broke out I was in London. I shared Trotsky's view that the conflict was an imperialist venture on all sides, so revolutionary socialists and workers of all belligerent countries should refuse to support it.

In London I took part in the discussions of a group of fifteen or twenty left-wing socialists, most of them committed Trotskyists or Trotskyist sympathizers; they were all refugees from Germany or other continental countries. We conducted our debates in German and called ourselves *Marxistische Arbeitsgemeinschaft* (Marxist Working

Group). In January 1940, as a contribution to our discussions, I wrote (in German) a paper entitled 'Theses on the War and the Situation in the Labour Movement'. Broadly reflecting the views prevalent among socialists of the extreme Left, it defined the war as imperialist, like the First World War, and asserted that neither camp deserved socialist support, but there was no unanimity on the character of the war or whether we should defend the country that had given us sanctuary. Some comrades favoured support for the anti-nazi alliance, arguing that a German victory would be an immeasurable disaster for our cause: it would destroy for decades the rights and liberties workers still enjoyed in the countries of bourgeois democracy, let alone any prospect of socialist revolution.

I stuck to the anti-war line during the initial, 'phoney' phase of the war, but was converted to the pro-Allied, 'defencist' position (in Marxist parlance) in the summer of 1940, after the Germans had vanquished and occupied several democratic capitalist countries in Scandinavia and Western Europe. Having come to the conclusion that the defeat of Hitler and his intention to invade Britain must be the over-riding objectives for a socialist, I volunteered for the British army, and served from August 1940 to November 1945.

In 1942 my unit was stationed in Scotland, first near and later in Edinburgh, and I made contact with the Workers International League (WIL), the strongest Trotskyist group in Britain, and with left-wing, near-Trotskyist members of the Independent Labour Party (ILP). Discussions with WIL and ILP militants led me to write another paper in April 1943, 'The Present War and the Policy of Revolutionary Internationalism'. I reasoned that although not only the Axis powers but Britain and the US were waging an imperialist war, the Leninist concept of 'revolutionary defeatism' must be rejected for a capitalist democracy at war with a fascist power. Three and a half years of war had shown that defeat by the nazi armies engendered not revolution but counter-revolution in the defeated countries – the imposition of fascist or near-fascist régimes. Read side-by-side with the 'Theses' of January 1940, this paper illustrates the change in thinking of many left-wing socialists during that period. (Edited versions of both papers will be included as Appendices I and II in the second volume, War and Twentieth-Century Socialists, which covers the inter-war period and the Second World War.)

The Edinburgh Trotskyists took my arguments seriously but were not wholly convinced. A leading member intended to submit my paper as a discussion document to the scheduled WIL conference in London, but before then my services were required in another theatre of war. I was posted away from Scotland and lost touch with the Edinburgh Trotskyists. I never did find out if my paper had figured at the London conference: the group's journal, *Workers' International News*, which reported on the proceedings and contained the main speeches, did not go into the details of the discussion.

At that stage, socialists' attitudes towards the war had again become a subject of purely theoretical debate. In 1940, after the fall of France, the support of the overwhelming majority of Britain's socialist labour movement was essential in the national crisis. That support was still there in 1943, when the outcome of the war was no longer in doubt, especially after the Italian surrender. Victory for the Anglo-Soviet-US alliance, and the downfall of nazism, seemed assured, whatever socialists in Britain or elsewhere in the West might say or do. Yet my interest in the potential impact of socialist views and policies about war persisted. It grew stronger after 1945 when new conflicts – the Chinese Civil War, the wars in Korea and Vietnam, and various Middle Eastern conflicts – provoked comments and actions from socialists.

This led me to study more intensively the historical aspects of the problem: the words and deeds of socialists from the middle of the nineteenth century, when Marx and Engels first commented on contemporary conflicts. *War and the Marxists* is the product of these investigations. It is intended as a straightforward factual account of what leading socialists said and did when faced with the threat or reality of war. It is not a theoretical treatise and, while mentioning certain obvious inconsistencies and contradictions, it does not try to judge the merits of the concepts and policies.

Although not all socialists mentioned or quoted in this volume were committed Marxists, the title *War and the Marxists* seemed appropriate. Marxist phraseology and idiom predominated in the debates, and most participants adopted Marxist criteria in defining their positions. Besides, the borderline between strict Marxists and non-Marxist socialists is by no means distinct and rigid. Karl Liebknecht's statements and actions during the First World War were generally indistinguishable in content and purpose from those of Rosa Luxemburg, and they were wholly approved by Lenin, who regarded himself as an orthodox Marxist. Liebknecht did not endorse the materialist conception of history or Marxist dialectics, but to treat him as a non-Marxist in the context of the debates on socialist policy in that war would be sheer pedantry.

This volume spans seventy years, to the end of the First World War. Marx died in 1883, halfway through this period. Engels was an active political writer until his death twelve years later. The presentation of the views of Marx and Engels shows that they often believed war would lead to revolution in a belligerent country, but never evolved a comprehensive theory about the link between war and revolution. They always hoped for the victory of the more 'progressive' side; when tsarist Russia was at war, they wanted her enemies to win. In the early twentieth century, when socialist parties existed in most capitalist countries and socialist revolution seemed a short-term possibility, the followers of Marx and Engels tried to hammer out a consistent policy to exploit the war-conditioned crises of capitalism and hasten its overthrow.

A further volume will deal with the inter-war period, the Second World War, and very briefly the years since 1945. The major powers have not confronted one another directly in any of the many wars of the last forty years, and the arrival of the nuclear age has invalidated socialist assumptions in their debates about war. Since Hiroshima and Nagasaki, most discussions about war, among socialists and non-socialists, have been concerned with preventing nuclear war and avoiding escalation of non-nuclear conflicts. Socialist attitudes have not been basically different from those of liberal or conservative politicians and commentators: the post-1945 debate about war and wartime policies has been devoid of a specifically socialist dimension.

S.F. KISSIN
London 1988

PART I
Marx and Engels, and the Wars of the Nineteenth Century

1 The 'Revolutionary Wars' of 1848–9

The Prussian-Danish War

The revolutionary tide which engulfed much of Europe in 1848 and 1849 provoked some minor wars involving German states, especially Prussia and Austria. Almost all Marx and Engels wrote about these wars was bound up with the expectation of early proletarian revolution. They believed that Europe was ripe for such a revolution. In the Communist Manifesto, which appeared at the beginning of 1848, they asserted – correctly, as it turned out – that Germany was 'on the eve of a bourgeois revolution' and went on to predict, erroneously, that this would be 'but the prelude to an immediately following proletarian revolution'. They must have felt sure that once proletarian rule had been established in Germany, it would not be confined to that country.

Marx and Engels believed, again mistakenly, that a great European or even a 'world war' would break out shortly and would hasten the process of European revolution. For this reason they actually hoped for a war waged by one or more European powers against tsarist Russia, the most reactionary and oppressive power, the *bête noire* of democratic and progressive elements of that time.

The first war the two friends commented on in detail was the Prussian-Danish war of 1848–9. The issue was the fate of the duchies of Schleswig and Holstein, with predominantly German populations but linked to the Danish crown. After a revolution had begun in Prussia and other parts of Germany in the spring of 1848, the Germans of Schleswig and Holstein set up a provisional government in Kiel, proclaimed secession from Denmark and appealed to the German Confederation (a loose association of states, with Austria and Prussia as the leading members) for the admission of Schleswig-Holstein as a single state. Thousands of young Germans enlisted as volunteers and went to the aid of the rebel armies.

On behalf of the German Confederation, Prussia went to war with

Denmark. In April 1848 Prussian troops occupied the whole of Schleswig and Holstein and invaded Jutland, but withdrew after reverses on the battlefield and a Russian threat to intervene. After more inconclusive fighting in 1849 an armistice was agreed, followed by a Danish-Prussian peace treaty in June 1850, which in all essentials restored the *status quo* of Danish rule over the duchies. The Germans in Schleswig-Holstein continued to resist but were defeated. The settlement was confirmed by the treaty of London of May 1852, which placed it under the guarantee of the main European powers.

Marx and Engels were wholeheartedly in favour of the war against Denmark, and they urged the German side to conduct it with energy and resolve. In their view, the armed rising of the Germans in Schleswig-Holstein was part of the revolutionary struggle for a united democratic Germany – a cause dear to their hearts. Engels wrote in the *Neue Rheinische Zeitung*, the radical newspaper they published in Cologne, that 'the war we (Germans) are waging in Schleswig-Holstein is a truly revolutionary war.'[1]

While approving of the Schleswig-Holstein rising and the war, Marx and Engels (both Prussian by birth) distrusted the royal Prussian government. They described its conduct of the war as inept and attacked the armistice and the 'treacherous peace'. But they dissociated themselves from the jingoist excesses of some Germans and part of the German press.

At the time Denmark enjoyed the support of Russia, and this was a further reason for wanting the Danes defeated. Marx and Engels thought that war, not only with Denmark but with Russia, was the prerequisite of a positive solution of the European revolutionary crisis. They also believed such a war to be inevitable. In June 1848, Engels accused Prussia of lacking 'the courage to accept . . . the long-awaited and unavoidable conflict with Russia'.[2]

In July 1850, Engels reiterated the indictment of Prussia for deserting the Schleswig-Holstein troops in battle and then signing a 'treacherous peace'. He elaborated a theory he had formulated on a previous occasion – that the Danes and some other small ethnic groups had no claim to independent nationhood. According to Engels, revolutionary democrats had to work and fight for the unification of 'the great nationalities hitherto cut up in small states' (like the Germans and Italians), but not for the independence of 'those small wrecks of nationalities, such as Danes, Croats, Czechs, Slovaks, and so on, counting from one to three millions each at the very outset, or ... those mongrel would-be nations, such as the Swiss and Belgians'. Only the 'great and equally powerful nations, such as the French, English, German, Italian, Hungarian and Polish' would belong to a future 'European confederacy of republics'. As for the people of Schleswig and Holstein, they should not be 'forced to follow the fate of small, impotent, half-civilized Denmark, and to be slaves of Russia for ever'; rather 'they should be allowed to re-unite themselves to a nation of forty millions, which was then just engaged in the struggle for its freedom, unity, and consequent recovery of its strength.'[3]

This startling and un-socialist contempt for the small and 'would-be' nations which the young Engels displayed in the late 1840s — apparently in agreement with Marx — is not found in the mature writings of the two friends. There is no trace of it in Engels's comments on the war of 1864, when Austria and Prussia defeated Denmark and Schleswig and Holstein were ceded to the German powers.[4]

It is clear from what Marx and Engels wrote during the Danish war of 1848–9 that they wanted their native Germany to be strong and united as a democratic republic. In this sense they were German patriots, but they were not chauvinists or even nationalists. In conflicts involving Germans they did not back the German side 'right or wrong'; their support went to the party they regarded as more progressive. Engels wrote that in recent history the Germans had usually played a reactionary role: they had supplied mercenaries to the British in the American revolutionary war; they had intervened against the French Revolution; Austria and Prussia had joined Russia in dismembering and plundering Poland, and Austria was guilty of repression in Italy and Hungary. He went on:

> The blame for the infamies committed with the aid of Germany in other countries falls not only on the governments but to a large extent also on the German people. But for the delusions of the Germans, their slavish spirit, their aptitude as mercenaries and jailers ... the German name would not have been so detested, cursed and despised abroad.

Yet a new era had dawned, he wrote,

Now that the Germans are throwing off their own yoke, their

whole policy *vis-à-vis* foreign nations must also change — or else the fetters with which we have chained other nations will shackle our own new freedom ... Germany will liberate herself to the extent to which she sets free neighbouring nations.[5]

Revolts against Habsburg Rule: Rising in Italy

Marx and Engels hoped for a German victory in the conflict with Denmark; they backed the non-German side in the wars which shook the Habsburg monarchy during the same revolutionary period — the Italian and Hungarian wars. The aim in Hungary was national independence and internal democracy. The Italian revolution had the same objectives, as well as the unification of Italy, which consisted of a number of states, most under direct or indirect Austrian control.

Marx and Engels sympathized with the Hungarians and the Italians, whose cause they considered was progress and revolutionary democracy. They also thought the defeat of Austria would hasten the downfall of the hated Habsburg monarchy. They welcomed actions by Austrian revolutionaries to help the insurgents, and applauded when the people of Vienna began an insurrection in October 1848 to prevent the departure of Austrian troops to the Hungarian front. They spoke with regret of the 'confusion' in the minds of some German Austrians who had taken part in the Vienna revolution of March 1848 but had then volunteered for the campaign against the Italians.[6]

A rising in Sicily against Neapolitan rule marked the beginning of the Italian revolution in January 1848. Unrest in other parts induced the princely rulers of several states to grant constitutions, but the revolution in Vienna on 13 March 1848 really brought things to the boil and ended Prince Metternich's forty-year dominance at the Austrian court. The news sparked armed rising in the two provinces under direct Austrian rule, Lombardy and Venetia. The citizens of Milan chased the Austrian garrison (mainly Croats) out of their town. The Austrian troops, led by the aged Fieldmarshal Radetzky, then evacuated most of Lombardy. In Venice the Austrian garrison was induced to leave, the 'Republic of St Mark' was proclaimed. King Charles Albert of Sardinia-Piedmont declared war on Austria. Patriotic enthusiasm gripped the whole of Italy, and volunteers streamed to the theatre of war in the north.

Progressive opinion both in Italy and abroad saw the ideal

framework for Italian independence in a unitary democratic republic; this was the solution championed by Giuseppe Mazzini and his radical-republican friends, and the one preferred by Marx and Engels. Certain Catholic and conservative elements favoured a federation of the existing Italian states, perhaps with the pope at its head. Others visualized unity under the house of Savoy, the reigning dynasty of the kingdom of Sardinia and Piedmont — which is how unification eventually came about. The one objective all patriots had in common was the total expulsion of Austria from the Italian peninsula.

In April and May 1848 the Piedmontese army scored some successes, but the Austrians gained the upper hand, and in August King Charles Albert was compelled to sign an armistice virtually restoring the *status quo*. The king resumed fighting in March 1849, but his army was decisively beaten at Novara, and he abdicated in favour of his son. The new king, Victor Emmanuel II, had to accept Austria's onerous peace terms; but he lived to fight again and, contrary to Marx's and Engels's predictions, became the first king of an independent Italy some twelve years later.

During the summer of 1849 unrest in all parts of Italy was quelled, largely by Austrian military intervention, and princely rulers were reinstated. Venice was retaken by the Austrians in August, and Sicily was subdued by the Neapolitans. The revolution had failed throughout Italy.

After the armistice between Austria and Piedmont which ended the first phase of the Italian war, Engels praised the Italian people's courage and devotion in the struggle for freedom. He attributed failure to the vacillation and cowardice of the pope and the native princes, and especially of the king of Sardinia and Piedmont. Charles Albert, this 'arch-enemy of Italian liberty', who had let himself be acclaimed the 'liberator' and the 'sword of Italy' (*la spada d'Italia*), had in fact been concerned only with territorial aggrandizement and with his own 'great power and magnificence'. The king's ambitions, his hatred of all truly liberal people, and his and his generals' military incompetence, had enabled the Austrians to score a decisive victory. But things would now change:

Henceforth the Italians can and will no longer entrust the cause of their liberation to a prince or king; to ensure their salvation they must get rid, as soon as possible, of this *spada d'Italia* which has turned out to be useless. Had they done this earlier, had they

superannuated the King and his system ... and established a
democratic union among themselves, not a single Austrian would
by now have remained in Italy. [7]

The Italian people would learn from bitter experience, would discard
their illusions and 'secure ... independence under a single democratic
banner'.

When the same King Charles Albert resumed fighting seven months
later, Engels ardently hoped for the victory of the Piedmontese army,
and he was bitterly disappointed by its defeat at Novara. He went
further than before in his denunciation of the Sardinian king's alleged
treachery, and in discerning a link between the monarchic system and
defeat in war. He declared that in a national crisis a monarchic system
was unable to wage war successfully. Only a republic could have taken
the requisite measures:

> A nation fighting for independence must not limit itself to the
> *ordinary* methods of warfare. *Levée en masse*, revolutionary war,
> guerillas everywhere − that is the only way for a small nation to
> stand up to a large one, the only means whereby a comparatively
> small army can be enabled to withstand an army that is stronger
> and better organized.

In a monarchy, even a constitutional one like the Piedmontese, an
initial military defeat (such as Novara) meant a lost campaign.

> But in a republic this defeat would have been *by no means
> decisive*. Monarchy is intrinsically craven, never dares to resort
> to extreme revolutionary means. Had Piedmont been a republic
> ... it would have found a way to conclude the campaign quite
> differently.

After outlining the military moves a revolutionary leadership would
have been likely to make, Engels continued:

> The *levée en masse*, with the whole people taking up arms − that
> is something royalty shrinks from doing. Only the republic will
> resort to such means, as the events of 1793 prove. [8] The appli-
> cation of such methods presupposes *revolutionary terror*, and
> where has a monarch ever been willing to resort to that? When a
> people needs to exert all its strength to save itself, nothing will
> hinder it so much as the monarchy. If Italy is not to perish because
> of the monarchy, then it is imperative that monarchy in Italy
> should perish. [9]

Engels foresaw that the defeat of the Piedmontese would mean reactionary restoration in Florence and Rome. He was wrong, however, in his repeated and emphatic assertion that a monarchic régime would be unable to lead Italy to independence and unity. He almost certainly misjudged Charles Albert of Sardinia-Piedmont when he accused him of treachery and suggested that the king had engineered his own defeat. Charles Albert reaped no reward for his alleged treachery. Defeat was a terrible blow to him. He abdicated, a broken man, at the age of 51 and died in his Portuguese exile a few months later.

How did Marx and Engels see the link between war and revolution in the Italian events of 1848 – 9?

In their eyes, revolution was not the likely consequence of defeat in war but the pre-condition of victory over the Austrians. Marxist advice to the Italians amounted to what was later called 'revolutionary defencism': determined resistance to the external enemy combined with internal struggle to replace a reactionary monarchy with a progressive, radical republic.

The fierce criticism which Engels levelled against the Sardo-Piedmontese king and his establishment, hand in hand with the expression of ardent hopes for the victory of the Piedmontese and all Italian insurgents, evokes a more recent example of revolutionary defencism: Trotsky's position on the correct 'Marxist' policy in the event of the Soviet Union (under Stalin) being involved in war with an 'imperialist' enemy. For all his denunciation of what he regarded as the counter-revolutionary treachery of Stalin – that 'gravedigger of the Revolution' – and of the ruling bureaucracy, Trotsky maintained to the end of his life that the Soviet Union was still a 'workers' state' and that all revolutionary socialists should be committed to her unconditional defence in the kind of war that started ten months after Trotsky's death.

Engels considered the monarchic system in Piedmont and other Italian states to be responsible for the disastrous outcome of the war with Austria; that is why he preached a republican revolution which, he argued, would lay the foundation of future victories. Similarly, Trotsky described the Stalin régime as the greatest obstacle to victory and urged the Russian working class to return to the Leninist and 'proletarian' form of government which had brought victory in the civil war. Both Engels and Trotsky erred in regarding a change of régime as essential for success; Italy achieved unity and independence under the same Piedmontese dynasty that had lost the war of 1848 – 9. The Stalin régime led the Soviet Union to victory against Hitler's Germany, with substantial territorial gains and a tremendous increase in world power.[10]

Hungary's Revolutionary War

At the time of the great European upheavals of 1848 – 9 the kingdom of Hungary, then inhabited by less than five million people, had been part of the Habsburg dominions for over a century. A Hungarian national movement fought for what is now usually called 'Home Rule' (a separate Hungarian government) without challenging Habsburg's dynastic reign. The great majority of Hungarian nationalists were ready to accept the Austrian emperor as king of Hungary.

In the autumn of 1847, a few months before the Vienna revolution, the Hungarian Diet meeting at Pressburg (now Bratislave, the Slovak capital; the city's Hungarian name is Pozsony) had adopted, under the influence of Lajos Kossuth, a number of progressive legislative measures. These included the commutation of feudal obligations, the emancipation of the Jews, and equal taxation of all classes of society. After the rising of March 1848 a weakened Austrian government could no longer refuse the more far-reaching demands for Hungarian autonomy. An independent Magyar administration then went beyond the Diet decisions and abolished all feudal rights and privileges, all tithes and labour services, and introduced universal suffrage.

A crucial feature of the Hungarian revolution of 1848 – 9 was the antagonism between the Magyars, the predominant ethnic group, and the Croats and other Slavonic races whose territory formed part of the Hungarian kingdom. The Croatian nobleman Jellačić, who had been appointed 'Ban' (governor and military commander) of Croatia by the king-emperor, strove to detach it from Hungary and turn it into an Austrian province, to be ruled from Vienna. He invaded Hungary with a Croatian army in September 1848. A few weeks later Emperor Ferdinand issued a manifesto dismissing the 'rebellious' Hungarian government (then headed by Count Batthyanyi and Lajos Kossuth) and empowering Jellačić to take action as governor of Hungary, but Jellačić was defeated by the Hungarians and retreated to the walls of Vienna. The Austrian government sent him reinforcements, which provoked another rising in Vienna on 6 October. It was crushed, and cruel retribution followed. A half-hearted attempt by the Hungarians to go to the aid of the Vienna rebels ended in failure.

In December 1848 the feeble-minded Emperor Ferdinand abdicated in favour of his eighteen-year-old nephew Francis Joseph, who went on to reign for sixty-eight years, until his death during the First World War. The Hungarians refused to recognize the new emperor as king of Hungary, since the changeover had no regard for the Hungarian constitution.

The war of independence began in earnest. After initial reverses the Hungarians drove the imperial army from their country. In April 1849 the Hungarian government severed all ties with the Habsburg monarchy: Kossuth was proclaimed head of the independent Hungarian state. But in May Russia intervened in support of the Vienna government and invaded Hungary, scoring decisive victories by early August. On 13 August the Hungarian supreme commander, Görgey, surrendered an army of 160,000 to the Russians. The Hungarians had lost their war of independence.

Engels and Marx gave unqualified support to the Hungarian revolution and its democratic leaders. Accusations such as they levelled against the Prussian leadership in the Schleswig-Holstein war, and against the king of Sardinia and his government in the conflict with Austria, are absent from their analysis of the Hungarian revolutionary war, written after a victorious campaign by the Magyars in the spring of 1849, on the eve of Russia's intervention.[11]

The sympathies which Engels and Marx felt and expressed for the Hungarian leaders and their revolutionary-democratic policies were enhanced by several factors. The intervention of reactionary Russia tended to confirm the progressive nature of the Magyar struggle, and a feature of the Hungarian war was its international dimension – the links the revolutionaries had forged with like-minded militants of other nations. An alliance with the Poles had been proclaimed in January 1849, and, according to Engels, over 20,000 Poles volunteered for the Hungarian army. A fighting alliance with the German revolutionaries of Vienna had taken practical shape in the Vienna rising of October 1849, and in the Hungarians' abortive attempt, in turn, to render military assistance to the German-Austrian insurgents.

11

The 'Imminence of World War and Revolution'

There was another reason why the two German socialists regarded the Hungarian struggle with sympathy. They believed and hoped that the conflict between Habsburg's autocratic reaction and the Hungarians' democratic radicalism would lead to a full-blown European war – and a European revolution.

Engels predicted an early collision between Britain and Russia as a result of the latter's armed intervention in central Europe, on the grounds that 'the English bourgeoisie cannot be expected to let Austria become a Russian province.' In the concluding paragraph Engels wrote:

> War will come. Paris is on the threshold of revolution ... While in southern Germany the core of a German revolutionary army is being formed, which prevents Prussia from taking an active part in the Hungarian campaign, France is on the point of playing an active role in the struggle ... Soon the French, the Magyar-Polish, and the German revolutionary armies will celebrate their fraternization on the battlefield before the walls of Berlin. [12]

Thus Engels expected Germany, Poland and Russia to be involved in a war originating in the Austrian-Hungarian conflict, Britain being drawn in by balance-of-power considerations. He was confident that this all-European war would culminate in the triumph of international revolution.

The interaction of war and revolution was the subject of an earlier article by Marx, which foresaw a new rising by the French working class, and 'world war' in 1849. Proletarian revolution in France, Marx argued, was the pre-condition for the liberation of Europe, but the chief obstacle to this liberation was British capitalism:

> England dominates the world market, and England is dominated by the bourgeoisie ... Old England can be overthrown only by *world war*, since war alone can provide the Chartists, the organized English working-class party, with the conditions for a successful rising against their all-powerful oppressors. When the Chartists take over the British government, then, and only then will social revolution pass from the realm of utopia to that of reality. Yet any *European* war in which Britain is involved is a world war ... A European war will be the first result of the victorious proletarian revolution in France. As in the days of

Napoleon, England will lead the armies of counter-revolution; yet that war itself will make her the leader of the revolutionary movement, and thus England will repay the debt she incurred by her actions against the revolution of the eighteenth century. [13]

He referred to these predictions in the last issue of the paper, in an article dealing with its suppression. 'In saying farewell to our readers we remind them of what we said in our first January issue: a revolutionary rising of the French working class and world war – that is what the year 1849 has in store for us.' [14]

Marx and Engels obviously agreed on the world situation and the immediate future. Once again their expectations were not borne out. The French workers did not rise, and when a major war broke out in 1853–4 it bore no resemblance to the 'world war' of Marxian prophecy, and produced no revolutionary upheavals.

Engels's vision (presumably shared by Marx) of the French, Hungarian, Polish and German revolutionary armies fraternizing 'on the battlefield before the walls of Berlin' seemed to presuppose that the reactionary camp would comprise the three powers of the 'Holy Alliance', Russia, Austria and Prussia. What is not clear is how Engels and Marx saw the position of Britain: her participation would assuredly impart a global character to the war. In his New Year article Marx had predicted that capitalist Britain would lead the counter-revolutionary camp, but after a Chartist-led revolution a British working-class government would be at the head of the revolutionary movement. Yet Engels, writing in the last issue of *NRZ*, regarded Britain's involvement as due to the fact that 'the English bourgeoisie cannot be expected to let Austria become a Russian province.' This suggests that Britain would feel compelled to intervene, from the start, as an enemy of the (Russian-led) counter-revolutionary camp, and a potential ally of the progressive coalition of republican France and revolutionary Germans, Magyars and Poles. It would seem that Marx and Engels, while agreeing on the outlines of impending events, were not in complete accord about the details concerning the 'world war' they considered inevitable.

The attitude of the Marxist journal towards its own country, Prussia, was defeatist inasmuch as it foresaw, and welcomed, a Prussian defeat in an imminent war. *Neue Rheinische Zeitung* does not spell out the exact relationship between revolutionary action and military developments. But it would have been logical for Marx and

Engels to argue — as Lenin did over sixty years later — that reciprocal interaction existed in that revolutionary militancy was apt to cause setbacks at the front and, *vice versa*, that the defeat of one's own reactionary government would further the cause of revolution.

In his article of 1 January 1849 Karl Marx predicted a Chartist takeover in Britain, due to her involvement in world war. Again, the mechanics of cause and effect were not explained. What he apparently meant was that reverses early in that war — with Britain leading the 'counter-revolutionary armies' — would weaken the bourgeois establishment and create a revolutionary situation. This too is in line with Lenin's notion of revolutionary defeatism in the First World War.

The Future of the Slav Races

During the Prussian-Danish war of 1848–9, Marx and Engels voiced their contempt for reactionary small 'would-be' nations like the Danes, the Dutch, the Belgians and the Swiss. More scathing still were their comments, in the context of the Hungarian revolutionary war and the predicted European war, on some of the Slav nations: the Czechs, the Slovaks, and above all the Croats.

When the people of Prague rose against Habsburg rule in June 1848, Engels stressed the democratic and revolutionary character of the rising; he denounced the brutal retribution meted out by the Austrian commander, Prince Windischgrätz, and once again condemned the perennial German policy of subjugating and enslaving other nations.[15]

Yet his — and Marx's — attitude changed completely when the Czech and Slovak nationalists showed willingness to come to terms with the Austrian rulers some months later, and displayed hostility towards the Hungarians and the revolutionary Germans. That, at any rate, is how Engels saw the situation. He contrasted the revolutionary role of the German and Hungarian democrats in 1848 with the help given to Habsburg reaction by Czechs, Slovaks and Croats:

All the South Slav races . . . placed themselves at the disposal of Austrian reaction . . . The Austrian *camarilla* found support only among the Slavs. It was the Slavs who played a decisive part in the downfall of Italy and who stormed Vienna, and it is the Slavs who now are staging a concerted attack on the Magyars.

14

A peculiar personal resentment or disappointment seems to have contributed to Engels's change of heart, for he added: 'This is their gratitude for the support which the whole German democratic press gave to the Czech democrats in June (1848), when they were shot down by Windischgrätz – the same Windischgrätz who is now their hero.'[16]

In passing judgement on certain nationalities or ethnic groups Marx and Engels did not normally formulate their views in 'class' terms, for example by blaming the capitalist classes but exonerating the workers, as present-day Marxists invariably do. In the East German (1956) edition of the *Collected Works* the editorial notes on Engels's article about the Prague rising assert that at the time in question (June 1848) 'the masses of the Czech people, peasants and proletarians' had played an active part in the revolutionary movement; later the 'Czech liberal bourgeoisie', which supported the Habsburgs in their fight against revolution and democracy, had given a nationalistic slant to the movement. In this respect Marx and Engels were less 'Marxist', or less in keeping with stereotype present-day Marxian concepts, than their twentieth-century interpreters. The condemnations by the two founding fathers were directed against the peoples as such, without distinctions between (good) proletarians and (bad) capitalists. The Czech, Slovak and Croatian workers and peasants are not exempted, either explicitly or implicitly, from Engels's statement that 'all the South Slav races' had aided Austrian reaction. In his article on 'The Revolutionary Movement', Marx accused 'Croats, . . . Czechs . . . and similar riff-raff' of having strangled the cause of freedom in Vienna.[17] In 'The Magyar Struggle', Engels declared that after a victorious proletarian revolution in France 'the Austrian Germans and Magyars will be free to wreak bloody vengeance on the Slav barbarians.'[18]

We encountered this contemptuous attitude towards small 'reactionary' or 'would-be' nations in their comments on the Danish war of 1848, where the Danes, the Dutch, the Belgians and the Swiss were deemed unworthy of national independence. Engels was even more explicit in condemning the Czechs and other Slavic entities to national extinction. He attempted a historical justification of the case for denying them independent nationhood:

Except for the Poles, the Russians, and perhaps the Turkish Slavs, no Slav people has a future, for the simple reason that all the other Slavs lack the elementary historical, geographical, political and industrial conditions. Peoples which have never had

15

a history of their own ... or which were *forced* to attain the first stage of civilization only by means of a foreign yoke, are not viable and will never be able to achieve any kind of independence.

And that has been the fate of the Austrian Slavs. The Czechs, among whom we would include the Moravians and Slovaks, ... never had had a history of their own ... Bohemia and Moravia passed definitely to Germany and the Slovak regions remained with Hungary. And this historically absolutely non-existent 'nation' puts forward claims to independence? [19]

This is not unlike some of Hitler's utterances during the Sudeten crisis of September 1938, when he denied the existence of a Czechoslovak nation. But if these reactionary Slav peoples, according to Engels, have 'no claims to independence' and 'no future', what is to become of them?

The impending general war will ... wipe out these petty hide-bound (Slavic) nations, down to their very names. The next world war will bring about the disappearance from the face of the earth *(vom Erdboden verschwinden machen)* not only of reactionary classes and dynasties, but also of entire reactionary peoples. And that, too, is progress. [20]

In conjunction with other Engelsian passages on the history and the future of the various European races, the context seems to indicate that 'disappearance' will be the result not of genocide but of absorption by stronger and more progressive neighbours, followed by assimilation. That is the usual interpretation, but it is not undisputed. Karl Kautsky, a great Marxist authority of the late nineteenth and early twentieth centuries, believed that Engels was speaking of the necessary *extermination* of the 'reactionary' Slav races.

Kautsky quoted the above passage and commented:

One reads such remarks with utter amazement, indeed with horror. In many respects they reflect not just a totally fallacious view of actual conditions but also — which is still more objection-able — an abandonment of principles which form the basis not only of international socialism but particularly of Marxist thought.

We are told that, except for the Poles, the Slavs are all counter-revolutionary by nature; hence they would not only have to be fought in the present situation ... No, they must be exterminated

... The only solution was to fight and destroy them ...
Actually Marx and Engels displayed this terrible hatred of the Slavs only for a very brief period. [21]

The curious thing about Kautsky's criticisms of this advocacy of genocide (as he understood Engels's remarks) is that, a long time before this criticism, he had echoed Engels's 1848 dicta in a different context; in respect of barbarian tribes in Asia.

In a letter to Engels, dated 11 May 1882, Kautsky (then twenty-eight years old) dealt with the question of what would happen to India and other British possessions after a successful proletarian revolution in Britain. After suggesting that under the guidance of a socialist Britain India might be able to skip the capitalist phase and proceed directly to socialism, Kautsky continued, 'Those savage tribes *(die wilden Voelkerschaften)* which cannot be assimilated to modern culture, will probably have to disappear from the face of the earth.' [22] It can hardly be an accident that Kautsky used exactly the words *(vom Erdboden verschwinden)* which Engels had used of the impending fate of some Slav peoples thirty-three years earlier. It would seem that Kautsky had read the 1849 article without being horrified by its sentiments, and that as a young man he did not scruple to express similar feelings regarding other ethnic groups; but as an octogenarian he saw matters in a different light. It would probably have been a shock to him, towards the end of his life, had his attention been drawn to his cruel words more than half a century before.

Whatever Engels meant when he predicted the 'disappearance' of entire reactionary peoples, it is an atrocious statement to make, apart from being wide of the mark as a prediction. Small wonder that Kautsky and other twentieth-century Marxists have felt uneasy about this wholesale death sentence. This is one of the rare instances of the communist editors of the *Collected Works* repudiating the views of the masters:

It must be evident to us today that the articles 'The Magyar Struggle' and 'Democratic Pan-Slavism' contain some erroneous judgements on the past and future of the small Slav peoples incorporated into Austria ... History has not confirmed Engels's opinion that the small Slav peoples of central Europe were doomed to be absorbed and assimilated by their larger and more civilized neighbours.

By way of furnishing a 'Marxist' explanation for the master's un-Marxist views, they continue:

> In these pronouncements, Engels was probably influenced by the gravity of the political situation at the time, and this accounted for the sharp polemical tone of his articles . . . A certain part was played in this by the idea which Marx and Engels entertained at that time of the nearness of a simultaneous victory of the proletarian revolution in the developed countries, a revolution which would have put an end to both social and national oppression . . . [23]

This interpretation is not quite in keeping with Engels's prediction of a workers' rising in France which would set the Austrian Germans and Hungarians free to 'wreak bloody vengeance on the barbarian Slavs'. However, it is certainly true to say that Marx and Engels believed proletarian revolutions to be imminent at that time. Their expectation of an impending European war reflects the belief in the close link between revolution and war, but they thought that, apart from furthering the cause of revolution, war would tidy up and simplify the map of Europe, by eliminating a number of small countries.

Engels's prophecy of the disappearance of 'entire reactionary peoples' ostensibly refers to the Austrian Slavs; but in view of what he wrote in a different context about the 'small wrecks of nationalities', the 'mongrel would-be' or 'miserably powerless so-called nations' which could never form part of 'a European confederacy of republics', we may assume that the Danes, the Dutch, the Belgians and the Swiss − not to speak of the people of Luxembourg or Liechtenstein or Andorra (not even mentioned in this context) − likewise have no chance and no right to survive. [24] The Marx-Engels version of post-revolutionary Europe − to the west of Russia − would seem to be a confederation comprising six republics: France, Britain, Germany, Italy, Hungary and Poland. The list does not include the four nations inhabiting the Iberian or the Scandinavian peninsulas − Spain, Portugal, Norway and Sweden. They are not specifically doomed, but apparently are not regarded as potential members of the coming confederation of European republics.

2 The 'Eastern Question' and the Crimean War

The Crimean War (1854–6) might well have gone down in history as the 'War of the Empires'. It was a conflict between the Tsar's empire and a coalition comprising the Ottoman empire, the British empire and the French 'Second Empire' of Napoleon III. The Habsburg empire, though not a belligerent, intervened diplomatically in opposition to Russia: Austrian pressure induced the Tsar to make important concessions which facilitated the peace treaty of Paris in March 1856. The only non-imperial state involved was the kingdom of Sardinia-Piedmont which sent a contingent of troops to aid the West in 1855, and thereby made a marginal military contribution.

If ever a war could be termed 'reactionary' it was the Crimean War. The friction that led to its outbreak arose from a dispute about control of the holy places in Palestine and the protection of the sultan's Christian subjects. Deeper issues had to do with the 'Eastern Question': the weakness and chaotic condition of the Turkish empire which still included much of the Balkans. Crucially, how would the decline and possible disintegration of this empire affect the international balance of power, and the military, political and commercial interests of Russia, France, Britain and Austria? The Western powers feared the encroachment of Russia on Turkey (primarily European Turkey) and Russian attempts to dominate the Bosphorus and the Dardanelles, which would turn the Black Sea into a Russian lake.

None of the countries involved was waging a 'national' war; none fought for national independence and unity. If Lenin was right in 1914–15, in asserting that socialists should support only national but not reactionary wars for power-political interests, Marx and Engels should have called upon their fellow socialists in the belligerent countries to oppose the Crimean War. This was not the line adopted by the founding fathers. They took sides, not so much *for* the Western powers as *against* Russia. They were critical, and at times abusive, of the governments and leading politicians of the countries involved; but above all they wanted a Russian defeat. They also hoped and believed that the war would revive the European revolution which had lain dormant after the 1848–9 upheavals; and that the prospects of this cause depended upon the victory of Russia's enemies.

At the time of the crisis that led to war Marx and Engels were living in England and were regular contributors to the *New York Daily Tribune*. They reported and commented on current British and European events. Most of the articles on the Crimean War were written by Engels, especially those dealing with the military aspects; some of them appeared under Marx's name. The American paper was progressive but not socialist; yet the two friends could speak their minds freely and voice their hopes for the resurgence and success of 'revolutionary democracy'. It is true that the articles which appeared in the *New York Daily Tribune* lacked the inspired perorations which marked many of the articles in *Neue Rheinische Zeitung*, but there is no reason to assume that either felt they had to pretend to hold views not their own or suppress views they held.

In an article on the 'Eastern Question', written in March 1853, about a year before the Anglo-French declaration of war, Engels denounced Russia's designs of 'annexation and aggrandizement' which would exclude Britain from the Black Sea and injure her commercial interests. For economic as well as military and political reasons Britain must be 'the earnest and unyielding opponent of Russia's power policies'. A Russian victory over Turkey would enable the tsar's 'gigantic and swollen power' to advance towards the domination of eastern and central Europe. After subduing Turkey, Engels argued, Russia would annex Greece and Albania, and turn the Habsburg dominions into a vassal state. He went on:

> Then another question is possible, is even probable. The broken and undulating western frontier of the empire, ill-defined in respect of natural boundaries, would call for rectification, and it would appear that the natural frontier of Russia runs from Danzig or perhaps Stettin (now Gelansk and Szczecin) to Trieste. And as sure as conquest follows conquest, and annexation follows annexation, so sure would the conquest of Turkey by Russia be only the prelude for the annexation of Hungary, Prussia, Galicia, and for the ultimate realization of the Slavonic empire which certain fanatical panslavistic philosophers have dreamed of.[1]

Here Engels presaw a development which began to acquire reality only after the Second World War. If the east European satellite countries are seen as part of the Russian empire, which in a way they are, it would be true to say that Engels's fears have largely materialized — without Russian conquest of Turkey. In fact, the western frontier of the most westerly satellite, the (east) German Democratic Republic, is far to the west of what Engels considered Russia's possible 'natural frontier'. From his assessment of Russian expansionism Engels drew a remarkable conclusion:

> Russia is decidedly a conquering nation...Let Russia get possession of Turkey, and her strength is increased nearly half, and she becomes superior to all the rest of Europe put together. Such an event would be an unspeakable calamity for the revolutionary cause. The maintenance of Turkish independence, or in case of a possible dissolution of the Ottoman empire, the arrest of the Russian scheme of annexation is a matter of the highest moment. *In this instance the interests of revolutionary democracy and England go hand in hand.* Neither can permit the tsar to make Constantinople one of his capitals, and we shall find that when driven to the wall, the one will resist him as determinedly as the other.[2] (Emphasis added.)

Engels's and Marx's hatred of Russia made them hope for Turkey's success, but it did not blind them to the repressive character of Ottoman rule, especially in Europe. A few weeks later Engels wrote that Turkish repression in the territories inhabited by Christians directly benefited Russia. For the Greek Christians the tsar, however wicked his rule might be in other respects was *'their natural liberator and protector'*, but once the Turks ceased to dominate a large part of the Balkan peninsula, the Christians there would no longer look upon the tsar as a friend and ally. Hence, a 'simple and final solution' offered itself: the creation of 'a free and independent Christian State on the ruins of the Moslem empire in Europe'. This would probably be achieved by the progress of the European revolution. From that conflict Britain could not keep aloof. In order to prevent Russia from seizing Constantinople she must undermine the tsar's influence in the Balkans by promoting the solution suggested by Engels.[3]

In this context Marx put forward, somewhat later, the possible alternative of 'the establishment . . . of a federal republic of Slavonic states',[4] roughly what materialized in the shape of the Yugoslav federation. During the first quarter of this century the 'Eastern Question' was settled broadly on the lines envisaged by Marx and Engels.

International tension increased during the summer of 1853 and, as normally happens in such situations, public opinion began to polarize.

There were heated debates and meetings for and against hard line policies, for and against risking war with Russia. Where did Marx and Engels stand? They did not shilly-shally or compromise. They were both *in favour of war*, as is clear from their articles in *NYDT* and other utterances.

Marx and Engels had predicted and hoped for war prior to the Crimean War. They favoured war with Denmark in 1848 and hoped that it would spread to engulf Russia. In 1849 they expressed similar hopes for war with Russia − as an aspect of imminent 'world war' − in connection with the Hungarian rising. In 1853−4 their bellicose viewpoints were even more emphatic. Before and after the outbreak of the Crimean War they castigated successive British governments for their reluctance to go to war and, subsequently, for not waging it vigorously enough.

In an article published on 14 July 1853, Marx denounced 'the naked and shameful subserviency' of Western diplomacy in the face of Russian aggressiveness.[5] Eleven days later, he pressed the need for war even more openly. After writing that the British aristocracy and bourgeoisie were lying 'prostrate before the barbarian autocrat', while the proletariat 'alone protests against the impotency and degradation of the ruling classes', Marx reports on a great 'peace meeting' at Halifax, called by the Manchester School ('laissez-faire' economists and politicians). 'The hall was crowded, and many thousands could obtain no admittance.' The Chartists of Halifax summoned Ernest Jones 'by electric telegraph', and he had arrived just in time for the meeting. Marx's report continues:

> Already the gentlemen of the Manchester School believed they would carry their resolution, and would be able to bring home the support of the manufacturing districts to their good Aberdeen[6] when Ernest Jones rose and put an amendment pledging the people to *war*, and declaring that before liberty was established peace was a crime. There ensured a most violent discussion, but the amendment of Ernest Jones was carried by an immense majority.[7]

Karl Marx and Frederick Engels obviously sided with Ernest Jones and the war party. They wanted war because they thought it would lead to defeat for tsarist Russia and produce a revolutionary situation in the West. The ebbing of the revolutionary tide in and after 1849 had not shaken their faith in the early revival and success of 'revolutionary democracy'. Marx in particular was optimistic about the prospects for revolution, and felt that the cause would prosper whichever policies Western governments pursued. As he put it in the New York paper,

> The Western powers . . . commence by encouraging the Sultan to resist the Czar from fear of the encroachments of Russia, and terminate by compelling the former to yield, from fear of a general war giving rise to a general revolution . . . The revolutionary party can only congratulate itself on this state of things. The humiliation of the reactionary Western governments, and their manifest impotency to guard the interests of European civilization against Russian encroachment cannot fail to work out a wholesome indignation in the people . . . [8]

Thus a Western hard line would result in war and possibly revolution, while moderation − or 'appeasement' as it is now usually called − would revolutionize the people's consciousness; either way the revolutionary party would gain.

War between Russia and Turkey started in October 1853, and first reports on the fighting said that the Russians had suffered some reverses, both in Europe and in the Caucasus. Engels joyfully commented, 'The war everywhere opens with disasters for the tsar. Let us hope that such may be its history to the end, and that the Russian government and people may be taught by it to restrain their ambition and arrogance, and mind their own business thereafter.' [9]

In March 1854, after Britain and France had entered the war, Engels again recorded his wish for a Russian defeat. He wrote to the editor of the London *Daily News* offering his services as a military commentator and saying that he hoped the Russians would be thoroughly beaten, but that as a general rule he would try to keep politics out of his articles. (The letter contained details of Engels's military studies and expertise; he mentioned that he had served with the Prussian artillery and 'seen some active service during the insurrectionary war in South Germany, 1849' − but he omitted to say on which side he had fought. His offer to write for the paper was not accepted.) [10]

Marx and Engels were over-optimistic about the prospects of revolution and the ability of the anti-Russian coalition to achieve quick major successes. In January 1854, two months before Britain and France declared war, Engels had 'no doubt' that the Allies could destroy Sevastopol and the Russian Black Sea fleet, could take and hold the Crimea and occupy Odessa, and that all this need take no more than a month from the beginning of active operations. (In the event Sevastopol fell after seventeen months of war; the Allies never took Odessa.) But in the same article he warned the five great European powers – Britain, France, Russia, Austria and Prussia – that there was a sixth power, mightier than any of them: the revolution, which was 'now again called to action by the commercial crisis and by the scarcity of food'. The symptoms of its return were visible everywhere 'in the agitation and disquietude which have seized the proletarian class'. The impending European war would be the signal, 'and this sixth and greatest European power will come forward, in shining armour, and sword in hand...Then all calculations as to the balance of power will be upset by the addition of a new element which...will as much baffle the plans of the old European powers, and their generals, as it did from 1792 to 1800.'[11]

During the period of pre-war tension the two socialists had expressed doubts about the seriousness of British statesmen in preparing for war. In January 1854 Engels referred mockingly to Lord Aberdeen's 'prayers for peace' and, less mockingly, to Lord Palmerston's 'collusion with Russia'.[12] (Palmerston was not at the time a member of the government; he succeeded Aberdeen as prime minister in January 1855.) In February Marx darkly hinted, without explanation, that 'treachery lurks behind the clamorous war preparations of the coalition.'[13] As the war dragged on without tangible results, Marx and Engels grew more impatient and outspoken. In a joint article written in June 1854 they accused Lord Aberdeen of intending to make peace on a *status quo* basis but added, with obvious satisfaction and approval, that the British people would have none of this: 'They hold the crippling of Russia to be indispensable, so that she cannot soon again thus upset the world; and they expect impatiently some brilliant feat of arms, such as the capture of Kronstadt or Scvastopol.'[14]

This notion of the war being a war of the people, with the ruling classes dragging their feet, was a recurring theme in the Marx-Engels reports and comments. Thus, reviewing the events of 1854, Marx wrote that while 'the oligarchy' had led Britain into the great war with France some sixty years previously, 'it was the people that forced the English oligarchy into the current war with Russia.'[15] Somewhat later, when Russian aggression against Turkey began, he explained that 'the national hatred broke forth in a blaze, and never, perhaps, was a war as popular as this.'[16] The middle classes had lost their enthusiasm for the war, but not the workers and small farmers. It was similar in France, where the bourgeoisie had been against the war from the start: 'Both British and French proletarians are filled with an honourable national spirit.'[17]

One of Engels's forecasts which history failed to confirm was that the Crimean War would spread and that Austria would join in, as either Russia's ally or enemy. A 'real war on a large scale, something like the grand wars of Napoleon' would develop in 1855, and 'other battles far more fierce, far more decisive...the battles of the European peoples against the...European despots', resulting in the great European showdown between progress and reaction. 'Then the struggle will be only between the democratic revolution on one side and the monarchical counter-revolution on the other.'[18]

Sevastopol fell in September 1855, but the war was not over. In the Caucasus in November, the Russians captured the fortress of Kars in Turkish Armenia, which strengthened their bargaining position in the ensuing peace talks. After lengthy negotiations in Paris, in which Austria also took part, a peace treaty was signed on 30 March 1856. Its main provisions were the neutralization of the Black Sea, which involved the closure of the Dardanelles and the Bosphorus to foreign warships, and a ban on the maintenance of navies and naval arsenals in the Black Sea by Russia and Turkey. Kars was returned to Turkey, and Sevastopol and other Allied-held Crimean towns to Russia. Russia had to abandon, for the time being, any designs she might have had on the Straits and Constantinople, but the terms were not as onerous as Marx and Engels had wished them to be. The 'crippling' of Russia, which they said 'the people' of Britain would insist on, was not a facet of the post-war settlement.

Nor had the other Marxian predictions come true. The war had not spread, let alone reached Napoleonic levels. It had acquired no revolutionary dimensions, and produced no battles in which 'European peoples' confronted 'European despots'. The result was substantially a return to the *status quo*, both in international power relations and in revolutionary potentialities.

In April 1856 the *NYDT* and the Chartist *People's Paper* carried articles by Marx on the fall of Kars. He argued that this last-minute Russian success was the fault of British Prime Minister Palmerston and Foreign Secretary Lord Clarendon. He no longer spoke of their indecision or reluctance to fight energetically. He accused them of deliberate action in the interests of the enemy: they had planned the

Russian capture of Kars. In a further article (for the *People's Paper*) he suggested that the British government had deliberately thwarted a Turkish plan for the relief of the siege of Kars, and called its fall 'the turning point in the history of the sham war against Russia', an event without which there would have been 'no treaty of Paris...no sham peace'.[19]

What Marx apparently intended to prove was that the war was some kind of shadow-boxing as far as Russia and the West were concerned − a 'phoney' war, we would call it today. The two revolutionaries who had originally thought that 'in this instance the interests of revolutionary democracy and of England go hand in hand' concluded that the British government, by conducting a 'sham war' and in the end helping the Russian enemy, had harmed the interests of Britain and of 'democracy'. Marx and Engels must have felt that the failure to fight an all-out war was why their predictions of international and revolutionary consequences had not come true.

The Crimean War, its preceding crisis and aftermath gave Marx and Engels their one opportunity, while living in England and in active contact with the British working-class movement, to comment on a major war in which Britain was involved. The judgements they passed form a basis for assessing their general attitudes to wars between capitalist − or at any rate non-socialist − powers.

Marx and Engels were certainly not defeatist for Britain; they wanted her to wage offensive war against Russia and to conduct it with the utmost determination. A crushing Russian defeat seemed to them to be both in the power-political interests of Britain and in the revolutionary interests of 'European democracy'. They believed that the British people wanted all-out war but that their rulers were guilty of treachery.

3 Britain's Wars against Persia and China 1856−60

The harmony of interests between Britain as a world power and what Marx and Engels called 'revolutionary democracy' had caused the two friends to support the war against Russia; they were, as we saw, more pro-war than the British establishment.

However, they felt no sympathy for Britain in her colonial and semi-colonial ventures in Asia. In Marx's eyes, the Anglo-Afghan war of 1839−42 was 'infamous' (although the containment of Russian expansion was one of Britain's motives), and the Burmese war of 1852 'senseless'.[1] In the summer of 1853, when the war against Burma seemed to flare up again, Marx remarked that 'of all the warlike expeditions of the British in the East, none has ever been undertaken on less warranted grounds that those against Burma.'[2] Neither he nor Engels attempted a political analysis.

In Britain's wars against Persia and China, between 1856 and 1860, Marx and Engels backed the Asian side against what Marxists would now call 'British imperialism'. But they never feigned affection for the régimes or the ruling strata of the Asian enemies of Great Britain; nor did they play down the atrocities committed by the Chinese or by the sepoys in the Great Mutiny.

War with Persia 1856−7

Persia's occupation of the principality of Herat on the Persian-Afghan border in October 1856 led to war, waged by Britain on behalf of the East India Company. Britain maintained that Persia's action violated a treaty, and despatched an expeditionary force which landed at the Persian port of Bushire. The ensuing British-Indian campaign was successful.

Commenting on the British declaration of war, Marx described the occupation of Herat as a mere pretext for British armed intervention. Her real objective, he asserted, was territorial gain, and especially the acquisition of the island of Kharg in the northern part of the Persian Gulf. Marx characterized Britain's expansionism:

> So soon as the East India Company casts a greedy look on any of the independent sovereigns, or on any region whose political and commercial resources or jewels are valued, the victim is accused of having violated this or that ideal or actual convention, transgressed an imaginary promise or restriction, committed some nebulous outrage, and then war is declared, and . . . the perennial force of the fable of the wolf and the lamb is again incarnadined in national history.[3]

This is the style in which a twentieth-century 'Marxist-Leninist' might have commented on an 'imperialist' venture such as Italy's 1935–6 war against Abyssinia. Marx did not express a wish for the defeat of the British campaign, but we may assume he would have welcomed it. He was, incidentally, wrong in asserting that the acquisition of the island of Kharg was Britain's real objective. Kharg had been occupied by British-Indian forces but, by the treaty of Paris, Britain obtained only Persia's evacuation of Herat and her recognition of Afghan independence; Kharg Island was returned – and still belongs – to Persia. A few years after the war Herat, town and province, became – and still is – part of Afghanistan.

The 'Second Opium War' and its Aftermath

Another conflict between Britain and an Asian country began simultaneously with the 'little war' against Persia (as some contemporary writers called it), but it had far greater impact on British consciousness and opinion. This was the so-called 'Second Opium War' against China. The 'First Opium War' (1838–42) led to the treaty of Nanking in 1843, by which China made substantial concessions to Britain's foreign trade interests.

This second conflict arose from an incident in Canton harbour in October 1856: the boarding by Chinese officials of a Chinese ship which at one time had held a British registration, and the arrest of twelve (Chinese) members of the crew on charges of piracy and smuggling. Protests lodged by British representatives in Canton and Hongkong, which spoke of an 'insult to the British flag', induced the Chinese governor to release the twelve sailors; but he rejected the British demand for an official apology, insisting that no insult had been intended or committed (no flag was shown at the time of the boarding). Thereupon the British fleet began a bombardment of Canton which lasted three weeks and caused many casualties and great damage.

Marx commented on these events in the articles he wrote for the *New York Daily Tribune.* The news from China had caused a considerable sensation in Britain, and Marx was not alone in voicing indignation at Britain's actions. His statements that 'the British are in the wrong in the whole proceeding,' and that this was 'a most unrighteous war'[4] were echoed by leading British politicians and newspapers. Actually Marx's initial reaction was restrained. He recapitulated the facts which showed British action to be contrary to international law, and concluded, somewhat tamely, that 'the civilized nations of the world' were likely to disapprove this act of aggression, since the second Chinese war, unlike the first, might obstruct trade with China 'for an indefinite period'.[5] The London *Daily News*, in a passage quoted in Marx's article, denounced the bombardment of Canton far more harshly than did Marx. The paper said it was 'monstrous' that Britain should have been engaged in 'the wicked work of carrying fire and sword, and desolation and death, into the peaceful homes of unoffending men, on whose shores we were originally intruders'.

Later Marx used stronger language: 'the unoffending citizens and peaceful tradesmen of Canton have been slaughtered...and the claims of humanity violated,' and he listed previous acts of 'English ferocity' in China.[6] He also accused the British press of silence about such shameful aspects of British policy as broken treaties, bribery and corruption, the illegal opium trade, and so on, but the Marxian denunciation of the aggression is on much the same lines as his attacks on Lord Palmerston's government by members of parliament and other British politicians. In the House of Commons, Cobden tabled a motion of censure which was carried by 263 votes to 247; in the debate on this motion Cobden was supported by Disraeli and Gladstone among others, neither of whom had yet reached the pinnacle of his fame.

Marx and Engels, then, were in respectable company in their opposition to Britain's official China policy. They expressed views which reflected the attitude of at least a substantial section of the British public and, writing about this conflict, Marx did not draw any theoretical conclusions regarding the link between war and revolution. He did not dwell on the potential impact of the war on domestic developments in either country. His articles could have been written by any radical journalist opposed to the war but not primarily interested in revolutionary domestic upheavals which might result from it.

A more 'Marxist' approach can be discerned in an article by Engels on Britain's wars with Persia and China. As usual he dealt at length with the military problems, but it was he, rather than Marx, who set the conflict in the social and political tendencies of the age. For Britain, this minor war against a weak opponent was not likely to affect events to any appreciable extent. But China was in a state of turmoil and civil war. The revolutionary Taiping movement, launched in 1851, had not yet spread to the southern provinces where the war

29

with Britain had so far been confined. But, according to Engels, a heightened national consciousness, resulting in fanatical action, had gripped the masses in the areas affected by the conflict. Their mood differed completely from that which prevailed at the time of the First Opium War, when the people had left the struggle to the military. He went on:

> But now . . . the mass of the people take an active, nay, a fanatical part in the struggle against the foreigners. They kidnap and kill every foreigner within their reach. The piratical policy of the British Government has caused this universal outbreak of all Chinese against all foreigners, and marked it as a war of extermination. Instead of moralizing on the horrible atrocities of the Chinese . . . we had better recognize that this is . . . a popular war for the maintenance of Chinese nationality. [7]

Engels took the view that China's war with Britain, whatever its outcome, would be a catalyst for social and political revolution within China, and that it would hasten the advent of a new era for China and the whole of the Far East.

This was an interesting departure in the theoretical sphere. Comments by Marx and Engels on the repercussions of war had previously been concerned either with its possible impact on the international balance of power, or − as in the case of King Charles Albert of Sardinia − with the success of constitutional régimes in fighting wars of national liberation. Engels's article on the Anglo-Chinese war, written in May and published in June 1857, is significant because the assessment of the war's inevitable effects on China's internal situation marks a stage in the emergence of a 'Marxist' concept regarding the interaction of war and social revolution.

The Second Opium War dragged on until 1858. It led to the signing of the treaties of Tientsin which China concluded with Britain and France, Russia and the USA, and whereby she had to make further concessions regarding foreign trade.

There was a further conflict with China in 1859−60; like the Crimean War, it was waged jointly by Britain and France. Under the treaties of Tientsin, Britain and France were entitled to have official envoys in Peking. In June 1859 a British and a French envoy arrived together at the mouth of the river Peiho with a naval escort of nineteen vessels and over 1000 soldiers. They intended to go by river to Tientsin and thence to Peking. The Chinese, who were willing to receive the missions but objected to the passage of a naval squadron on the Peiho, blocked the entrance to the river, and fighting ensued when the British fleet tried to remove the obstructions. Several ships were sunk or disabled, and 470 British and French troops were killed or wounded. The Allies withdrew, but the British and French governments resolved upon war. After some Chinese resistance, the Allies occupied Tientsin and entered Peking, where the British destroyed the summer palace; this was done in retaliation for the capture and killing of British and French plenipotentiaries who had gone under a flag of truce to negotiate with the Chinese commissioners.

Following the Anglo-French 'victory', China had to pay a war indemnity and compensation to the families of the murdered prisoners; she had to sign a convention confirming the right of British and French envoys to reside in Peking, and providing that the port of Tientsin should be open to trade and to residence by foreigners.

Karl Marx commented on these events in four articles published in the *New York Daily Tribune* in September and October 1859, when the war was just beginning. He pointed out that the despatch of warships to Tientsin was contrary to international law. 'Does the right of the French ambassador to reside in London involve the right of forcing the river Thames at the head of an armed French expedition?'[8] A number of other (non-socialist) writers and politicians took the same view.

Marx denounced the hysterical and chauvinist reaction of part of the British press to the conduct of the Chinese, who were faced with what amounted to an invasion. As an extreme example he singled out the observations of the London *Daily Telegraph*:

> Great Britain must attack the seaboard of China ..., invade the capital, expel the emperor from his palace .... Everyone of them (the Chinese generals) must be hanged as a pirate and a homicide to the yard-arm of a British man-of-war .... The Chinese must now be taught to value the English, who are their superiors, and ought to be their masters .... We might retain Canton,... and lay the basis of a new dominion.[9]

There is little political analysis in Marx's articles on this war. He does not suggest that Britain might derive material advantage from renewing hostilities with China. According to him, this new Chinese war was 'anything but popular with the British mercantile classes'. In 1857, at the beginning of the previous war, these classes 'expected great commercial profits from the forcible opening of the Chinese market'. But in 1859 they would be angry to see the fruits of the earlier victory jeopardized by a new conflict, launched 'for the purpose of pestering China with the nuisance of permanent embassies at its capital': in other words, for reasons of great-power prestige.[10]

There is little of a 'defeatist' angle to Marx's comments. He spoke with satisfaction of the defeat of the Anglo-French expedition at the Peiho, saying that the engagement had resulted 'in the utter discomfiture of the aggressors'.[12] But he was aware that the two Western powers would attain their objectives, and that even the failure of the campaign would not have had major political repercussions in France or Britain.

4 The Indian Mutiny

Britain's 'little war' with Persia had ended, but the Second Opium War was still in progress when the British empire was shaken by a crisis which overshadowed Middle and Far Eastern conflicts. A massive mutiny of the native troops in India broke out in the spring of 1857, and the ensuring war lasted until 1859, when the mutiny was suppressed. For obvious reasons this rebellion, and Britain's actions in quelling it, figure much more prominently than the Anglo-Chinese war in the articles Marx and Engels wrote for the *New York Daily Tribune*.

A spirit of resentment and revolt had been rife in parts of India for some time; it was reflected in acts of indiscipline among the 'sepoys', the native Indian troops. This became open mutiny in May 1857, ostensibly because of a rumour affecting the religious sensibilities of both Hindu and Moslem soldiers. On Sunday, 10 May, the native troops in Meerut, who had assembled on the parade ground, shot and killed several British officers. The British troops rallied and drove the mutineers from their barracks. The sepoys fled along the road to Delhi where they were joined by the native garrison. All Britons within reach were murdered, and the aged heir of the late mogul, who resided in the vast palace of Delhi, was proclaimed emperor of India. The standard of rebellion was planted on the battlements of the palace. The mutiny spread over large areas of northern and central India.

Marx's first article, written at the end of June, was chiefly an account of the mutiny and of the capture of Delhi by the rebels. Marx pointed to the uniqueness of the events and the significance of the revolt in the wider Asian context:

> The present revolt is distinguished by fatal features. It is the first time that sepoy regiments have murdered their European officers; that Mussulmans and Hindus, renouncing their mutual anti-pathies, have combined against their common masters; ... that the mutiny has not been confined to a few localities; and lastly, that the revolt in the Anglo-Indian army has coincided with a general disaffection exhibited against English supremacy on the part of great Asiatic nations, the revolt of the Bengal army being, beyond doubt, intimately connected with the Persian and Chinese wars.[1]

Most of the articles on the mutiny were written by Marx. Engels's contributions were largely reports and assessments of the military operations and military prospects; but he also castigated the brutality of the retribution meted out by British troops, the massive looting (especially after the recapture of Delhi and of Lucknow), and the iniquities of British colonial administration. Engels had praise for some of the British commanders but contempt for others. Towards the end, he said that the British had won the war, but lost the battle for the hearts and minds of the Indian people; Britain would, in future, be hated more fiercely than before, by both Hindus and Moslems.[2]

Marx's articles were also mainly factual reports on the progress of the insurrection and of the British campaign of reconquest. Like Engels, he welcomed the insurrection, but neither saw the conflict in terms of right and wrong. They listed the crimes committed by the East India Company and by individual British officials in India, but did not try to depict the sepoys or the leaders of the revolt as heroes. Marx, in particular, did not play down the atrocities of the insurgents. When the Lucknow residency was besieged by rebels in September 1857, Marx spoke of the 'gloomy prevision' of 'the capture of the place by starvation, and the massacre of its brave defenders with their wives and children'.[3] Another article begins with the statement: 'The outrages committed by the revolted sepoys in India are indeed appalling, hideous, ineffable.' But Marx adds that the 'infamous' conduct of the sepoys was 'only the reflex, in a concentrated form, of England's own conduct in India'.[4] And Engels, writing about the recapture of

33

Lucknow by the British in March 1858, commented that the revolt would now 'subside into its concluding, chronic period, during which the insurgents would finally take the character of dacoits or robbers, and find the inhabitants of the country as much their enemies as the British themselves'.[5]

No direct expression of pro-Indian sympathies, or of hopes for the success of the revolt, are to be found in the articles or in the letters Marx and Engels exchanged at the time of the mutiny. But there is a significant passage in one Marx wrote to Engels in January 1858. 'India,' Marx declared, 'with the drain of men and bullion it must cost the English, is now our best ally.'[6] This dictum contains an element of 'defeatism': it considers the weakening of the capitalist establishment to be the result of protracted and costly warfare, and implies that this will enhance the prospects of revolution in Britain.

Marx and Engels would apparently have welcomed a long continuance of the insurrection which they (like Disraeli before them) described as not just a military mutiny but a 'national revolt'. But they do not seem to have wished for its complete success, which would have meant the end of British rule in part or the whole of India. For one thing, they probably did not consider such an outcome a serious possibility. Furthermore, they do not appear to have thought the total or partial liberation of India a desirable consequence of the mutiny, or as a desirable short-term objective in itself.

Implicit in a number of Marx-Engels utterances is the view that British rule in India, however base and mercenary its motivation, however reactionary and oppressive its character, had in the past and would have in the future an essential role in the sub-continent's social and economic development. Some of its functions were destructive of features and phenomena which once had a positive value but had become an obstacle to progress in the nineteenth century. Thus, in the first volume of *Capital*, Marx describes the autarkic Indian village communities which, after the coming of the British, had fallen victim to modern European-style commerce and industry.[7] In a series of articles on British rule in India which he wrote for the *New York Daily Tribune* in 1853, he explained the historical necessity for their disappearance:

We must not forget that these idyllic village communities, inoffensive though they may appear, had always been the solid foundation of oriental despotism. We must not forget that this stagnatory, undignified and vegetative life, that this passive sort of existence evoked on the other hand, in contradistinction, wild, aimless, unbounded forces of destruction and rendered murder itself a religious rite in Hindustan. We must not forget that these little communities were contaminated by distinction of caste and by slavery.

England, it is true, in causing a social revolution in Hindustan, was actuated only by the vilest interests, and was stupid in her manner of enforcing them. But . . . the question is: can mankind fulfil its destiny without a fundamental revolution in the social state of Asia? If not, whatever may have been the crimes of England, she was the unconscious tool of history in bringing about that revolution.[8]

Marx went on to list certain regenerative aspects of British domination in Indian society: greater political unity, the emergence of a native army, a free press, and an educated Indian class 'endowed with the requirements for government and imbued with European science'. Above all, there was a modern system of communication.

That was written four years before the mutiny; but what Marx and Engels wrote about the revolt and its leadership in 1857 and 1858 leaves little doubt that in their opinion the pre-conditions of Indian self-government had not then materialized. The educated Indian class 'endowed with the requirements for government', which took over from the colonial administration ninety years after the mutiny, was not yet in place when the two founders of modern socialism commented on those events. Hence it must be regarded as certain that the 'defeatism' Marx and Engels displayed at the time was limited to domestic weakening of the colonial power and did not extend to total British defeat in the colonial war − a defeat which would have meant the loss of India or a substantial part of it.[9]

5 The Italian War of 1859 and its Aftermath

The cause of Italian unity recovered more speedily from the frustrations and disasters of 1848−9 than was generally expected.

Within a dozen years of the defeat of the Italian revolution, unification was substantially achieved. In March 1861 King Victor Emmanuel II of Sardinia was proclaimed king of Italy. His independent kingdom comprised the whole peninsula with the exception of Venetia, which was ruled by Austria for another five years, and Rome, where the pope continued as a secular ruler until 1870.

Patriots of all shades had worked for the goal of an independent Italy. They included revolutionary democrats like Mazzini and Manin, and Garibaldi with his volunteer army, but the chief architect of Italian unity and independence was a conservative nobleman, Count Camillo di Cavour, a native of Turin, the Piedmontese capital. When he became prime minister of Sardinia in 1852, he set course for the achievement of unity by the incorporation of all states and provinces within the kingdom of Sardinia.

Cavour was convinced that Austria's expulsion from Italy would result only from Austria's defeat by a major power. In 1858, when relations between Austria and France became strained, he reached agreement with Napoleon III on a joint war against the Habsburg monarchy. After victory, Sardinia was to annex Lombardy, Venetia and parts of central Italy; France's reward would be Savoy and Nice, the Piedmontese provinces on the French side of the Alps.

War broke out in April 1859, and the Austrians were beaten within a few months. But Napoleon, who felt that Cavour would not accept French dominance, went back on the agreement and granted the Habsburg emperor an armistice; under a peace treaty of November 1859, Sardinia-Piedmont obtained only the larger part of Lombardy. Cavour then encouraged risings against the old ruling houses and their Austrian garrisons, and Napoleon soon realized that control of Italy was beyond his grasp. In March 1860 he agreed to help Piedmont gain Tuscany and other parts of central Italy. A rising in Sicily in April 1860, against the Bourbon 'King of the Two Sicilies', induced Garibaldi to land there in May 1860. He overcame Bourbon resistance, crossed to the mainland and victoriously marched north; in September he took Naples, where Bourbon rule collapsed. Cavour and Garibaldi, not originally friends and allies, agreed that Victor Emmanuel be recognized as king of Italy. This happened in March 1861 after plebiscites in southern Italy, where the people voted massively — much to the chagrin of Mazzini — for annexation to Sardinia-Piedmont.

The war of 1859 found Marx and Engels in a dire dilemma. In March, when war between Austria and the Sardo-French alliance seemed imminent, Marx said in an article with a Berlin dateline that the common people in Prussia sided with Italy in her conflict with Austria, but could not help supporting Austria against Napoleon III.[1]

Marx and Engels, who were hoping for the downfall of both the Habsburg dynasty and the Bonapartist régime in France, did not commit themselves to either camp. They sympathized with the Italians' struggle for unity and independence, and would have supported them against Austria, even under Victor Emmanuel, had not that struggle been vitiated, for them, by the French alliance. They considered this alliance even more obnoxious because of an understanding which apparently existed between France and Russia; the Sardinian kingdom thus seemed linked, at least indirectly, to tsarist Russia; for Marx and Engels, then as always, the epitome of oppression and counter-revolution.

Marx outlined his views in an article for the *New York Daily Tribune* in January 1859, when it still seemed possible that the Italians would fight alone, without the help of Bonapartist France. According to Marx, a 'small clique' in Italy hoped for help from the French emperor; another party, 'small but sincere', put its trust in the Sardinian king. But the 'Italian national party' would regard the launching of a war of independence 'under the auspices of France and Piedmont' as a national misfortune. They believed that Cavour's plans would not lead to genuine independence but would merely result in the Austrian yoke being replaced by a French one. The national party was convinced that the Italian people could win a national war against Austria on their own, at the right time, and within the framework of national revolution, which would be a signal to all oppressed nationalities to fight for their own emancipation. In conclusion Marx – apparently speaking in his own name – expressed the hope that a war, if it should come, would lead to a just settlement of the Italian and other questions which continued to impede progress and prosperity throughout the civilized world.[2,3]

Marx shared the opinion of the national party, one of whose leaders was Giuseppe Mazzini. He made this clearer still in 1859, when war had begun, in an article which included a textual translation of the lengthy 'manifesto' Mazzini had issued from his London exile.[4] Marx and Mazzini did not normally see eye to eye: Marx's private correspondence does not lack expressions of sarcasm and even contempt for the Italian revolutionary. Yet in this case the two men seemed in complete harmony. Marx stressed that any pronouncement by Mazzini at that juncture deserved general attention. He had performed 'an admirable deed of moral courage and patriotic dedication': his exposure of the plans hatched 'between Bonaparte, (Tsar) Alexander and Cavour, the agent of the two autocrats', should be taken very seriously.

Mazzini's manifesto tallied broadly with Marx's exposition of the opinion and the programme of the 'Italian national party'. Mazzini confessed himself unhappy about the enthusiasm most Italians had shown for the French alliance, and their acceptance of the dictatorial powers the Sardinian parliament had conferred upon King Victor Emmanuel. The French emperor, Mazzini went on to say, did not want a united Italy. Now the war had started, all republican patriots should prepare insurrections all over Italy, to 'Italianize' the war and ensure the defeat of Austria.

A few weeks later, on 25 June 1859, the radical German-language paper *Das Volk* (which appeared in London) published an article by Marx speculating about alleged Prussian plans for intervention at the side of Austria. Prussia had mobilized, and Marx asserted that the mood of the Prussian people made it likely that participation in the war would bring about a revolution, and not only within Prussia:

> The absolute necessity of revolution is universal. . . . Where and how the revolution will come is of minor importance. Come it will, and that is what matters. This time Prussia seems to be destined to give a reluctant expression to this urgent general need for revolution.... Prussia's...alliance with Austria *means revolution.* [5]

Marx does not specify the causal relationship between war and revolution. He does not predict Prussia's defeat, nor does he regard her defeat as a pre-condition for revolution. In his view it is Prussia's entry into the war which will spark off revolution – in Prussia or elsewhere: another example of the wishful thinking in which he and Engels so often indulged. During the twelve years following Marx's prophecy Prussia fought three victorious wars, two of them against a major power: only the third provoked a revolution – in vanquished France.

Since the link between war and revolution in the Marxian historical perspective is the main theme of this book, it seems apt to point out that there is an element of vagueness and inconsistency in many of the Marx-Engels pronouncements on their interaction. No comprehensive theory on this was ever formulated. Marx and Engels regarded the war against Denmark in 1848 as revolutionary because, like the American war of independence, it resulted from a revolutionary secessionist rising. The revolution which began in France in February 1848 and quickly spread to central Europe was the cause (not the effect) of the wars of 1848–9 which the peoples of Hungary and Italy waged against the Habsburg empire. In the Marx-Engels analysis, the Hungarian war, which was linked with an internal social revolution, had assumed European dimensions by 'involving' Poland, Germany and Russia; shortly a new – proletarian – revolution in France would herald France's entry into the war. Then, the prediction went on, British participation, initially on the side of counter-revolution, would lead to world war and to a successful Chartist-led revolution in Britain.[6] The Marxian vision of the constellation in this impending world war was ambiguous and self-contradictory; but Marx and Engels were consistent in voicing confidence in the ultimate triumph of revolution and progress.

A similarly involved reciprocity between war and revolution is foreshadowed in their 1859 writings, and as in 1848–9 nearly all their forecasts proved erroneous. Prussia did not enter the war, possibly because Louis Napoleon feared its intervention and concluded a hasty and lenient peace with the Austrians. And no revolutionary crisis developed in Europe outside Italy.

The two socialist friends had expected Austria's setbacks to lead to a renewal of the events at the end of the preceding decade, in Italy as well as throughout the Austrian empire. Writing in *Das Volk* in July 1859, where he could give vent to his revolutionary feelings and hopes, (he had to be cautious in the *New York Daily Tribune*), Engels referred to the fact that Emperor Francis Joseph had personally taken command of his troops at the unlucky battle of Solferino. He attributed defeat to poor generalship and concluded, 'An important result has been achieved. One of our (German) chief sovereigns has made an utter fool of himself, and his entire old Austrian régime now totters. Discontent is rife throughout Austria, and the people want the overthrow of a system marked by internal oppression and defeat in war.'[7]

Engels also hoped that the mistaken policies of other German princes would have revolutionary consequences. After the revolutionary events of 1848 the German people had acquired enough strength 'to settle accounts, not only with the French and the Russians, but also with thirty-three (German) monarchs'.[8]

Later, in 1861, Engels discussed the possibility of an early European war, with Austria and Prussia opposed by France, Italy and, possibly, Denmark. Whatever happened in that war, Engels concluded, there would be revolution – in France if Napoleon III were beaten, in Prussia and Austria if those monarchies suffered defeat.[9] Here and on other occasions Engels, and Marx, underestimated the resilience of legitimate, hereditary monarchies. The downfall of a king or emperor who had usurped a throne and lost a war has always been normal; this is also the usual fate of a usurping uncrowned dictator. But a great many legitimate sovereigns, throughout history, have lost wars and kept their crowns; it would appear that the first Bonaparte emperor showed greater insight than Marx and Engels when he told Metternich in 1813 (according to Metternich's memoirs), 'Your monarchs who are born in the purple can be defeated twenty times over yet return to their capitals; I, the son of fortune, cannot do that. My rule will end on the day on which I shall have ceased to be strong and to inspire fear.'

During the 1859 war and its aftermath a change of emphasis can be discerned in the way Marx and Engels viewed the problems connected with the conflict. This change is reflected in two anonymous pamphlets by Engels. The first was entitled *Po and Rhine*, and it was written early in 1859, before the Italian war had begun. Engels restated, in essence, the position he and Marx had taken in 1848−9 about Italy's right to unity and independence. The stress was on the military aspects of Austria's domination of northern Italy. Engels rejected a view canvassed by influential press organs in Austria and other parts of Germany, that the possession of Lombardy was a strategic necessity for Germany as a whole. Speaking as a German to his German compatriots, he explained that the possession of those Italian provinces by a German monarchy was, on balance, more harmful than beneficial, and was anyway doomed to early evanescence. Austrian rule in Italy was the rule of violence and terror.[10]

The German people should ask themselves whether the limited military advantages of retaining parts of Italy were not outweighed by the political drawbacks. Engels formulated the issue in strangely un-Marxist terms, admitting the national interest as the only criterion:

Does the possession of Lombardy outweight the hatred, the

fanatical hostility it has earned us throughout Italy? Does it outweigh the fact that we all now share the guilt for the measures by which Austria secures her rule in Italy — in the name and in the interests of all of Germany, as we are told?...So long as we hold on to Lombardy, Italy will definitely be an ally of France in any French war against Germany. Once we leave Lombardy this will no longer be the case. But is it in our interest to retain these four (Lombardian) fortresses, and thereby assure for ourselves the fanatical emnity, and for the French the alliance, of twenty-five million Italians?[11]

Besides, if strategic considerations could form a basis for claims to foreign territory, then the French could, with equal or greater justice, lay claim to the German-populated left bank of the Rhine. As a defensive frontier the Rhine would be more important for France than the Mincio and the Po for Germany. And just as the Germans would not contemplate the cession to France of German territory west of the Rhine, they could not expect the Italian people to tolerate foreign rule in an Italian-populated part of their country.

Po and Rhine as a pamphlet is devoid of socialist or even radical-democratic ideology, so much so that the author was widely believed to be a German general. Moderation is counselled in the power-political interest of a future united Germany[12].

Engels's second anonymous pamphlet, headed *Savoy, Nice and the Rhine*, discusses similar military-political problems from a different angle. Written in February, it was published in April 1860. Armed conflict with tsarist Russia was one of its main themes. In *Po and Rhine* Engels had treated Austria as the chief villain. In the second pamphlet the Germans are called upon to defend their own against the aggressive designs of Bonapartist France and tsarist Russia. A united, independent Italy was still in Germany's interests, but, according to Engels, this was not what Louis Napoleon and his ally Cavour wanted. The kingdom of Sardinia-Piedmont was now on the wrong side of the front line. In 1848—9 Marx and Engels had hoped for the success of the Piedmontese armies, while denouncing the king as a traitor. In 1860, Piedmont was a potential ally not only of France but of Russia — and everything was changed.

Savoy, Nice and the Rhine, like its predecessor, lacks ideological content. German policy was to be dictated by national interest, not by the requirements of progress and radical democracy. The essay begins

41

by ominously bracketing France, Piedmont and Russia, and by asserting that Germany, not Italy, was now the real issue:

It is now a year since the Bonapartist-Piedmontese-Russian plot went into action...The initial instinctive reaction throughout Germany was that it was no longer Italy but our own destiny that was at stake...The ultimate aim of all Bonapartist wars must be the reconquest of France's 'natural frontier' − the Rhine. [13]

After explaining how, in military terms, the possession of Nice and Savoy was paving the way for France to obtain the Rhine frontier, the pamphlet lists Germany's age-old grievances against Russia and calls for their redress. Engels's language is strangely nationalistic. He recalls that in 1807, in order to reach agreement with Napoleon, Russia had betrayed her ally Prussia and annexed Prussian territory. In 1814 she had annexed parts of the Austrian and Prussian provinces of Poland, 'and she thereby assumed an offensive position which will continue to threaten us until we have driven her from this position.' The German people are exhorted to take a firm stand against the Russo-French deal which would assure France of the Rhine frontier and Russia of a free hand in the East.

How much longer are we to stand for the game they are playing with us? Should we forty-five million (Germans) tolerate that one of our richest, most beautiful and industrially advanced provinces is constantly being used as a decoy by Russia, to lure the praetorian régime in France? Is it the Rhineland's only destiny to be a theatre of war, so that Russia may have a free hand on the Danube and the Vistula?

That is the question. We hope Germany will soon answer it, sword in hand. Let us stick together, and we'll send them all packing, the French praetorians and the Russian cabbage-eaters. [14]

Yet Russia too was due for revolution in Engels's opinion. Incompatibility of the existing social structure with industrial and agricultural development was bound to produce confict between the ruling class and the peasant-serfs. That structure would fall, and with it Russia's traditional foreign policy. But the change would inevitably be a violent one: 'It would seem that it will be Germany's task to drive these facts home to the Russians − not only with the pen but with the sword. If and when *that* happens it will be a rehabilitation for Germany, compensating for centuries of political humiliation.' [15]

What Engels felt was that the revolution Russia needed, which would change her foreign policy, would be the result of war with Germany. Something of the kind did occur over half a century later, in entirely different circumstances.

While condemning the foreign policies of the Turin government, Marx and Engels welcomed the progress of the anti-Bourbon and anti-Austrian revolution in 1860, and praised the achievement of Garibaldi and his volunteer army. There is no reaction on record from either to the proclamation of Victor Emmanuel II as king of Italy in March 1861. Their contributions to the New York paper were in abeyance between February and October of that year, frustration that an event had come to pass so contrary to their expectations and hopes might account for their failure to seek other avenues of written expression.

The leading spirits of the socialist movement in the nineteenth century were no more united in their interpretation of events than their heirs in our own time. Marx and Engels had minor differences of opinion but usually agreed after discussion. Other socialists, British and continental, often disagreed vehemently with the two founding fathers.

The German socialist leader Ferdinand Lassalle, for example, saw the 1859 Italian war in a completely different light. After the outbreak of war he expounded his views in a pamphlet entitled *The Italian War and the Tasks of Prussia*. Lassalle gave unstinted support to the Italian cause, and was not at all put off by the alliance with Bonapartist France: 'Italy is waging the most just, the most sacred war any nation could wage: she is fighting for her national independence and existence against Austria's coercive rule.'[16] Like Marx and Engels, Lassalle disliked Napoleon III and his régime, but unlike Marx and Engels — and Mazzini — he did not feel that the Italians should have rejected French assistance and fought Austria alone. France's help, he argued, was just as legitimate for the Italians as it had been for the German people, to regain national independence in 1813 with the help of tsarist Russia.

Lassalle's purpose in writing the pamphlet was largely to counter the anti-French propaganda of part of the Prussian press which favoured alliance with Austria and war against France. He reasoned against this course of action in similar vein to Engels's *Po and Rhine*. Lassalle wrote:

Should we, for Austria's sake, draw upon ourselves the deathly hatred of the French nation – and of twenty-five million Italians? Should we not now at last cease to play the part Germany played throughout the Middle Ages – to oppress other nations and thereby to forfeit the ability to establish freedom here, in our own country? [17]

While opposing the Prussian press clamour for war against France, Lassalle did not urge Prussia to join the French-Piedmontese alliance against Austria. Prussia had declared her neutrality and 'this is almost the first time we agree with a move made by a Prussian government.' He added that Prussia should also ensure that none of the smaller German states, where sympathies with Austria were strong, would succour the Habsburg war effort. Yet he did not want Prussia to remain militarily inactive. He argued for renewing the war with Denmark and wresting Schleswig-Holstein from foreign domination. The Prussian government ought to proclaim: 'If Napoleon revises the map of Europe in the south, in accordance with the nationality principle, well, then we shall do the same in the north. If Napoleon liberates Italy, well, then we shall take Schleswig-Holstein.' [18]

It is a matter for speculation whether Lassalle's bellicose outlook exerted any influence on Bismarck who, some seven years and two victorious wars later, annexed Schleswig-Holstein to Prussia. We do know that after Bismarck had become Prussian prime minister in 1862 he had several secret meetings with Lassalle, and the two also exchanged letters. When the crisis over Schleswig-Holstein broke in 1864, Lassalle supported Bismarck's line in favouring not only war with Denmark but Prussia's annexation of the duchies, rather than setting up a new German state of Schleswig-Holstein under Prince Frederick of Augustenburg, who claimed to be the rightful heir.

Lassalle's pamphlet understandably found no favour with Marx and Engels. In a latter to Engels on 18 May 1859, Marx described it as an 'enormous blunder'. [19] He made no mention on this occasion of Lassalle's advocacy of war against Denmark or of the attempt to justify the French-Italian alliance; his criticism was that Lassalle had failed to react to the anti-French press campaign by emphasizing that the antagonism between Germany and Russia was more important than the German-French antagonism.

The German-Russian antagonism and the possibility of military confrontation figures in another passage of the same letter, which throws an interesting light on Marx's view of the interaction of war and revolution. He speaks of certain 'vulgar democrats' who honestly believed that Austria's defeat in the war against France and Piedmont, together with revolutions in Hungary and Austrian Poland, would lead to revolution in Germany. Marx makes it clear that he is not hoping for a German revolution at that stage: 'These blockheads forget that *now* a revolution in Germany, that is, the disorganization of her armies, would benefit not the revolutionaries but Russia and Boustrapa.'[20]

Read in conjunction with Engels's *Savoy, Nice and the Rhine*, where he mentioned the prospect of revolutionary developments in Russia and, in that context, Germany's task to explain the facts to Russia 'with the sword',[21] the Marxist position in 1859–60 could be defined as follows: Marx and Engels thought that the states of the German Confederation, and especially Prussia, should, in the German national interest, take a firm line against Russia's aggressive policies reflected in the expansionist plot with France; they considered war between Germany and Russia to be likely and desirable; they hoped for a German victory in that war, facilitated by, and promoting, revolutionary events in Russia; they believed that the movement within Russia for the emancipation of the serfs would cause a revolutionary change in Russia's social structure and in her foreign policy, which would then cease to be aggressive.

From the German angle, there is not a trace of revolutionary defeatism in this attitude. The 1859 position of Marx and Engels regarding the desirability of a German revolution is unclear and possibly inconsistent; but they did not anticipate revolutionary events in Prussia, Austria or any other German state as a result of military defeats at the hands of tsarist Russia. They wanted Germany to be strong enough to defeat the Russians on the battlefield.

6 Conflicts in the Western Hemisphere in the 1860s

The American Civil War 1861–5

Civil War broke out in the United States of America in 1861, after the secession from the Union of most of the southern slave states, and ended in 1865 with the victory of the North, followed by the re-integration of the rebel states in the Union and the abolition of slavery throughout the USA.

Marx and Engels were not ambivalent about the Civil War: no 'other side', no intermixture of rights and wrongs. They were both emphatically and unreservedly for the North, though frequently critical of the political actions and strategy of the Union's leaders. The North, they believed, stood for free labour against southern defence of negro slavery. This was by no means the general or even the prevalent view in Britain at the time. Leading newspapers and politicians, including a number of prominent Liberals, refused to regard the conflict as a clash betwen northern progress and southern reaction. Sympathies for the South were largely due to economic considerations like the dependence of the Lancashire cotton industry on imports of raw materials from the southern plantations. Yet even now liberal historical opinion is not unanimous in holding the North to have been the champion of progress and humanity, and the southern 'Confederacy' the unmitigated upholder of evil. For example, a generally pro-Marxist publication of a selection of articles by Marx and Engels on the Civil War had this to say, in an editorial introduction, about Marx's contributions (mainly for the Viennese paper *Die Presse*) on the Civil War:

> Nevertheless, matters were not as simple as Marx portrayed them. From today's perspective it is impossible to ignore both the popular character of the resistance of the southern smallholders and the imperialist dimension of the war aims of the North, of which the devastation and exploitation of the Southern territories were an inevitable by-product.... The populist rhetoric of American capitalism veiled a reality which was predatory and imperialist even in the 1860s, and the war against the South was undoubtedly part of its imperialist expansion. [1]

Marx tried to answer similar arguments by contemporary critics of the Union's policies. In an article published in *Die Presse* on 25 October 1861, he dismissed the thesis of *The Times* and other British papers that the war was primarily a tariff war between northern protectionism and southern free trade, and that Britain must naturally side with the champions of free trade. Marx pointed out that the protectionist tariff had been passed by the US Congress after, and because of, the outbreak of the rebellion. He also tried to demonstrate that the war had been started by the South, and that the North was on the defensive. For several months running, the secessionists had seized forts, arsenals, shipyards and other federal assets, had taken northern troops prisoner and insulted the Union flag, without provoking a military reaction from the North. But the bombardment of Fort Sumter on 11 April, 'a blatant act of war', had compelled President Lincoln to issue the proclamation for the protection of the Union, and thus to 'answer war with war'.[2]

Marx recapitulated the pre-history of the conflict in an attempt to refute the view of some pro-southerners that slavery was not the real issue. He argued that it was the policy of the slave-holders, whose number did not exceed 300,000 but who virtually ruled the South, not merely to perpetuate slavery in their part of the USA but to extend it to new territories. A factor precipitating the conflict was the growth of the Republican Party in the years preceding the election (in 1860) of Abraham Lincoln as president. The Republicans were committed to territorial limitation of slavery and opposed to aggressive foreign policies. The pro-slavery politicians realized that further increases in slave territory were not possible within the framework of the Union, especially as the population of the anti-slavery north-west (at that time Wisconsin, Michigan, Minnesota, Iowa) was growing faster than the white population of the slave states. This decided the South to force an immediate showdown after Lincoln's election. As Marx put it:

> From the southern point of view the Union remained valuable only inasmuch as it provided the South with federal power for implementing its slave policy. When this was no longer the case it seemed better to break right away rather than to watch the progress of the Republican Party and the upsurge of the north-west for another four years and then to begin the struggle under less favourable conditions. This is why the slave-holders' party decided to play for the whole stake.[3]

The alleged wish of the secessionists to spread slavery figured in a further article by Marx, in which he dealt with the advice many British and some American opponents of slavery had given the federal government: to accept secession and let the South go, thereby purging itself of complicity in the vile institution of slavery. This advice, Marx said, ignored the fact that the South was fighting not only for its independence but for conquests. It wanted to repossess the border states — Kentucky, Missouri, Maryland and Delaware — which had retained slavery side by side with free labour, but had remained within the Union. The South's attempt to annex Missouri and Kentucky showed that, while it insisted on the right of the individual state to leave the Union, it would not acknowledge a state's right to remain within the Union. Moreover, the Confederacy laid claim to large areas beyond the border states, and if the North abandoned the contested area it 'would surrender more than three-quarters of the United States to the slave republic'.[4] If Missouri, Kansas, New Mexico, Arkansas and Texas went to the South, California would have to follow. Southern possession of the mouth of the Mississippi would force the great agricultural states of the north and north-west to join the South for economic reasons. Marx went on:

> The Union would thus not actually be dissolved, but rather *reorganized...on the basis of slavery*, under the acknowledged control of the slave-holding oligarchy....The slave system would thus contaminate the whole Union. In the northern states, where negro slavery is not practicable, the white working class would be gradually reduced to the level of helotry....The present struggle between South and North is...nothing but a struggle between two social systems, the system of slavery and the system of free labour. These two systems can no longer peacefully co-exist on the North American continent: this is why the struggle has broken out. It can only end in the victory of one system or the other.[5]

Emphatic partisanship for the northern cause did not make Marx and Engels uncritical *vis-à-vis* the policy of the northern leaders or the way they waged their campaigns. Marx attacked the concessions which Lincoln and his government felt constrained to make to the 'loyal' slave-holders in Kentucky and other border states. Anxiety to retain the allegiance of these doubtful allies, and undue respect for their sensibilities, had 'afflicted the Union government with incurable weakness,...forced it to conceal the real issue in the war and prevented it from attacking the enemy's most vulnerable spot – the root of the evil, *slavery itself*.'[6] Yet Marx felt sure that developments would compel the North to take the decisive step and proclaim *the emancipation of the slaves*.

On 30 August 1861 General Frémont, the 1856 Republican Party's candidate for the presidency and now commander of the Union forces in Missouri, proclaimed the confiscation of the property of all persons in the state of Missouri who had taken arms against the Union, and the emancipation of their slaves. In his limited sphere he had done what Marx and Engels thought desirable on a national scale from the outset. President Lincoln endorsed the confiscation of property but ordered Frémont to revoke the freeing of the slaves. When Frémont refused, he was removed from his post as commander of the Missouri army.

For Marx and Engels the attitudes of the president and his administration highlighted the timidity and vacillation of the northern leaders on the slavery question. Marx claimed that Lincoln's pusillanimous decision to annul the emancipation had been taken 'in deference to the noisy protests of the "loyal" slaveholders of Kentucky'.[7] Whether this interpretation of the Frémont-Missouri episode is correct, or not, the northern leadership did exercise extreme caution on the question of slavery and emancipation in the initial phase, and adopted bolder methods only when the tide had turned and victory was a less distant propect. The transition from the 'constitutional' to the 'revolutionary' stage of the Civil War – in Marx's phrase – came in September 1862 when Lincoln proclaimed the emancipation of the negro slaves in the rebel states. Clearly Lincoln approached the inter-relation of civil war and abolition from pragmatic considerations which were, in a way, opposite to those formulated by the two socialists. Marx and Engels believed that an early proclamation on emancipation and the integration of negro soldiers in the Union forces would hasten a northern victory. Lincoln took the view that substantial military successes would have to be scored before he could afford to take any irrevocable steps towards abolition.

A serious incident in the first year of the conflict brought Britain, where Marx and Engels lived, to the brink of war with the North, and might have made her the ally of the southern Confederacy.

On 8 November 1861 the US frigate *San Jacinto* stopped and searched the British steamer *Trent* in the Atlantic and arrested four of her passengers: James M. Mason and John Slidell, the Confederacy's commissioners to Britain and France respectively, then en route to England, and their two secretaries. Both France and the United Kingdom had recognized the Confederates as belligerents without recognizing the southern government and establishing diplomatic relations. The two commissioners were taken to Boston in the US warship and treated as prisoners-of-war. The feat of the *San Jacinto* and her commander, Captain Charles Wilkes, was hailed as a great triumph in the northern states. In Britain the action provoked an out-cry and bellicose comments in most daily papers; Lord Palmerston's government demanded reparation and despatched troops to Canada, but eventually counsels of moderation prevailed on both sides. The United States government officially disavowed Captain Wilkes's action, and the two commissioners were released and allowed to proceed to England.

In his articles in the Austrian paper dealing with the *Trent* affair Marx showed less impassioned partisanship than in most of his writings about the Civil War. He suspected Palmerston of seeking a pretext for war, but felt that the incident was unlikely to provoke it. According to Marx's interpretation of international law, the American ship was entitled to stop and search the British steamer but had infringed procedural rules by seizing the southern envoys. He also pointed out that, quite apart from the legal aspects, the arrest of these men had been pointless since Confederate representatives were already established in London.

Marx dealt with the possibility of war between Britain and the northern states in several articles for the *New York Daily Tribune* in December 1861. For obvious reasons the paper could not be an outlet for what Marx had to say from London about the progress and pros-pects of the war in the United States. But it did publish contributions dealing with the state of British public opinion regarding events connec-ted with the war, such as the *Trent* affair and its possible repercussions.

'The friends of the United States on this side of the Atlantic,' Marx said, 'anxiously hope that conciliatory steps will be taken by the Federal government.'[8] War between the USA and the United Kingdom was what the southern 'slavocracy' and its northern tools had wanted from the beginning. Britain possessed 'overwhelming maritime power' in the Western hemisphere. If war should come, her first moves would be diplomatic recognition of the Confederacy and action to terminate the blockade of the Confederate ports. The people of the USA should therefore 'be...ready to turn the tide of popular opinion in England by openly avowing, and carefully making up for, an international blunder the vindication of which might realize the boldest hopes of the rebels'.[9]

In beating a retreat after the *Trent* incident the United States took what Marx considered the right action. He was jubilant at the peaceful settlement of the incident, and claimed that his feelings were shared by the majority of people in Britain:

Events proved Marx right and 'General' Engels mistaken in his 'expert' predictions of the military outcome. In September 1862 the Confederacy's attempt to conquer Maryland, one of the 'border states', ended in failure; and the decisive northern victory at Antietam Creek was the signal for Lincoln to do what Marx and Engels had urged the North to do from the start. The Presidential Proclamation of 22 September declared that all slaves would be free from 1 January 1863 in all states still in rebellion.

In an article published in *Die Presse* on 12 October Marx called the proclamation 'the most important document of American history since the foundation of the Union'.[14] And to some extent he revised his opinion of Lincoln. He still referred to him as an average man, devoid of intellectual brilliance and greatness of character. Marx found his style without idealistic spirit or fervour, and 'he always does the most significant things in the most insignificant manner.' Lincoln's most decisive declarations were couched in pedestrian terms and read like lawyers' briefs.[15] His policies were inconsistent, his actions often objectionable or ridiculous. 'Yet in the history of the USA and of mankind he will have his place next to Washington.' Herein, Marx added, lay the greatness of the political and social organization of the New World, that it enabled average people to carry out actions which in the Old World only heroes could perform.

Engels was less enthusiastic. He agreed that the failure of the Maryland campaign was a severe blow the Confederacy; but he attached overriding importance neither to this event nor to Lincoln's proclamation. In a letter to Marx of 5 November 1862, he maintained that a truly revolutionary spirit was still absent in the North; he was far from impressed by the performance of its people: all they had achieved after eighteen months of war was 'the discovery that all their generals are asses and all their civil servants scoundrels and traitors.'[16]

After Lincoln's re-election in November 1863 Marx drafted a panegyrical address of congratulation, on behalf of the General Council of the International Workingmen's Association (the First International). It read in part:

We congratulate the American people upon your re-election by a large majority. If resistance to the Slave Power was the reserved watchword of your first election, the triumphant warcry of your re-election is, Death to Slavery.

From the commencement of the titanic American strife the working men of Europe felt instinctively that the star-spangled banner carried the destiny of their class.... While the workingmen, the true political power of the north, allowed slavery to defile their own republic, ... they were unable to attain the true freedom of labour or to support their European brethren in their struggle for emancipation; but this barrier to progress has been swept off by the red sea of civil war.

The workingmen of Europe feel sure that as the American War of Independence initiated a new era of ascendancy for the middle class, so the American anti-slavery war will do for the working classes. They consider it an earnest of the epoch to come, that it fell to the lot of Abraham Lincoln, the single-minded son of the working class,[17] to lead his country through the matchless struggle for the rescue of an enchained race and the reconstruction of a social world.[18]

This eulogy contrasts oddly with the contemptuous sarcasm which marked most of Marx's previous references to the American president. Odder still are some 'un-Marxist' statements about the American workers being 'the true political power of the North', and about the 'anti-slavery war' having initiated a new era of ascendancy for the working classes. As Marx well knew, the northern industrial bourgeoisie fought the war because it was materially interested in the preservation of the Union and the replacement of slavery by free, mobile labour. Yet he seems to consider the northern capitalists' victory as the beginning of proletarian revolution in the United States: a thesis he never spelt out elsewhere in letters or articles.

Marx was also author of the message of condolence which the General Council of the International addressed to President Andrew Johnson in May 1865, after Lincoln's assassination. It was even more effusive in praise of Lincoln than the congratulatory message of November 1864. The murdered president was now described as

a man neither to be browbeaten by adversity nor intoxicated by success, inflexibly pressing on to his great goal, never compromising it by blind haste, slowly maturing his steps, never retracing them, carried away by no surge of popular favour, disheartened by no slackening of the popular pulse, ... in one word, one of the rare men who succeed in becoming great without ceasing to be good. Such indeed was the modesty of this great and good man that the world only discovered him a hero after he had fallen a martyr.[19]

Marx may mentally have included himself among those making the belated discovery.

Surprisingly, the General Council's message also contained some flattering remarks about W.H. Seward, the secretary of state, who had been wounded in another terrorist attack. In 1861 Marx had called him a conciliator and appeaser of the South; by 1865 Seward had become a man of sagacity who, it was hoped, would soon be restored 'to health, public activity, and well-deserved honours'. As for the new president, the message exhorts Andrew Johnson 'to uproot by the law what has been felled by the sword' – enactment of abolition – and concludes, 'A profound sense of your great mission will save you from any compromise with stern duties. You will never forget that to initiate the new era of the emancipation of labour, the American people devolved the responsibilities of leadership upon two men of labour – the one Abraham Lincoln, the other Andrew Johnson.' But this second 'man of labour' did not enjoy the sympathies of the two socialists much longer. Within months they found that he had not shunned 'compromise with stern duties'; they accused him of 'hatred for negroes' and of making weak-kneed concessions to former slave-holders and secessionists.[20]

The actual and potential interaction of war and revolution played a major part in the comments of Marx and Engels on the American Civil War, in which social revolution or at least fundamental change in social organization was a paramount issue.

Again and again they stressed that the progressive side should ensure victory by employing 'revolutionary' methods. This led Engels to formulate a concept which could be called 'defeatist' although it had no affinity with the Leninist variety of revolutionary defeatism. Engels believed that temporary setbacks and lost battles which did not spell ultimate defeat and collapse could have a beneficial effect in rousing the government and the masses to fight an all-out revolutionary war, as the French did in 1792–3. Engels had invoked the French Revolution on previous occasions, and especially in 1849, when the Piedmontese forces were beaten by the Austrians and the Italian revolution faced defeat. In the French revolutionary war the methods embodying the slogan of 'the Fatherland in Danger' had the dual effect of propelling the Revolution towards its climax and of bringing victory in battle; similar policies would produce similar desirable results in all wars of that kind.

The American Civil War did not follow that pattern. Transition from what Marx called the 'constitutional' to the 'revolutionary' phase was the result not of reverses but of successes which had averted the danger of an early defeat. And the US government's cautious (or, according to Engels, 'cowardly') approach did not lead to a northern defeat or a 'rotten peace', as Engels had feared and predicted. The Civil War ended in overwhelming victory for the North, followed by the disintegration of the Confederacy and the full restoration of the Union; within a few months a constitutional amendment abolished slavery on the whole territory of the United States.

It is a moot point whether, if Lincoln had adopted from the outset the radical revolutionary methods advocated by Marx and Engels, the North would have won the war earlier; its victory could not have been more complete. Indeed, we cannot be sure that Lincoln was wrong when he refused to antagonize the people of the other border states by radical policies – such as Frémont's Missouri proclamation – because he felt that their defection to the Confederacy might have resulted in a southern victory. It would seem that Marx (though apparently not Engels) came to realize in retrospect that Lincoln's opportunist step-by-step tactics had been right. This is suggested by the passage in the General Council's message to Andrew Johnson in which Marx lauds the dead president for 'inflexibly pressing on to his great goal, *never compromising it by blind haste, slowly maturing his steps*, never retracing them...' That reads very much like a repudiation of the impatient criticisms which Marx, and to a greater degree Engels, had levelled at Lincoln and his government during the early stages of the Civil War. It is obvious that in the course of those four years Marx had gradually but thoroughly revised his judgement of Lincoln's character and his stature as a leader and statesman.

A nuance of unacknowledged disagreement between the two friends is noticeable in the statements quoted in this chapter. While Engels's criticisms of the northern government were harsh to the point of implying at times that they did not deserve to win or to enjoy the sympathies of progressive opinion, Marx never wavered in his commitment and passionate hope for the triumph of the Union's cause.

War in Mexico 1861–7

The outbreak of the American Civil War coincided with an acute crisis in neighbouring Mexico, where prolonged civil commotion had produced near-anarchy and economic chaos. The country was heavily indebted — not for the last time in its history — to foreign financial institutions. When the Mexican government suspended the payment of interests on its foreign debts in July 1861, the three main creditor countries, France, Britain and Spain, agreed on joint intervention.

Troops of the three powers landed in Mexico; but in April 1862 Britain and Spain withdrew. The French remained, and in June 1864, when nearly the whole country was under their control, including the capital, they installed an Austrian archduke as a puppet emperor. But after the American Civil War pressure exerted by the government in Washington induced the French to evacuate Mexico in 1867. The Mexican republicans under the liberal President Juarez reconquered the country, and the 'emperor' was captured and executed after a summary trial.

Marx wrote two articles on 'The Intervention in Mexico' in November 1861, before European troops had actually landed; one was published in the Viennese paper *Die Presse,* [21] the other in the *New York Daily Tribune.* [22] In 1862 co-operation with both journals ceased, and no comments by Marx or Engels exist on subsequent developments.

In both articles Marx strongly condemned the intended invasion which he claimed no one in Britain wanted, except perhaps the bankers to whom the Mexican government owed money. The real reason for the intervention was that the interventionist powers wanted to take advantage of the Civil War to torpedo the Monroe Doctrine, which made impermissible European interference in an American state recognized by Washington. The American Civil War, Marx went on, had created 'an opportunity for European monarchs to secure an intervention precedent on which they could build later'. This was their ultimate objective; the immediate and intended result of the intervention would be a return to anarchy in Mexico, which had been subsiding due to the military successes and the policies of President Juarez. [23] The two articles make it clear that Marx's sympathies were entirely with the Juarez government.

The war that followed the intervention was, of course, a kind of colonial war, similar to the fighting in India which began with the

Mutiny. Yet while Marx conceded that British rule in India had some unintended beneficial and progressive effects, he discerned no redeeming features in the European intervention in Mexico, which he denounced as 'one of the most monstrous ventures in the annals of international history'.[24]

Disturbances in Jamaica 1865

An insurrection of sorts in the British crown colony of Jamaica in 1865 provoked few comments from Marx and Engels who, as we noted, had lost their regular outlets for journalistic activity in 1862. They referred to the Jamaican events in their correspondence, without attempting to analyse them.

Slavery had been abolished in Jamaica – and throughout the British Empire – in 1833, but many white planters continued to exploit negroes ruthlessly. In October 1865 discontent led to rioting in the small town of Morant Bay, and spread out from there, but disturbances ceased when British troops arrived, and the soldiers did not have to fight. The rebellion, such as it was, was over within days, but the British authorities, from Governor Edward John Eyre down, exacted a bloody revenge. Negroes were flogged, some hanged, and many had their houses burned down. A Royal Commission later found that 439 persons had been put to death, mostly without any justification; over 600, including many women, had been flogged, and about 6000 houses had been wantonly burned.

Reports of the repression caused an outcry among liberal opinion in Britain. A 'Jamaica Committee' was formed to ensure that those responsible were brought to justice: J.S. Mill, Thomas Huxley, John Bright, Herbert Spencer and Frederic Harrison played leading parts in the campaign. Governor Eyre was dismissed, but there were no prosecutions or judicial punishments.

As might have been expected, Marx and Engels sided with the protesters. 'What do you say to the nigger insurrection in Jamaica and the brutalities of the English?' Engels asked on 17 November 1865.[25] Marx replied that the affair was typical of the 'vile beastliness' of the so-called 'true Englishman'. He quoted a *Times* remark that the Jamaican rebels had 'enjoyed all the liberties of an Anglo-Saxon Constitution' and commented: 'Indeed, they enjoyed the liberty of being taxed almost to death, so as to enable the planters to import coolies and thereby to repress the local labour market to below subsistence level.' English hypocrisy was unmasked by what was happening in Ireland, and by the 'Jamaican butcheries'.[26] A few days later Engels returned to the subject, expressing disgust at the boasts of British officers about 'their heroic exploits against unarmed niggers'.[27]

Marx and Engels used harsh words, but their strictures were akin to those of non-socialist radicals. Marx and Engels supported the cause of the oppressed in nearly all instances of foreign domination. They stood for the freedom of the Irish, the Poles, the Hungarians and the Italians, but they did not call for a British withdrawal from India at the time of the Mutiny, not did they consider the possibility of a transfer of power to the negro majority in backward Jamaica or voice hopes for the success of the rebellion.

7 Rising in Poland 1863

On 23 January 1863 a revolt broke out in the 'Kingdom of Poland' – that part of Poland, which under the decisions of the 1815 Vienna Congress was in union with Russia, with the tsar as king of Poland; to all intents it was a Russian province, and independence was the aim of the revolt.

Russian repression was harsh: the imposition of Russian as an official language, and harassment of the Roman Catholic church, to which the great majority of Poles have always belonged, were two of its aspects. The revolt achieved some initial success but lost its momentum after a few months, and by June the Russian army had quelled the rising, although in some parts of the country resistance continued into 1864.

Marx and Engels had always abominated Russian tsarism and eulogized Poland as a progressive and potentially revolutionary nation; small wonder that they greeted news of the insurrection with enthusiasm.

Marx's first reaction, in a letter to Engels of 13 February 1863, was to express certainty that a new era of revolution had opened in Europe: he hoped that 'the lava will this time flow from East to West and not the other way round'.[1] Engels was again over-optimistic: 'The Poles are magnificent fellows,' he wrote on 17 February.[2] Marx felt sure that revolutionary upheavals within Russia might be an early consequence. The abolition of serfdom, decreed in 1861, was to come into effect on 15 March 1863. Russian revolutionary circles believed that the peasants were bitterly disappointed at certain details of the reform, and that risings were likely. Engels apparently shared this belief; if the Polish rising was still going strong on 15 March, 'the balloon will go up in Russia'. He added that he had not been sanguine: 'At first I had an infernal fear that the whole thing would be a fiasco. But now there almost seems to be a greater chance of victory than of defeat.' Once again his and Marx's forecasts were proved wrong.

Marx also expressed the view (and Engels did not dispute it) that the revolution would spread to Prussia. Under a 'convention' signed with Russia, the Prussian government, already headed by Bismarck, was helping the tsarist authorities to suppress the Polish rising; this included the extradition of insurgents who had crossed the Prussian border. 'The Prussians, as usual, are behaving dastardly,' Engels wrote. 'Monsieur Bismarck knows that he is in for the high jump if Poland and Russia are revolutionized.'[3] But on 18 February the Prussian Diet, whose Liberal majority had been at loggerheads with Bismarck's administration, denounced the convention and called upon the government to observe neutrality *vis-à-vis* the Polish revolt. Marx again indulged his over-sanguine hopes: 'I just read in *The Times* that the Prussian 2nd Chamber has at last done a good thing. We shall soon have a revolution.'[4]

This correspondence expressed, in emotional rather than analytical terms, the pro-Polish sympathies of the two men and their hatred of tsarist oppression. A theoretical interpretation of the Polish issue – primarily from the German angle – is given in a resolution drafted by Marx and adopted by the German Workers' Educational Association in London in October 1863.[5] It calls upon members and sympathizers to donate money for Polish revolutionaries and asserts that 'without an independent Poland there can be no independent and united Germany, no emancipation of Germany from Russian supremacy.'[5]

This theory was refuted seven years later, when, under Bismarck's leadership, Germany became a united empire, free from Russian hegemony if indeed such hegemony had ever existed. Poland remained part of the tsar's possessions for more than half a century.

In defining the inter-relationship of the Polish and German issues, Marx did not call for war with Russia, as on previous occasions. An oblique suggestion about war as a solution came from Engels in December 1863, when after the death of King Frederick VII of Denmark the Schleswig-Holstein question had again become topical on the world political agenda. Engels wrote that 'the only chance' for Germany to liberate the two duchies was 'to start a war against Russia for the benefit of Poland'.[6] What Engels seemed to have in mind was that a Prussian and/or Austrian attack could prevent Russia from backing Denmark's claim to Schleswig and Holstein.[7]

Engels reiterated this demand for war with Russia on Poland's behalf a few years later, more directly and in a European rather than a specifically German context. In 1866, Polish independence came up in the debates of the Central Council of the International Working-men's Association. At the behest of Marx, a member of the Central Council, Engels wrote several letters to *The Commonwealth*, organ of the International, in which he emphasized that the workers of Central and Western Europe wanted war with Russia to restore an independent Poland.[8]

Marx and Engels ardently hoped for the success of the Polish revolt. They felt that Russia's defeat would open the floodgates to revolution all over Europe.

The idea of supporting the Polish rising by war against Russia was put forward by another German socialist, Ferdinand Lassalle, who had played a prominent part in the foundation of the first German socialist working-class party, the 'General Association of German Workers' *(Allgemeiner Deutscher Arbeiterverein)* early in 1863. Lassalle drafted a resolution for this organization on the Polish rising. It paid tribute to the Polish revolutionaries, whose heroic action was said to have special significance for Germany, because it could promote German national unity by being the issue of a German-Russian conflict.

> The restoration of an independent Poland under the aegis of Germany would be the most glorious and the most legitimate task facing Germany. A war to this end is in Germany's direct interests; it would be the only possible atonement, on Germany's part, for her share in the injustice of Poland's partition. At the same time Germany would rid herself of the pressure to which she is being subjected both from the East and from the West.[9]

This restored Poland would not, however, include all the Polish territory belonging to Prussia. The draft resolution stressed that, unlike Russia, Germany had made a large proportion of her Polish conquests part of the German ethnic and cultural sphere.[10]

Lassalle's German patriotism was perhaps one reason why he disliked the idea of handing back all of Prussian Poland. Another and perhaps weightier reason probably originated in his secret understanding with Bismarck, who had become Prussian prime minister in 1862. By the time of the draft resolution, Lassalle had been in contact with Bismarck for some months, and it seems that there was a secret pact for Lassalle's support of Bismarck's annexation of Schleswig-Holstein in return for Bismarck's introducing universal suffrage and making other concessions to the workers.[11] Such an agreement would have precluded any advocacy of major territorial concessions by Prussia.

Reluctance to antagonize Bismarck may also account for the omission from Lassalle's resolution of condemnation of Bismarck's help for the tsar in crushing the Polish rising – a policy fiercely denounced by Marx and Engels. Had Lassalle been alive in 1866 he would not have wanted the defeat of the Prussian government, as Engels did, in the belief that defeat would spark off revolution in Prussia. He would have supported Bismarck in the Austrian war, and might even have backed his entire policy of unifying Germany under Prussian hegemony.

8 The Wars of German Unification 1864–71

Austria and Prussia against Denmark 1864

Attempts by the Danish monarchy in 1863 to change the status of Schleswig and Holstein, and to link the northern duchy of Schleswig more closely to the Danish crown, led to a renewal of the dispute apparently settled by the London treaty of 1852. The issue was complicated by the claim of the Duke of Augustenburg to sovereignty over the two 'Elbe duchies', which was recognized by several German princes. Most Germans in Schleswig-Holstein wanted the two provinces to become a single German state within the Confederation, or within a future united Germany, while Bismarck envisaged their annexation to Prussia.

Early in 1864 Austria and Prussia, in alliance — and in disregard of the German Confederation's official decisions — declared war on Denmark. Their forces occupied Schleswig-Holstein, and soon crossed into Denmark proper. Attempts at mediation by Britain and France were unsuccessful, and Denmark was defeated by the summer of 1864. By the treaty of Vienna (October 1864) the king of Denmark ceded the Elbe duchies to Austria and Prussia jointly.

There was little comment from Marx and Engels on the 1864 war. They did not, as in 1848–9, have their own radical mouthpiece in which to interpret its character and significance. Unlike the earlier conflict about Schleswig-Holstein, the war was not part of a revolutionary wave that swept across the continent. In 1848–9 Marx and Engels had been in favour of war and wanted it to spread and engulf Europe. Not so in 1864. Marx hoped for peace because 'any war would delay the outbreak of revolution in France.'[1] Both he and Engels were still in favour of the separation from Denmark of Holstein and the German-speaking part of Schleswig, but they did not characterize this war as revolutionary.

The Marx-Engels position of 1863–4 differed in another respect from the stance they took in 1848–9. They had evidently abandoned the contemptuous view of Denmark which enabled Engels to claim that Germany was entitled to seize Schleswig by 'the right of civiliz-ation as against barbarism'.[2] In the letter to Marx of 3 December 1863 — where he claimed war with Russia over Poland was the only way to free the duchies — he listed the conclusions he had reached after studying the Schleswig-Holstein question, including its legal aspects and the problem of dynastic succession. He concluded that 'Germany's claim to Schleswig is confined to the *south*, which is German by nationality and the people's free choice, which means that Schleswig ought to be partitioned.'[3] Marx's reply contained a friendly reference to Germany's northern neighbours. 'One should not irritate the Danes. They must be made to realize that the Scandinavians and the Germans share *the same* interests against Russia, and that the secession of the German element would be the best solution from their own point of view.'[4]

In the autumn of 1864, with the fighting over and Schleswig under Prussian-Austrian occupation, Engels toured the Elbe duchies and found that German influence was stronger even in northern Schleswig than he had expected. He added, 'I wish it were more Danish, for in fairness one will have to cede some territory to the Scandinavians.'[5] A far cry from his earlier contemptuous thesis.

As on many other occasions, Marx and Engels misread the international situation in connection with the German-Danish war. On 3 January 1864 Engels wrote to his friend that in the likely event of war with Denmark 'we (Germans) shall have Denmark, Sweden, France and Italy against us, and possibly England as well,'[6] and shortly before the second campaign which crushed Danish resistance, Marx thought that Britain would probably declare war in defence of Denmark. As we know, Engels also believed that Schleswig-Holstein could not be prised away from Denmark without war against Russia.

The soundness of their political judgement may be questioned, but their views on the resolution of the Schleswig-Holstein issue were in line with the principles of international justice and self-determination. Marx and Engels were certainly not defeatists in this war: they wanted the German side to win and to end Danish rule in Holstein and the ethnically German part of Schleswig. But at least Engels was in favour of Denmark retaining, or regaining in due course, Danish-speaking northern Schleswig. They did not seem to care whether Schleswig-Holstein was to be a member state of the German Confederation or part of an existing state. Since they were in favour of replacing the Confederation by a united and indivisible German republic, they cannot have attached any significance to this aspect.

Ferdinand Lassalle who had urged the Prussian government in 1859 to liberate Schleswig-Holstein by war with Denmark repeated the exhortation at the end of 1863. He declared it to be the duty of all German governments to obtain the secession of the duchies from Denmark and their incorporation into Germany, 'by force of arms if need be'.[7] He also – like Marx and Engels – displayed indifference regarding the question of sovereignty of the duchies after they became part of Germany: 'The reorganization of Germany as a united state would automatically solve the Schleswig-Holstein question...it is comparatively unimportant whether, so long as thirty-three princes continue to reign in Germany, one of them is a foreign sovereign.'[8]

Yet Lassalle stressed that it would be undemocratic to back the claims of the duke of Augustenburg, and that the creation of a thirty-fourth princely state would militate against German national unity.[9] He had apparently embraced Bismarck's plan to make the Elbe duchies a Prussian province. This is confirmed in a note by Eduard

Bernstein, editor of Lassalle's writings. According to Bernstein, Lassalle (who died on 31 August 1864) had intended to address a mass rally in Hamburg in the autumn and to sponsor a resolution inviting Bismarck to annex Schleswig-Holstein to Prussia in defiance of Austrian protests. [10]

Austria against Prussia 1866

Denmark's cession of Schleswig-Holstein was followed by an Austrian-Prussian condominium over the Elbe duchies. From the start there were quarrels, largely provoked by Bismarck. In June 1865 the two powers agreed to end the condominium and to assign the administration of Holstein to Austria and that of Schleswig to Prussia.

The new arrangement worked no better – it was not meant to, as far as Bismarck was concerned. Austria tolerated pro-Augustenburg agitation in Holstein, which Prussia declared incompatible with the maintenance of law and order in Schleswig. Growing tension caused both sides to make diplomatic preparations for war early in 1866. Bismarck succeeded in neutralizing Napoleon III (with vague promises of territorial compensation which were not kept), and in concluding an alliance with Italy. Austria was supported by most member states of the German Confederation. Faced with an adverse vote in the Confederate Diet (*Bundestag*), Prussia invaded Holstein and declared the Confederation dissolved.

Austria fought the ensuing war in alliance with Bavaria, Saxony, Hanover, Württemberg and some other west and south-west German states; Prussia's allies were Italy and some minor north German states. The Italians were beaten at Custozza, but the Prussians were victorious against Austria's allies, and on 3 July 1866 inflicted a crushing defeat on the Austrians at Königgrätz in Bohemia. This decided the war, which had lasted only about seven weeks. Peace was concluded in August: Austria agreed to a new German Federation from which she would be excluded. Prussia annexed Schleswig-Holstein and other German territory, including the kingdom of Hanover and the city of Frankfurt. The new 'North German Federation' (*Norddeutscher Bund*) comprised Prussia and twenty-two small and medium-sized German states. Its constituent 'Reichstag' was elected by universal manhood suffrage in February 1867. Its constitution became the model of Bismarck's 'Reich', which emerged from Germany's victory over France in 1871.

The comments of Marx and Engels on the war of 1866 again reflected their views of the relationship between defeat in war and revolution. The war was the subject of intense debates in the Central Council of the International Workingmen's Association, the First International founded in 1864. In July 1866 the Council — of which Marx was a member — unanimously adopted a resolution describing the war as 'a conflict between governments' in which the working classes should stay neutral. Marx and Engels, who had wanted war to start and to spread in the late 1840s and the 1850s, now felt that there was nothing to choose between the warring powers. They regarded the war as reactionary on all sides, and were pessimistic about the prospects if the war should not lead to revolution.

'All those responsible for this war — if there is to be war — deserve to be hanged,' Engels wrote to Marx, and he added that this applied to Bismarck as well as the Austrian leaders.[11] Marx commented gloomily, 'Without a revolution in Germany those Hohenzollern and Habsburg dogs with their dynastic civil war will put the clock back in our country by fifty to one hundred years.'[12]

Between 20 June and 6 July 1866 the *Manchester Guardian* published five articles by Engels under the title 'Reflections on the War in Germany', in which Engels commented on the campaign 'from the purely military point of view'.[13] In the first four articles Engels declared himself convinced of a clear-cut Austrian victory; the Prussians were better armed, with breech-loader instead of muzzle-loader rifle guns, but Engels thought this far outweighed by superior Austrian leadership and morale. The Prussian soldiers, Engels claimed, were going to the war reluctantly, and their morale was low. Besides, the Prussians had made terrible strategic blunders. In the fifth and last article, written after Königgrätz, Engels explained that the Prussians had won a decisive victory, and presumably the war, because the Austrians had blundered even more disastrously.

'Military expert' Engels also predicted in his letters to Marx that the Austrians would win the war. In the likely event of the first decisive battle going against the Prussians, nothing would stop the Austrians from marching on Berlin; they might then 'dictate the peace in Berlin within a fortnight'. His wish was father to that thought. 'It is my dearest wish,' he went on, 'that the Prussians will get a terrific thrashing.'[14] He hoped for this because a speedy Austrian triumph would forestall foreign intervention, especially by Napoleon III, and would mean the fall of Bismarck's régime. This in turn might spark off 'another movement which runs counter from the start to specific Prussianism'.

On the eve of the war, Engels quoted conversations with German visitors who had told him of the revolutionary atmosphere in Prussian towns. He predicted a rebellion by the Prussian *'Landwehr'* (the territorial reserve or militia), and said, 'I think the balloon will go up in Prussia within a fortnight. If this opportunity passes without being used, and if the people stand for that, then we might as well pack up our revolutionary bag and baggage and concentrate instead on abstract theory.' [15] When the balloon failed to go up and the Prussians were victorious, Engels did not admit that he had been wrong, and neither he nor Marx ceased to talk and write about revolution.

Marx agreed that a Prussian defeat might have meant revolution in Berlin; but he was still optimistic about the general situation: 'Apart from a big Prussian defeat which would perhaps...have led to revolution, nothing better could have happened than a tremendous Prussian victory' [16] — not least because such an outcome must weaken the Bonapartist régime in France. Marx argued that Napoleon had hoped the war between Prussia and Austria would result in mutual exhaustion, when he could have played the arbiter. Now, in view of Prussia's victory, the emperor was in danger of being overthrown.

Engels, whose prophecies had all gone astray, was not dismayed either. Bismarck's success would have to be acknowledged, 'we may like it or not'. [17] He correctly foresaw that German unity on Prussia's terms would be achieved, and that imperial Germany would include the south-west, — Bavaria, Baden and Württemberg. He wrongly forecast the inclusion in Bismarck's Reich, 'in the not distant future', of the German parts of the Habsburg empire, and he discerned positive features in the result of the 1866 war:

The business has its good side in that it simplifies the situation and facilitates revolution, by ending the bickering between small capitals, and in any case by speeding up developments. After all, an all-German parliament differs completely from a Prussian Diet...The most noxious parochial influences will come to an end, and the political parties will at last be national instead of merely provincial.

The main disadvantage — and it is a very big one — is the inevitable swamping of Germany by Prussianism...There is, in my opinion, nothing we can do but simply to accept the facts without approving them, and to make the best possible use of the greater opportunities which must now exist for achieving the *national* organization and unification of the German proletariat.[18]

For once Engels did not predict trends towards early revolution, but described conditions which he thought would make the emergence of a revolutionary situation easier at some unspecified future date. The German empire which emerged from what historians have called Bismarck's 'revolution from above' was a fairly stable society; the revolution of 1918 was the result not of inherent weakness but of disastrous defeat in war. On the other hand, the spectacular growth — unrivalled in any other country — of the German Social Democratic Party between 1890 and 1914 tended to confirm Engels's view that national unification and centralization created more opportunities for the successful organization and progress of a nationwide socialist party of the working class.

In 1866, for the first time since Marx and Engels began to write and exchange views on contemporary political events, they were faced with a war which they assessed as a conflict between governments, in which the workers had no reason to take sides. Marx and Engels did not declare any of the warring powers more progressive or less reactionary, as they had done previously when war had broken out or was about to break out.

In 1866 they simply hoped for *that* result from which the revolutionary cause might benefit. Thus Engels wanted his native Prussia to lose the war, not because he preferred the Austrian chief minister Belcredi to Bismarck, or the Habsburgs to the Hohenzollerns, but because he believed (wrongly) that a revolutionary situation existed in Prussia, which would erupt in open revolution following a Prussian military defeat. Both he and Marx were 'defeatists' in the sense that they emphasized the connection and interaction between defeat in war and revolution. But they did not invite the workers, or the socialist leaders, to work for the defeat of the Prussian government. Nor did they argue, on Leninist lines, that one could want the defeat of one's own reactionary government without wanting the victory of the (reactionary and imperialist) enemy. When Engels stated unambiguously in April 1866, that Prussia's crushing defeat would be the fulfilment of his 'dearest wish', he left no doubt that he saw this defeat as tantamount to an Austrian victory. When Marx said, after the battle of Königgrätz, that failing a Prussian defeat (which might have led to revolution) a tremendous Prussian victory was the next best thing, he implied that — apart from other positive consequences — an Austrian defeat might unleash revolution within the Habsburg empire. The upshot, in plain terms, is that where they felt total antipathy to both belligerents, they would have welcomed any result which offered better chances for an early proletarian revolution.

The Franco-German War and its Aftermath 1870–1

Austria was treated leniently in the peace treaty of 1866. Schleswig-Holstein and the reorganization of Germany had been the issues, so Austria had to agree to the Elbe duchies' becoming part of Prussia, and to acknowledge the demise of the German Confederation and the inevitability of a Prussian-inspired solution to the German question. Emperor Francis Joseph ceded Venetia to Napoleon III, who passed it on to the kingdom of Italy. But Prussia demanded no frontier changes in her favour. It was Bismarck who insisted, very much against the king's original wishes, that Austria be left territorially intact. He wanted to make sure that Austria would stay neutral in Prussia's war with France which he thought, and hoped, would break out soon.

War did break out in July 1870. The crisis began with the vacant Spanish throne being offered to a Hohenzollern prince, scion of the Roman Catholic branch of Prussia's ruling house. The prince accepted, and the Prussian king, as head of the house of Hohenzollern, endorsed his decision; both the prince and the king probably acted on the promptings of Bismarck. The French were horrified at the prospect of a Hohenzollern monarch both east and south of their borders. They protested furiously, which Bismarck had expected; what he had not expected was that the French protests would cause the candidate and King William to have second thoughts. On 12 July it was announced that the prince would not accept the Spanish crown.

Bismarck was in despair and thought of resigning, but the French inadvertently helped him by pushing their luck. The French ambassador went to Ems where King William was taking the waters and asked him for an assurance that the candidature would never be renewed. The king refused to commit himself, and eventually turned down the ambassador's request for a further audience. The incident was reported by telegram to Bismarck, who published the 'Ems Despatch' in an edited, incisive form, calculated to infuriate the French by the insult to their national honour. Bismarck's stratagem worked. On 19 July France declared war, only to find herself confronted not only by Prussia and the North German Federation but by the whole of Germany, except Austria. The south German states, Bavaria, Württemberg and Baden, joined on Prussia's side.

The war lasted a little over six months, but it was virtually decided after a six-week campaign. The French had the worst of a number of battles and finally sustained a crushing defeat at Sedan on 2 September 1870, resulting in the capitulation of the French marshal MacMahon and his army of 80,000 officers and men. Napoleon III, who was with his army, surrendered to King William. On 4 September the (Third) Republic was proclaimed in Paris. A 'Government of National Defence' continued the struggle for several months but had to sue for an armistice at the end of January 1871. Before it was signed King William was proclaimed German emperor at Versailles on 18 January 1871: Bismarck's united Germany was born. At the peace treaty of Frankfurt, in May 1871, France ceded Alsace and part of Lorraine to Germany, and undertook to pay an indemnity of 5000 million francs (200 million pounds sterling.)

In the Franco-German War Marx and Engels, and the General Council of the First International, did not take their neutral stance of 1866. They sided first with Germany, which in their opinion was fighting a national and defensive war; but the two friends and the General Council shifted their position after the battle of Sedan and the fall of the Second Bonapartist Empire. From September 1870 onwards they regarded France as the country fighting a war of defence and emphatically denounced Germany's annexation of Alsace-Lorraine.

Marx and Engels gave a variety of reasons for their attitude, ranging from points of principle to practical considerations of the likely political effects of the war. In his first comment after the outbreak of the war, Marx said:

> The French need a thrashing. If the Prussians win, the centralization of *state power* will help promote the centralization of the German working class. Moreover, German predominance would shift the centre of gravity of the West European labour movement from France to Germany, and one only has to compare

the French and German movements between 1866 and the present to see that the German working class is superior to the French, both theoretically and organizationally. The German workers' superiority on the world stage over the French would also mean the superiority of *our* theory over that of Proudhon...[19]

On 28 July, with the war not yet ten days old, Marx wrote to his daughter Laura and her husband Paul Lafargue in Paris, explaining his position in different terms:

For my own part, I should like that both, Prussians and French, thrashed each other alternately, and that — as I believe will be the case — the Germans got *ultimately* the better of it. I wish this, because the definite defeat of Bonaparte is likely to provoke revolution in France, while the definite defeat of Germany would only protract the present state of things for twenty years...[20]

Engels was more certain of Germany's victory: 'I have no doubt at all...that the Germans will be victorious in the end....'[21] He expounded his view of the character and perspectives of the war, more 'Marxist' in that it was more closely linked to theory and principle than Marx's short-term, somewhat opportunistic considerations. Engels maintained that a war for Germany's national existence had been forced upon her by the French emperor. A German defeat would stabilize Bonapartism and cripple Germany for years or perhaps for generations:

An autonomous German labour movement would no longer be possible; the struggle for restoring national existence would absorb everything, at best the German workers would be towed along by the French. If Germany wins, French Bonapartism will be finished in any case, the perpetual squabble about how to achieve German unity will be at an end, and the German workers will be able to organize themselves on a much more distinctly national level than hitherto; as for the French workers, no matter what kind of government will take over there, they will certainly have more scope for free action than under Bonapartism.[22]

Engels criticized those German socialists who, like Wilhelm Liebknecht, 'preach total abstention and allow all sorts of secondary considerations to prevail over the paramount issue'. This referred to Liebknecht's defeatist attitude about the war. He had intended to vote

71

in the Reichstag of the North German Federation, against the war budget, but was persuaded by August Bebel, the only other Social Democratic member of the Reichstag, to abstain. There is a more direct attack on Liebknecht's defeatism in the postscript of the letter. 'The wretched Wilhelm,' Engels wrote, had 'obviously banked on Bonaparte's victory, only because he wants Bismarck to be sunk. You will remember that he always kept threatening Bismarck with the French.' Liebknecht is here charged with the kind of defeatism which Lenin considered the correct revolutionary policy in the Russo-Japanese war, some twenty-four years later.

Another reason for wanting Germany's victory was, according to Engels, the chauvinistic atmosphere in France. Engels argued that Napoleon III could not have waged the war but for the chauvinism of the mass of the French population: the bourgeoisie, petty-bourgeoisie, the peasants and certain sections of the working class: 'So long as this chauvinism has not been knocked on the head, and decisively, peace between Germany and France is impossible. One might have expected a proletarian revolution to do this job; but since war has come the Germans have no option: they must do it themselves, and forthwith.'[23] It was regrettable that Bismarck and his king would, at least temporarily, reap some glory from a victorious war; but that could not be helped:

> But to elevate for that reason anti-Bismarckism into the sole guiding principle would be absurd. In the first place Bismarck is now, as he was in 1866, doing some of our work for us − in *his own* way, and without intending to: nevertheless he does it. He makes things easier for us...Anyway, to try, à la Liebknecht, to put into reverse the whole process that has been going on since 1866, just because he (Liebknecht) does not like that process, is utter nonsense.

Engels arrived at guidelines for the policies the German socialists would pursue:

Our people should
1 Join the national movement in so far and so long as it is limited to the defence of Germany (which in some circumstances does not exclude a military offensive until peace is made);
2 At the same time emphasize the difference between German-national and Prussian-dynastic interests;

3 Oppose any annexation of Alsace-Lorraine...;
4 Work for an honourable peace with a republican, non-chauvinist government as soon as such a government takes office in Paris;
5 Constantly stress the unity of interests between the German and the French workers, who did not approve of the war and are not at war with each other.[24]

This programme foreshadowed the change of front which Marx and Engels showed a few weeks later, when a republican French government was willing to pay a war indemnity under a peace settlement without annexations.

Liebknecht's 'defeatist' attitude was not shared by the majority of the leaders of the German Social Democratic Workers' Party. On 24 July 1870 the party's 'committee' (*Ausschuss*) issued a manifesto calling upon the German workers to support the war so long as it remained defensive. Liebknecht, who was then editor of the party organ *Der Volksstaat*, sharply criticized the manifesto. He regarded the war as a purely dynastic one between the imperial Bonapartist and the royal Prussian monarchy, and felt that the party's position should be one of complete neutrality.

In this dispute between Wilhelm Liebknecht and the other leaders of the German party Marx and Engels, of course, sided with the latter. Marx was the author of the first 'Address' on the war, issued by the General Council of the International on 23 July 1870, which declared that Germany was waging a war of defence. It appealed to German workers not to 'allow the present war to lose its strictly defensive character and to degenerate into a war against the French people'; for, if that happened, 'victory or defeat will prove alike disastrous' for Germany.[25] This was of course a disavowal of Liebknecht's approach, yet Marx's utterances lacked consistency. When Bebel and Liebknecht abstained from voting on the war budget, they declared:

> We *cannot grant* the financial resources demanded for the conduct of the war, because this would be a vote of confidence in the Prussian government...It is equally impossible for us to *refuse* the money demanded, for this might be taken as a justification of the vicious and criminal policy of Bonaparte. As opponents on principle of every war, as *social-republicans and members of the International Workingmen's Association*, which fights against all

oppressors without distinction of nationality..., we can neither directly nor indirectly declare ourselves for the present war, and we therefore abstain from voting... [26]

This is obviously the neutralist position, tinged with some un-Marxist pacifism. The declaration, though implicitly rejecting defeatism, does not support Germany's war of defence — the official position of Marx and the General Council. Yet on 29 July Marx wrote to Liebknecht, 'At last Tuesday's meeting of the General Council I translated into English yours and Bebel's statement of protest in the Reichstag. It was received with strong applause.' [27] And in his letter to the Lafargues of 28 July, Marx emphasized that Liebknecht and Bebel had 'behaved extremely well' in the Reichstag.

Whatever indecision or vacillation Marx may have felt, the 'Addresses on the War' he drafted for the General Council were unambiguous in defining the council's attitude to the conflict. The first Address was followed by a second on 9 September — written after Sedan and the fall of Bonaparte — and a third, issued on 30 May 1871, after the French government under Thiers had crushed the Paris Commune.

According to these 'Addresses', Germany, though led by odious and reactionary politicians and monarchs, was at first fighting a just war of defence for her national existence and unification. But by September 1870 these objectives were no longer in jeopardy, and Germany's war became one of aggression and conquest, aimed at the annexation of the French provinces of Alsace and Lorraine. Marx and Engels did not like the French 'bourgeois' government which emerged from the revolution of 4 September any better than they did Bismarck and his gang, or the German princely rulers in league with Prussia; yet they regarded France's struggle for her territorial integrity as legitimate and worthy of support, and they campaigned for the recognition of the French republican government by Britain (which was granted in February 1871).

Even before the French *débâcle* of 2 September Marx and Engels felt that Germany's war would not stay defensive much longer. The Alsace-Lorraine issue was raised in Germany soon after war was declared. As early as July 1870 Engels mentioned a revival of 'the old clamouring for Alsace-Lorraine' [28] and when he exhorted the German party comrades to oppose all annexations, he added that Bismarck was already hinting at the annexation of these provinces to Bavaria and Baden. [29]

Marx agreed that Germany's annexation of Alsace-Lorraine 'would be the greatest disaster that could befall Europe and Germany in particular'.[30] And in a letter Marx wrote to the Brunswick executive of the German Social Democrats, he again asked them to strive for an honourable peace with France, without annexations; in this letter he correctly prophesied that the seizure of those provinces by Germany would 'force France into the arms of Russia', a prediction he repeated in the Address of 9 September.[31]

Engel's military analyses and predictions were more successful than in the past. He expected from the start that Germany would win, and in a series of articles he wrote for the Liberal London *Pall Mall Gazette* in July and August 1870 he anticipated an early French disaster. Neither he nor Marx was surprised by Sedan and the immediate downfall of the Bonapartist régime.

After the French defeat at Sedan, Engels thought the war was over: 'The war is at an end. There is no army left in France.'[32] He quoted correspondents' reports in British papers that the members of the provisional government and 'the bourgeois in Paris' knew perfectly well that France could not go on fighting.[33]

Within a few weeks of the Sedan *débâcle* German forces had invested Paris. Marx and Engels did not expect the city to withstand a prolonged siege. In an article in the *Pall Mall Gazette*, Engels predicted (wrongly) the impending fall of some outer forts, after which he felt the city ought to surrender: a refusal to do so would mean doomed resistance on the barricades and pointless sacrifices.[34]

Marx shared the view that Paris would fall very soon. He spoke of 'the imminent and *unavoidable* capitulation of Paris',[35] but earlier he had written to Edward Spencer Beesly and argued that the fall of Paris need not spell final defeat for France. This appears to be one of the occasions when Marx did not accept the 'General's' military judgement. The regular correspondence between the two men ceased at this time because Engels, having retired from his business activities in Manchester, moved to London on 20 September, and the friends met almost daily. Any disagreement between them was not reflected in an exchange of letters.

Engels did not believe that Germany's victorious progress could be thwarted by a French proletarian revolution; in fact, he feared a premature workers' rising before peace was concluded. He explained why such a rising was bound to harm the cause of the French working class:

> If one could do anything at all in Paris one should stop the
> workers starting a revolt before peace has come...if a rising were
> to succeed now...they (the workers) would be burdened with the
> legacy of Bonaparte and the present lousy republic, and would be
> pointlessly crushed by the German armies and again thrown back
> twenty years. They themselves have nothing to lose by marking
> time...[36]

It was regrettable, Engels went on, that so few people in Paris dared to
face realities:

> Who in Paris has the courage to consider the fact that France's
> power of active resistance in this war has been broken, and that,
> therefore, *there is no prospect of expelling the invader by means
> of a revolution* (emphasis added). Just because the people do not
> *want* to know the real truth I am afraid that something like that
> will happen.

In their comments on previous conflicts, especially the Italian
liberation struggle and the American Civil War, Marx and Engels
urged the side they supported to resort to revolutionary policies and
methods − *levée en masse*, guerilla warfare, and so on − which had
saved the First French Republic in 1793. Engels proffered no such
advice to the French workers after Sedan; on the contrary, he hoped
they would resist the temptation to take revolutionary action which
would hurt their own interests but not stave off defeat by Germany.

Engels was already thinking in terms of the next war: a French war
of 'revanche' to recover the lost provinces. In an article entitled 'How
to Beat the Prussians', he advocated the adoption of short training
periods for all able-bodied men in France, so as to have the largest
military reserve in the shortest time. If, as then seemed likely, the war
ended with the partial dismemberment of France, this would soon
enable the French nation to settle accounts with the Germans and
restore their territorial integrity.[37]

Marx's appeal to the German Social Democratic Workers' Party to
advocate an honourable peace with the French Republic and to oppose
all annexations was heeded. On 5 September 1870, the party's executive in Brunswick published a manifesto in complete accord with the
Marx-Engels line on the war: it called for an immediate peace without
annexations. A few days later several members of the executive were
arrested on treason charges and taken, in chains, to a fortress in East
Prussia.[38]

Marx and Engels applauded the actions of their German friends. Marx paid tribute to the German workers who were 'behaving admirably, despite the terror and the bourgeois-patriotic howling'.[39] He sharply criticized 'our French comrades' who, in an absurd and chauvinistic manifesto, had called upon the German invaders to 'withdraw across the Rhine' as though, Marx commented, the Germans could not get back to Germany without crossing the Rhine. Marx apparently saw a chauvinistic aberration in the backing French members of the International implicitly gave to the demand for the Rhine frontier. 'The entire tenor of this manifesto,' Marx concluded, 'is absurd and conforms by no means to the spirit of the International.'

The 'Government of National Defence' which was set up in Paris on 4 September 1870, with General Trochu as its head and Jules Favre as foreign minister, thought at first that the Germans, in accordance with the Prussian king's declarations, would agree to a peace without territorial changes.[40] But a meeting with Bismarck on 18 September convinced Jules Favre that France could not obtain peace without territorial concessions, so the government decided to continue the unequal struggle. All able-bodied men up to the age of sixty were called up; large armies of partially trained men were raised; guerilla units were improvised, and spontaneous popular resistance created problems for the German invaders.

Marx and Engels, who now sided with republican France, soon overcame their apparent disagreement about the military prospects. For once it was Engels who came round to Marx's view that France still had a fighting chance. At the end of October, when the Germans took Metz and Marshal Bazaine surrendered with his army of 170,000, Engels still felt that France might sue for peace.[41] A few weeks later he took a radically different view. On 9 November the French routed a Bavarian army corps at Coulmiers, and Engels, who had been unduly pessimistic in September, now fell into the opposite extreme of over-optimism about French chances of recovery. He wrote that France, through her stubborn resistance, had gained much international sympathy. Together with widespread European distrust of Prussia as a potential accomplice in Russian expansionist designs, this might change the situation in France's favour. Neutral powers might attempt mediation or even intervene militarily on the side of France.[42] Engels was certainly indulging in wishful thinking when he suggested in the same article that if 30,000 British soldiers were to disembark at

Cherbourg or Brest to join the valiant French 'Army of the Loire', French resistance would receive an immeasurable moral boost. And in even more fantastic vein: Italy and Austria might also send troops in support of France, and 'the Scandinavian kingdoms' might stage diversionary attacks on the Prussian frontier: if and when the Parisians learnt that such aid was forthcoming, they would discard any thought of surrender. None of the countries concerned showed any desire to act on Engels's fanciful suggestions.

Engels was soon reiterating that 'since the surrender at Sedan the prospects of France (have) much improved'; he added that 'even the fall of Metz. . . does not now look the crushing disaster it appeared to be at first'.[43] He wrote that although French attempts to raise the siege of Paris had failed, the city had supplies enough for at least two months. Even if Paris should fall, France would fight on, provided the people's spirit of resistance did not flag; surrender in present circumstances would be plain treachery.[44] Finally, he discerned signs of demoralization and exhaustion among the Prussian troops.[45]

A letter Marx wrote on 13 December to Ludwig Kugelmann in Hanover contained a similarly positive appraisal of France's prospects. He stressed that spontaneous resistance by the French masses had turned the war into a 'people's war' (*Volkskrieg*). Prussian reaction had been excessive reprisals – burning down of villages, taking of hostages, shooting of *franc-tireurs* – and these atrocities had radically swayed British public opinion, which had been 'ultra-Prussian' at the beginning of the war but was now definitely pro-French. 'However the war may end,' Marx commented, 'it has given the French proletariat practice in using arms, and that is the best guarantee of the future.'[46]

In January 1871 the French sustained a series of defeats, and on 28 January Paris capitulated after a siege of over four months. An armistice was agreed, and peace negotiations began. A French National Assembly, to be elected forthwith, was to decide on making peace.

Marx and Engels were still not prepared to consider France's cause as hopeless. In a letter to Paul Lafargue Marx denounced the capitulation of Paris as an act of cowardice, forgetting perhaps that four months earlier he had regarded the same act as 'imminent and unavoidable'. He added that if France made use of the armistice to reorganize her armies and realized 'that the waging of revolutionary war requires revolutionary measures and revolutionary energy', she could still be saved.[47] He wrote, in the same vein and in much the same terms, to Kugelmann. In spite of appearances to the contrary, Marx asserted, 'the position of the Prussians is anything but pleasant,' and could get even worse if the French gave the war 'a truly revolutionary character'. He accused General Trochu, commander of the Paris army, of having conducted the defence of Paris in a purely passive way: he had obviously found it 'much more important...to curb the Reds in Paris than to beat the Prussians'.[48]

In February 1871 Marx and Engels were hoping that the harsh conditions laid down by Bismarck at the beginning of the peace talks would induce the French capitalists (the workers anyway favoured continued resistance) to resume the war when the three-week truce expired. The conditions included a war indemnity of £400 millions.[49] Such demands, Marx said in his letters to Lafargue and Kugelmann, might convince the French bourgeoisie that yielding would be more costly than continuing the struggle. Engels expressed the same view: the 'peace party', consisting of urban capitalists, big landowners and parts of the peasantry would see no advantage in a peace settlement just as ruinous as continued war.[50]

But the war was not resumed. The bellicose mood in France had given way to a yearning to end the bloodshed. In the elections to the National Assembly on 8 February, an anti-republican, pro-peace majority was returned, except in Paris where most votes were for left-wing candidates in favour of war to the bitter end. The armistice was extended, and the National Assembly eventually approved the peace treaty of Frankfurt.

Before the treaty was signed, the rift between Paris and the provinces led to a rising in the capital and the establishment of the revolutionary *'Commune'* in March 1871. Similar proletarian revolts had broken out and been quelled in Paris and other towns the preceding autumn. This revolt was initially successful and for just over two months Paris was in the hands of a governing body of revolutionary socialists.

The immediate cause of the Paris rising was a government attempt to disarm the city's National Guard. When the Prussians entered Paris — where they occupied only a small area, and only for a few days — all regular army units had to surrender their arms, but the National Guard, comprised mainly of radical republican workers, was allowed to keep its weapons, including guns. On 18 March the Thiers government, then at Versailles, sent troops to seize the Guard's artillery. The

National Guard resisted and seized power in the capital where a *Commune* government was elected by universal suffrage. Few if any of its members were Marxists; the majority were followers of Blanqui or Proudhon. But Marx, though critical of many of the *Commune's* policies, acknowledged its socialist character; and Engels, twenty years later, concluded his 'Introduction' to a new edition of Marx's *Civil War in France* with the words: 'Look at the Paris *Commune*: that was the dictatorship of the Proletariat.'[51]

The rise and fall of the *Commune* was the main theme of the 'Address on the War', which the General Council of the International issued after the *Commune* had been crushed at the end of May by the troops of the Versailles government. This document by Marx was later published under the title *Civil War in France*.[52] Marx dealt at great length with the *Commune's* policies, actions and omissions, and with the bloodthirsty repression by the Thiers government after its forces had reoccupied the capital. He reiterated the accusations of treachery previously levelled at the members of the 'Government of National Defence'. Apart from heaping personal abuse upon Thiers and his ministers, Marx tried to show that they had planned capitulation from the start. He quoted from a statement General Trochu had made just before the capitulation that he had already told his colleagues in the government, immediately after the proclamation of the republic, that Paris could not stand a siege by the Prussians.[53] Marx, who had held and expressed exactly the same view in September – as had Engels – regarded this as proof that Trochu had intended all along to surrender Paris, and that this had been known to all the ministers: clearly, 'national defence' had been a pretext for the personal rule of those 'infamous impostors'. Marx then gave his explanation for this resolve to surrender Paris:

> Paris...was not to be defended without arming its working class...But Paris armed was the revolution armed. A victory of Paris over the Prussian aggressor would have been a victory of the French workman over the French capitalist and his state parasites. In this conflict between national duty and class interest, the Government of National Defence did not hesitate one moment to turn into a Government of National Defection.[54]

In other words, Marx charged the French bourgeoisie with having adopted a policy of *counter*-revolutionary defeatism: a policy of deliberately provoking defeat at the hands of the external enemy, because victory might have meant the victory of proletarian revolution in France.[55] Considering the desperate measures taken by Gambetta and other ministers to prolong resistance even after the disasters of Sedan and Metz, this Marxist theory must be said to lack plausibility.

In the same 'Address on the Civil War' in May 1871 Marx asserted that the capitulation of Paris had meant the surrender not only of the French capital but of all of France. This view was somewhat at variance with the position he and Engels had taken in February, when they argued that despite the surrender of Paris the French could reorganize their forces and resume the war with some chance of success. Marx also speaks of the attempt by the French ruling class 'to break down the revolution by a civil war carried on under the patronage of the foreign invader'.[56] There was some truth in the suggestion of German aid to the Versailles government in its fight against the *Commune*: even before peace was concluded, Bismarck had begun to release French prisoners-of-war to make them available for the onslaught on revolutionary Paris.

When Marx and Engels had come to the conclusion, in about November 1870, that France had a chance of avoiding ultimate defeat and that she was fighting for her national existence and her territorial integrity, they espoused her cause with far greater enthusiasm than they had shown for Germany during the pre-Sedan phase. Their fervent hope that republican France could resist the German invaders shows that in their maturity Marx and Engels had purged themselves of all traces of the German nationalism noticeable, for example, at the time of the Prussian-Danish war of 1848–9.

Of course, the impact of victory or defeat upon internal political developments also entered into the equation. Marx and Engels had come to believe that in the circumstances in France at the time, a French victory would be more likely to promote the cause of proletarian revolution. When France had lost the war and the 'proletarian revolution', after briefly triumphing in Paris, had succumbed to bourgeois reaction, Marx (in his retrospective assessment in *Civil War in France*) asserted that the bourgeoisie had turned defeatist because its leaders had realized that victory could be obtained only by arming the working class, which seemed bound to result in the overthrow of capitalist class rule.

9 The 'Russian Menace' in the 1870s and the 1880s

A by-product of the Franco-German War of 1870–1 was what Engels called 'the re-emergence of the "Eastern Question" ', which had lain dormant since the end of the Crimean War. In November 1870 Russia took advantage of the West European upheavals and the weakening of France to declare herself no longer bound by the 1856 Paris treaty provisions which debarred Russian warships from the Black Sea and Russian arsenals from its shores.

Engels expressed the hope that this unilaterial Russian action, undertaken (he suspected) with Prussian connivance, would induce Britain and other European powers to intervene in the Franco-German War to save Paris from surrender and France from ultimate defeat.[1] But Marx and Engels went beyond hoping for vigorous Western reaction. They wanted the British government to make full use of the empire's naval power to neutralize the threat emanating from Russia, and they raised this matter in the General Council of the International.

The peace treaty in March 1856 had been followed by international negotiations in the French capital about the laws of naval warfare; the talks culminated in the 'Declaration of Paris', signed by representatives of France, Britain, Russia, Austria, Prussia, Turkey and Sardinia on 16 April 1856, and subsequently acceded to by most other powers. The declaration abolished privateering and laid down that enemy goods on neutral ships, and neutral goods on enemy ships should be inviolate – with the exception, in both cases, of contraband of war.

Marx and Engels felt strongly that Britain should repudiate this declaration to regain her freedom of naval action in the event of war with Russia. They feared that the restrictions imposed upon Britain as the foremost naval power would give undue advantage to Russia. This was discussed by the General Council in January, February and March 1871, after Engels (co-opted on to the Council on his move to London) had tabled three resolutions on topical issues. The first two dealt with the campaign for the recognition of the French republic by the British government, which took place shortly afterwards, and with British intervention in the war to help France, for which Engels thought the right moment had passed. The third draft resolution stated that England could regain her freedom of action on the high seas only if she repudiated the Declaration of Paris; without this freedom she would be incapable not only of playing an effective part in continental affairs but of defending herself against 'continental military despotism'.[2]

This draft resolution illumines in an extraordinary way the attitude of Marx and Engels to war – not, in this case, to a war in progress but to a potential war between Britain and Russia, which they expected to break out in the near future. At first glance the wording of the resolution appeared to reflect the outlook not of international socialists but of British imperialists, implying that Britain had the right to intervene on the continent of Europe and should retain or regain the power and liberty under international law to use her naval strength to this end.

It is a fact that Marx and Engels never flinched from the thought of an alliance, or at least of co-belligerency, between the workers' movement and a bourgeois power when their interests happened to coincide. Eighteen years previously, on the eve of the Crimean War, in considering the necessity of countering Russia's expansionist designs, Engels said that 'the interests of revolutionary democracy and of England go hand in hand'. He and Marx reasoned to the same effect in 1871: that Britain was the only power capable of warding off the threat of Russian aggression, and that it was in the interests of the international labour movement and of socialism that she should be strong enough to do so.

In the discussions on the draft resolution, Engels, propounding his and Marx's view, told the General Council that it was imperative that Britain should be able to cripple Russia's foreign trade in a war; the Paris agreement, which paid excessive respect to private property at sea, conflicted with this need. Its repudiation would not be a breach of international law, because it had never been ratified by the British parliament and was therefore not binding on the government.[3] The working class, which owned no property, had no interest in securing its safety. But the workers were interested in Britain's recovery of her naval supremacy and in preserving it until the dissolution of the Russian empire. Engels added that all states based on force must disappear; the British empire was no exception, but that was not an immediate problem, and it could perhaps – here is one of Engels's luckier prophecies – be resolved peacefully. Meantime, Britain had to be strong enough to foil Russia's plans of conquest.

There is no doubt that in the event of war between Britain and Russia (or the Russo-German alliance which Engels believed to be in existence) the two friends would have supported the British war effort wholeheartedly; and they would have impressed upon the General Council that a British victory was in the interests of the international proletariat. Their policy in such a contingency would have been without a trace of defeatism, revolutionary or otherwise.

The first two of the three resolutions were overtaken by events; the third, encouraging Britain to denounce the Paris Declaration, was carried unanimously by the General Council in March 1871. Not surprisingly, the British government ignored it. What is more, Russia's repudiation of the treaty provisions was eventually accepted by the powers. An international conference, held in London from January to March 1871 and attended by Russia, France, Germany, Britain, Austria-Hungary, Italy and Turkey, agreed on a convention which repealed some clauses of the 1856 treaty and permitted Russia and Turkey to maintain warships in the Black Sea and arsenals along its shores.

If Russia's repudiation of the 1856 treaty provisions for the neutralization of the Black Sea marked 'the re-emergence of the Eastern Question', a rising of the Christian Slavs of Bosnia and Hercegovina in 1875, and a Bulgarian revolt in 1876 caused that 'question' to erupt into violent conflict once again.

In the summer of 1876 war broke out between Turkey and the Christian Balkan states of Serbia and Montenegro. The Serbs were soon defeated and made a separate peace, but in April 1877 Russia declared war on Turkey.

The treatment by the Turks of the sultan's Christian subjects was the main issue; Russian propaganda presented the tsar as the protector and liberator of these subject nations, and especially of the Slav peoples under Turkish rule. This line achieved some success, largely because of the barbaric methods the Turks used to crush the Bulgarian revolt. These 'Bulgarian atrocities' inflamed European public opinion and contributed to Turkey's isolation. The British government, led by Disraeli, made it clear that Britain's continued neutrality would depend on Russia's not seizing Constantinople. Russia had the support, from the outset, of Rumania and Montenegro; Bulgarian volunteers also flocked to join them. In December 1877 Serbia re-entered the war against Turkey, but the campaign went badly for the Russians at first.

Marx and Engels, who sided with Turkey from start to finish, rejoiced at the Russian defeats in the summer and autumn of 1877. In July Marx wrote to Engels (then on holiday in Ramsgate) that Russian setbacks in European Turkey were bound to 'lead directly to revolution in Russia'.[4] At the end of August Engels wrote that the Russians' military organization had collapsed; the mess they were in was 'worse than in the Crimea'.[5] Writing to F.A. Sorge in the United States at the end of September 1877, Marx said that Russia had been on the threshold of revolution for some time, and that 'the gallant Turks have hastened the explosion by years, with the thrashing they have inflicted...upon the Russian army and the Russian finances...' He added: 'This time the revolution begins in the East.'[6]

During the winter of 1877−8 the situation changed sharply. The revolution which Marx and Engels had confidently expected did not break out − not for another twenty-seven years. The Russians turned the tables on the Turks, and by the end of January 1878 had achieved overwhelming victory. Turkey was forced to sign the onerous peace of San Stefano by which Russia's Balkan allies were considerably enlarged and Russia gained new territory in Europe and Asia. The increase in strength and influence which Russia had obtained disturbed the other European powers: Austria, Britain and Germany demanded a revision. Russia yielded to pressure and accepted, at the Congress of Berlin in June/July 1878, a settlement which reduced her gains and reversed some of the territorial concessions Turkey had made at San Stefano.

The pro-Turkish sympathies of Marx and Engels were shared by their German party friends. Wilhelm Liebknecht, who had opposed the 1870 war with France and had wanted to vote against the war credits, now called for the intervention of the West and Central European powers, including Germany, against Russia. In a pamphlet entitled *On the Eastern Question, or Shall Europe Become Cossack?* he accused Bismarck of lacking 'a truly German spirit and German policy towards Russia'.[7] Liebknecht maintained that the discontent of the Christian Balkan people as whose champion the tsar posed, was 'ninety-nine per cent manufactured in Russia', and he denounced Gladstone, who campaigned for peace, as a Russian agent.

Marx read Liebknecht's pamphlet with approval. He defined his and Engels's attitude towards the Russo-Turkish war in two letters to Liebknecht in February 1878; both were published by Liebknecht as appendices to his pamphlet. The letter of 4 February 1878 − gave two reasons for the stance the two leaders in London were taking in 'emphatically siding with the Turks'. The first was odd – an argument that would hardly occur to a contemporary Marxist: 'We have studied the Turkish peasants – which means the bulk of the Turkish people – and we have found them to be unquestionably among the most efficient representatives, with the highest moral standards, of European peasantry.'[18] The second reason is more conventionally Marxist: 'A Russian defeat would have greatly hastened the social revolution in Russia...and with it a complete upheaval throughout Europe.' That had not happened, Marx added, because of England's and Austria's treachery. Both powers had, by devious means, helped Russia to win in spite of early setbacks; Bismarck, too, had contributed to Russia's success. Disraeli, the British prime minister, was apparently not one of the chief villains; according to Marx he was 'paralysed in his own cabinet by the Russian agent, the Marquis of Salisbury'.[9] Marx then reiterated a thesis he and Engels had propounded previously to explain why the side they favoured had done badly in battle: the main reason for the Turks' defeat was their failure to make a revolution in Constantinople and overthrow an incompetent and treacherous leadership.

During the last stages of the Franco-German War Marx and Engels had hoped for the intervention of Britain and other European powers on the side of France. In February 1878, they again felt that foreign intervention might save the day for the Turks. It appears from Marx's second letter to Liebknecht that they thought Britain might go to war against Russia.[10] Disraeli, apparently not as paralysed as Marx had assumed, had asked parliament to grant supplementary credits of six million pounds to prepare for possible war with Russia. A positive vote in the Commons was assured by the Conservative majority. In the division the government majority turned out to be larger than usual because only half the Liberal opposition voted against the credits while the rest abstained. To Marx's disgust, the only two working-class members of the House of Commons, Thomas Burt and Alexander Macdonald (officials of the Mineworkers' Union and originally miners themselves) voted with the Liberal rump against the credits. In his letter of 11 February, by way of explaining the attitude of the two men, Marx spoke of the demoralization of the English working class since 1848; it was now led by 'corrupt trade union leaders and professional agitators' who, like Gladstone and other prominent Liberals, were signing the praise of the tsar as the 'liberator of nations'. It is plain that in Marx's opinion the two Labour men should have voted *with* the Conservatives *for* the war credits, to enable the Tory government to make adequate preparations for war with Russia.

A curious postscript to Marx's second letter, as published in Wilhelm Liebknecht's pamphlet, speaks of 'a state of confusion' inside Russia, and continues, 'It seems desirable that, to begin with, peace will be established for a year or two. This would, in particular, foster the process of internal decay in Russia.'[11] Students of Marxist writings have expressed doubts about the authenticity of the passage. Some experts believe it was not part of Marx's original letter but an addition by Wilhelm Liebknecht.[12] If it was by Marx (which stylistic comparison makes likely), it would be a new departure, a break with the constant iteration of hope that Russia might be involved in war and be defeated.

On the other hand, this new line would be consistent with what Marx and Engels wrote from then on about the issue of war and peace. During the five-year period between the end of the Russo-Turkish war and the death of Karl Marx in March 1883, he and Engels repeatedly declared that peace would be more likely than external war to enhance the prospects of revolution in Russia, and in capitalist Europe generally. Thus, Engels said that Bismarck seemed to want war with Russia, if possible in alliance with England and Austria: 'But it would be better if in Russia the crisis quickly reached its climax, so that an internal upheaval eliminated the likelihood of war. A war against Russia and France simultaneously would be a struggle for (Germany's) national existence, and the chauvinism this would engender would put an end to our movement for years.'[13] A year later, Marx wrote, 'I hope there will not be a general war in Europe. Although in the long run the war would not be able to arrest social development (I am thinking of *economic* development), but would rather intensify it, it would still certainly result in useless exhaustion of strength for a more or less prolonged period.'[14]

In February 1882 Engels examined the question of war in Europe in connection with events in the Slav provinces of the Habsburg empire. The introduction of conscription for the southern Slavs in 1881 had sparked off a rebellion in the 'protectorate' of Hercegovina. Karl Kautsky and Eduard Bernstein, editors of the German party's official organ *Der Social-Demokrat*[15] took the side of the Slav rebels, stressing that without support from the western working class the Austrian Slavs would rely on help from the tsar. Engels disagreed, pointing out that the Slavs would anyway look to the tsar, and that it would not be in the interests of the West European workers to risk war for their sake. He wrote that Russia was on the threshold of revolution, but that (another) war might give tsarism a new lease of life.[16] On the anti-Austrian rebellion of the Slavs as a possible cause of war he said:

> . . . I do not wish to examine how it came about that the small Slav peoples regard the tsar as their only possible liberator. It is a fact that they do — we cannot change it, and things will remain like that until tsarism is overthrown. Should war come, all these curious mini-nations will take the side of tsarism, the enemy of the entire West. . . So long as this is the case I am not interested in their *instantaneous* liberation; they remain our direct enemies just as much as the tsar, their ally and protector.
>
> We have to work for the emancipation of the West European proletariat and to subordinate everything else to this aim — the Balkan Slavs may be an interesting lot, but whenever their striving for freedom conflicts with the interests of the proletariat I don't care for them in the least. The Alsatians too are oppressed, and I for one shall be pleased when we (Germans) are rid of them. But if they, on the eve of a clearly approaching revolution, should try to provoke war between France and Germany. . . and thereby delay the revolution, I shall say: Stop It! You could have as much patience as the European proletariat. Its emancipation will also be yours, but until then we will not allow you to frustrate the struggle of the proletariat. The same goes for the Slavs. The victory of the proletariat will inevitably give them genuine freedom — not the temporary and phoney freedom conferred by the Tsar. . . To unleash, for the sake of a handful of Hercegovinians, a world war which will cost a thousand times more lives than Hercegovina has inhabitants, that is not my idea of the policy the proletariat should pursue. . . [16]

Over three decades, Engels apparently had not revised in any essentials his low opinion of the smaller Slav peoples. However, in 1882 he did not repeat the sentence of doom he had pronounced in 1849 on 'entire reactionary peoples' (most Slav nations) whom the next world war (then a welcome prospect) would cause to 'disappear from the face of the earth'. In fact, in 1882 he promised the Slavs 'genuine freedom' as a result of the victorious revolution of the European proletariat. Of course, this did not necessarily mean that smaller Slav nations would enjoy full national independence, or that they would have 'a future in history'.

After dealing with the issue of the Balkan Slav rising, Engels dwelt on the possibility and the probable consequences of a confrontation between a German-Austrian coalition and tsarist Russia. His reasoning illustrates the new approach he and Marx had adopted after 1878 to the question of interaction of war and revolution: both men now regarded war as a retarding and regressive phenomenon rather than a promoter of revolution and progress.

Engels argued that once the two German monarchies were tied down in the east, chauvinism and revanchism would be rife in France, and the left bank of the Rhine would soon become a French war aim: 'It seems evident that Germany would then be engaged in a fight for her existence, which means that within Germany, too, jingoism will completely gain the upper hand...Once war is in progress, the outcome of such a European conflict...will be quite unpredictable; I would not wish for such a war at any price...' In Germany, Engels went on, a revolutionary situation was rapidly maturing, and once the Russian revolution had started (which was 'only a matter of months') Germany would follow suit. The only thing which might destroy the prospect of revolution in Russia was external war: it would undo all the splendid efforts of the Russian revolutionaries. Hence, socialists must hope that peace would be preserved.

If peace continues, the Russian Panslavists are checkmated and will soon have to leave the scene. Then the (Russian) emperor could make one last attempt with the old bankrupt bureaucrats and generals...That could not last more than a few months, and then there will be only one way out − to send for the liberals: this means some kind of National Assembly, which in turn...means revolution *à la* 1789. This being so, should I wish for war? Certainly not...[17]

Engels felt the same way ten months later, when he still believed revolution in Russia to be imminent if peace were maintained.

A European war I would consider a misfortune; this time it would be really frightful, it would kindle chauvinism everywhere for years to come, since every nation would be fighting for its existence. The whole work of the revolutionaries in Russia, who are now on the eve of victory, would have been wasted, destroyed; our party in Germany would, for the present, be swamped by the chauvinist flood and shattered, and it would be the same in France.[18]

It is obvious that for Engels, and for Marx in his last months, Russian tsarism was still the main enemy, and its overthrow still the first priority. But they had abandoned the view they had held and expressed repeatedly for over thirty years, that war would hasten revolution in Russia and elsewhere in Europe; they now felt, on the contrary, that peace would make an early revolution more likely. The reasons they gave for disliking the notion of war – that it would unleash a chauvinistic wave, that it would mean widespread exhaustion of energies, and so on – could have been adduced previously when they were welcoming the prospect of war and its outbreak. The only new factor was that war might have seemed marginally more destructive towards the end of the century, than in the fifties or sixties.

10 Colonial Conflicts and Problems 1882

The British Occupation of Egypt

The Russian-Turkish War of 1877–8 was the last major international conflict in the lifetime of Karl Marx. There were some minor wars between 1878 and Marx's death in 1883; not all of them elicited written comments from the two socialists. There is a casual reference, in Marx's correspondence, to the events which led to the Afghan War of 1878–9. Nothing exists on the first skirmish between the British and the South African Boers in 1881, when British troops were defeated at Majuba Hill and Laing's Nek. But both Marx and Engels did express their opinions on the armed clashes in Egypt in 1882.

Egypt was still nominally under Turkish suzerainty; in practice European influence was growing and Britain was particularly involved because of the purchase by Disraeli's government of the khedive's shares in the Suez Canal Company in 1875. Increasing foreign encroachment produced a nationalist reaction: a 'National Party' led by Arabi Pasha, who became minister of war in 1882, was pledged to anti-European policies. Anti-European riots in Alexandria, and the arming of the city's forts by Arabi, caused the British fleet to bombard Alexandria in July 1882 (after both the French and the Italians had refused to take part). Eventually a British force was landed, ostensibly to put down the rebellion and restore the khedive's authority; Arabi was defeated at Tell-el-Kebir in September 1882, and the nationalist revolt collapsed. British occupation of Egypt was the immediate consequence.

Socialists in France and Germany sympathized with the anti-imperialist struggle of the Egyptians and denounced Britain's armed intervention. Rallies were held in Paris, under the auspices of Jules Guesde and his followers (who included Marx's son-in-law Paul Lafargue), and resolutions of protest at British aggression were passed. The organ of the German Party, *Der Sozialdemokrat*, endorsed these resolutions and expressed support for Arabi and his party.

Marx and Engels felt strongly about British intervention but were not inclined to admire or support the Egyptian nationalist movement. The letters they exchanged at the time dealt primarily with the military aspects and the diplomatic background to the conflict. Engels believed Russia to be behind the whole affair. He suggested that Gladstone, British prime minister of the day, had agreed that Britain should take Egypt and Russia Turkish Armenia,[1] but Engels criticized the approval which the German socialists and their paper had given to the Guesdist declarations of sympathy for the Egyptian nationalists. 'It seems to me,' he wrote, 'that you come out too strongly in favour of the so-called National Party.' Arabi was most probably an ordinary pasha who begrudged foreign financiers their profits because he wished, in true oriental fashion, to pocket them himself. The Latin races were too prone to wax enthusiastic whenever somebody talked about 'revolution'.

> In my view we can very well plead the cause of the oppressed fellahin without sharing their illusions...and denounce the brutalities of the English without a show of solidarity with their present military opponents. In all questions of international politics extreme distrust is called for regarding the political sentimentalism of the French and Italian (socialist) party press; we Germans are in duty bound to demonstrate in this field, too, by our critical detachment, the theoretical superiority which, after all, we possess.[2]

Marx, who was plagued by illness and distressed after the death of his wife, did not put pen to paper as often as his friend. But there is no reason to doubt that he shared Engels's views, and that he agreed with the sceptical approach towards the Egyptian nationalists and the condemnation of Britain's aggressive expansionism. In one of the last letters he wrote, addressed to his daughter Eleanor on 9 January 1883, Marx had strong words for the British occupation of Egypt; he described it as a most scandalous 'hypocritical-Christian conquest undertaken in the midst of peace';[3] Britain had invaded and occupied Egypt without a prior declaration of war on Turkey.

Engels and Kautsky on Indian Independence

Colonial expansion was widely practised in those days by the European great (and some medium) powers. The division of the African continent and other backward parts of the globe came ever nearer to completion. The sympathies Marx and Engels always had for the native populations in the struggle against colonial oppression and their resistance to European encroachment are discernible in their comments on these crises and conflicts, but they were not generally hoping for the military defeat of the colonial power. Their basic attitude to the colonial problem and its long-term perspectives emerges from Engels's letter to Kautsky of 12 September 1882 – (where he also mentioned the Egyptian crisis).

It appears that Marx and Engels were in favour of complete 'decolonization' (to use the modern term). Engels wrote that the 'colonies proper' – countries with European populations, such as Canada, Australia, and so on – would become independent as soon as the working class assumed power in the mother country, while colonies inhabited by native peoples – India, Algeria, the Dutch, Portuguese and Spanish possessions, for instance – would be taken over by the proletarian régime and led to full independence.

> It is difficult to say how this process will develop. India will perhaps, indeed very probably, make a revolution, and since the emancipated proletariat cannot wage any colonial wars, the Indians would have to be given free rein... The same might happen elsewhere, for example, in Algeria or Egypt,...The half-civilized countries will automatically be taken in two;

92

economic necessities will see to that. The social and political stages which these countries will have to pass through before arriving at socialism — that, I think, is today but a matter of idle hypothesizing. One thing alone is certain; the victorious proletariat cannot, without undermining its own victory, impose any blessings upon a foreign nation.[4]

Engels wrote this in reply to a question raised by Kautsky about the fate of the colonies after a proletarian takeover in the metropolitan European state. Kautsky had suggested that India should continue to be ruled by a socialist Britain, in the interests of both the British and the Indian peoples.

Will the English proletariat...set India free? From the point of view of our doctrine the answer must be Yes, but I believe that our principles apply without qualification only in regard to the nations in our own cultural sphere.

I believe that if the British proletariat were to retain possession of India, both sides would benefit: the former by keeping a source of raw materials, and the latter inasmuch as the Indian people, if left to themselves, would succumb to the worst type of despotism...

Under the guidance of the European proletariat, on the other hand, India could...easily progress towards modern socialism without having to pass through the intermediate stage of capitalism....[5] In my view the question is of importance even now because it might then be in the interests of the proletariat that England does not lose India; for if she did, Russia, that is, the tsarist régime, would threaten the interests of the proletariat not only in Europe but also in Asia.[6]

Engels disagreed. He replied that the Indians would make a revolution anyway, and if they insisted on independence a British working-class government could not retain India by a colonial war.

Ironically, over half a century later, the same Karl Kautsky argued that the liberation of the colonies might come about peacefully while capitalism still held sway, at least where the colonial power was one of the European democracies where the working class could exert a measure of influence on government policies. In 1937, when Kautsky was in his eighty-fourth year, he had this to say about the prospects for decolonization:

It is a most fortunate fact that the greatest colonial power in the world is England, which is also the most democratic of the great powers of Europe. It is also the state which first, and most effectively, adopted methods of peaceful development. In England, the men and the parties standing for peaceful methods have always proved stronger and politically decisive in the last resort...We may expect the liberation of the colonies to be achieved peacefully.[7]

Yet Kautsky still counselled caution regarding India. He thought that despite her high standard of civilization she lacked the pre-conditions for democratic government: witness the survival of oriental despotism in many princely states. An immediate British withdrawal would result in complete anarchy: 'India with her strongly contrasting religions, nationalities and castes would be...an arena of endless religious, linguistic and caste conflicts.'[8]

Kautsky might have overestimated the difficulties of decolonization in India, but in the light of the bloodshed which accompanied British withdrawal ten years later his misgivings were not without foundation. However, he no longer believed, as fifty-five years previously, that even a proletarian Britain should try to keep India; nor did he repeat his statement about the disappearance of the 'savage tribes'. On the other hand, in 1882 Engels did not formulate the objections to Indian independence which Kautsky thought still existed in 1937.

PART II
Socialism after Marx –
the Approach of Armageddon

1 The Danger of European War in the 1880s and 1890s

Karl Marx died on 14 March 1883. Engels, who survived him by twelve years, continued with undiminished industry and energy to write and to comment on topical events and problems.

Colonial conflicts did not occupy a prominent place in Engels's pronouncements during that period. His published writings contain no mention of the African crisis of 1885: the Mahdist rising in the Sudan, resulting in the fall of Khartoum and the death of General Gordon. He did not take much notice of the tension between Russia and Britain over Afghanistan, which reached its climax in the spring of 1885, but some significant remarks occasioned by that crisis illustrate his views on the link between defeat in war and revolution.

According to Engels, the 'Socialist League'[1] was in a state of great excitement over 'the Afghan panic'; its militants were speculating about the probability of war, of Britain's defeat, of uproar in India, and of revolution in Britain itself with socialism triumphant. Engels confessed he was less sanguine about the prospects of a British revolution. He expressed doubts about the defeatist stance of the Socialist League, saying that Englishmen who had rid themselves of jingoism, tended to develop a hatred for their nationality. This was not necessarily wrong in itself, but was out of place when there was a question of war against the Russian tsar. The Socialist League, Engels concluded, would not set England aflame, but the Russian nihilists might succeed in doing that in Russia, with the help of an unsuccessful war.[2]

Engels clearly would not have been defeatist for Britain if war with Russia had broken out in 1885. What he wrote to Laura Lafargue makes it seem likely that he would have hoped, and possibly worked, for a British victory and Russia's defeat.

Another prominent socialist of the day, the Frenchman Jules Guesde — Engels's junior by twenty-five years — took a completely different view. He thought that Western socialists should welcome an Anglo-

Russian war, because their cause would benefit, whatever the outcome.

In an article entitled 'La Guerre féconde' ('The Fruitful War') Guesde visualized the possible revolutionary consequences of the defeat of Russia or Britain. A Russian military *débâcle* in Central Asia, he wrote, would lead to the collapse of the tsarist régime. The nobility and the bourgeoisie would then share power, in a western-style parliamentary system. Guesde did not think in terms of a Russian proletarian revolution; nor did he share Engels's view that the Russian nihilists would be the driving force. But he felt sure that the overthrow of tsarism would produce a socialist revolution, not in Russia but in Germany. Once the German working class realized that there was no longer a tsar backing the kaiser's efforts to thwart the progress of Social Democracy, the proletarian revolution would triumph on the ruins of 'the empire of iron and blood'. [3]

Guesde's approach to a British defeat was the same as the Socialist League. He thought the despatch of large British military contingents to the east might provoke a successful rising in Ireland even before battle was joined. Egypt and the Sudan would 'escape the blessings of civilization which Gordon and then Wolseley were sent to foist on them by force of arms'. The first British reverses would spark off the disintegration of 'the largest and most exploitative of all colonial empires'. The ultimate result would be the loss of India. The economic consequences of losing India and her market would make it impossible for the British workers to continue to rely on purely legal methods of political action. The British working class would have to fight for power; and in view of the high standard of its organization the struggle would not be prolonged or the outcome in doubt. Thus British capitalism might 'meet its Sedan on the banks of the river Oxus', and its downfall would herald the end of European capitalism as a whole. Universal revolution would ensue, 'with the English proletariat as its vanguard'.

The forces of reaction, Guesde went on, were aware of the threat; hence the frantic efforts in London and St Petersburg to avoid conflict. But socialists knew that such cataclysms must precede the birth of the society of the future, and hoped for the clash which would mark the beginning of the end of an intolerable system. The blood shed by the soldiers of the tsar and the soldiers of the queen would bear fruit for all mankind.

This was not how Engels viewed the threat of major war in the 1880s and early 1890s, when growing international tension heralded the division of Europe into two camps. Nearly all that Engels then wrote emphasized the atrocious character of modern war, the waste, devastation and bloodshed, and the harm such a war would do to the proletarian cause. He kept reiterating that there was no issue, in the circumstances then existing, which could justify a European war. He particularly tried to convince his socialist comrades in France, who felt strongly about the loss of Alsace-Lorraine, that there was no purpose in armed conflict for the recovery of those provinces: after a socialist takeover in Germany, which could not be long delayed, the question of Alsace-Lorraine and of North Schleswig would be settled peaceably on the basis of self-determination.

A brief Balkan war at the end of 1885 was the occasion for Engels to voice in stark terms his abhorrence of war at that stage. The belligerents were Bulgaria and Serbia.[4] Serbia had reacted to a voluntary union of Bulgaria and Eastern Rumelia (which nominally was still part of the Turkish empire) by demanding concessions to restore the balance of strength in the Balkans; when no concessions were offered she declared war. The Bulgarians had the better of the fighting, but were prevented by the great powers from making territorial gains.

Engels for once did not take sides. His overriding concern was that this conflict should not spark off a conflagration involving the major powers of Europe. When the war was but a few days old, he spoke of the likely consequences if it should spread:

There is now a serious danger of a European war. These wretched remnants of former nations, Serbs, Bulgarians, Greeks and other bandit scum...apparently begrudge each other the air they breathe and feel compelled to cut each other's greedy throats. This would all be very well but for the fact that every one of these mini-tribes could take decisions affecting the issue of war or peace in Europe...

Our movement is making such good progress...we need a few years of quiet and growing strength so badly, that we could not possibly wish for a political cataclysm. It would push our movement into the background for years to come, and afterwards we would probably – as after 1850 – have to make a very belated start from scratch...

If a great war breaks out it will lead to six million soldiers taking the field...The result will be bloodshed, devastation and eventually exhaustion as never before...One thing can be safely predicted: if that war comes it will be the last ever; it will mean the complete collapse of the class state...

Thus...whatever happens will in the end turn into something that helps our party to gain power and put an end to all that nasty old business *(dem ganzen alten Schwindel ein Ende zu machen)*. But I must confess, I wish it would be done without the killing which is not necessary. But if it has to be, I only hope that my old injury won't stop me mounting a horse now at the right moment.[5]

It is remarkable that the sixty-five-year-old Engels should have regarded his injury but not his age as an impediment to active service.

He had come to hate the idea of violent conflict, destruction and bloodshed; though still convinced of the ultimate victory of socialism, he hoped that the transition would be a comparatively peaceful process. This was not how he and Marx had assessed actual and probable conflicts twenty or thirty years previously, but Engels had not rid himself of the contempt for certain small nations which he and Marx had shown in their earlier writings. As for his predictions of the consequences of modern war, some but by no means all of them came true with the First World War, which unfortunately was not 'the last war ever'.

The Serbian-Bulgarian war did not spread, but tension did not subside. When speculation was rife again the following autumn, Engels wrote to Bebel in much the same vein, adding that a war would 'enflame chauvinism and national hatred', thus delaying the international proletarian revolution.[6]

In 1870–1 Marx and Engels had warned the Germans that the annexation of Alsace-Lorraine would lead to a Franco-Russian alliance against Germany. During the second half of the 1880s events seemed to move in that direction: a gradual rapprochement between France and Russia culminated in a formal alliance in 1893. Yet Engels was far from happy when he realized that their predictions were likely to be proved right in the near future. In an article in the French journal *Le Socialiste* in November 1886, he stressed that a French war of revenge, undertaken with Russian help and under her guidance, might produce a monarchist counter-revolution in France:

The tsar wants the restoration of the Orléans dynasty, i.e. of his close friends, whose régime would be the only one to offer him the right conditions for a sound and lasting alliance...Events in France, Russia and Germany move so much in our favour that, for the moment, we can only wish for the continuation of the *status quo.*[7]

General war, on the other hand, would make everything unpredictable again: 'Revolution in Russia and France would be delayed; our party in Germany would suffer the fate of the *Commune* of 1871.' There was no possible dispute over Alsace-Lorraine between the French and the German socialists, who had always protected against the annexations of 1871. 'The socialists of both countries are equally interested in the preservation of peace, since it is they who would have to bear all the expenses of the war.'

Engels returned frequently to the subject of European war. Every time he did so, he grew more apocalyptic about the consequences. He affirmed that for Prussia-Germany any future war would be 'a world war of never yet imagined dimension and vehemence'.[8] Eight to ten million soldiers would slaughter one another and devour all the food resources of Europe in the process.[9] Devastations would rival those of the Thirty Years' War, but compressed into three to four years, and spread over the whole continent:

There will be famine, epidemics, general brutalization – due to acute destitution – of the armies and the civilian masses...crowns will roll over the pavement by the dozens...only one result is absolutely certain: general exhaustion, and the emergence of the conditions required for the ultimate victory of the working class...At the end of the tragedy...the victory of the proletariat will either have been achieved or at least appear inevitable.

To sum up, Engels's view on the relationship of war and revolution was that the global catastrophe he feared would bring a proletarian victory in the long run, regardless of who was the winner, but only after unheard-of suffering, devastation and bloodshed. Engels believed, as we shall see, that military defeat facilitated revolution, but he did not suggest that socialists should therefore desire and promote their own government's defeat. While socialist revolution was inevitable, war or no war, it was likely earlier if peace were maintained.

In an article for the Russian journal *Sotsial-Demokrat* (published in Zurich by Plekhanov and Axelrod), which Engels began to write in December 1889 and finished in February 1890, he analysed the international situation in the specific context of Russia's foreign and domestic problems. The article, 'The Foreign Policy of Russian Tsarism', also appeared in the German periodical *Neue Zeit*, the French *Idée Nouvelle* and the English Socialist paper, *Time*. The formation of two big armed camps in Europe, Engels argued, was due to the policies of Germany and Russia. There were only two reasons why this great European war had not yet broken out. Firstly, the rapid progress in weapons technology, so that every newly-invented firearm was obsolete almost at once; secondly, uncertainty about the outcome of the gigantic struggle.

Engels maintained that the tsar's policy of conquest and aggrandizement was not popular with the Russian people. Fundamental changes were bound to take place soon, leading to the downfall of tsarist autocracy and the election of a national assembly which would represent the rural population – the vast majority of the Russian people. Then Russian foreign policy would undergo a fundamental change. The people would insist on abandoning the policy of world domination, so that pressing internal problems could be tackled and solved. Thus revolution in Russia – bourgeois-democratic not socialist, Engels believed – would also end the threat of world war. The transformation of the Russian political system would affect developments in other countries, above all Germany, where it would hasten the seizure of power by the socialists. Besides, the arms race would stop, and this would enable the advanced west to devote itself to its historic task, 'the conflict between proletariat and bourgeoisie, and the transition from the capitalist to the socialist system of society'. This revolutionary change in Russia was bound to come within a few years. 'May it come about in good time, before something else, then unavoidable, happens.'[10]

The right attitude of the proletariat to militarism and war was the main subject of debate at the Second International Socialist Congress, held in Brussels in August 1891. The First International, the International Workingmen's Association, had collapsed in the early 1870s, largely because of the antagonism between Marx and the anarchist leader Bakunin. The Second Socialist International was founded in Paris in 1889. Its congress in Brussels two years later was attended by some 370 delegates from all over Europe and the USA, most of them Marxists; anarchist delegates were excluded from the deliberations.

There was agreement that war – any war – would be a disaster and that it was the duty of the working class and all socialists to do everything to prevent a conflict in which the main European powers would be involved. No delegate showed any inclination to consider the positive effects a war might have from the socialist point of view, to suggest for example – as Marx and Engels did on several occasions after 1848 – that war against a profoundly reactionary country like Russia was desirable because it might benefit the revolutionary cause.

The Brussels congress adopted a resolution tabled jointly by a German and a French delegate, Wilhelm Liebknecht and Marie-Édouard Vaillant, which called upon the working masses to protest actively against war and military alliances, and to organize themselves internationally to ensure the victory of socialism.[11] But a Dutch delegate, former clergyman Domela Nieuwenhuis, who was later to embrace anarchism, did not consider this resolution sufficient. He asked the congress to proclaim that socialists in all belligerent countries would call on the proletarian masses to cease work on the outbreak of war. Only a small minority, which included some British and French delegates, backed Nieuwenhuis's proposals. Engels shared the view of Bebel, Liebknecht, Jules Guesde and Vaillant that it was unrealistic to hope to prevent war by calling a general strike, a view borne out by what happened when war began twenty-three years later.

Socialists in all countries continued to discuss the question of averting war, and of how a socialist party should behave if its country was involved. If a general strike was not practicable, what means of effective protest existed? It was widely felt that most working-class followers would not protest or resist; they would be swallowed up in the universal patriotic fervour which developed as a concomitant of the initial phase of modern war; and they would not listen to party leaders who proposed an anti-war campaign. But what about the élite, the vanguard: the socialist parties and their cadres? They should keep clear heads, swim against the tide if necessary, and devise their policies on the basis of unemotional, objective factors: the issues and aims of the war, its aggressive or defensive character, and the effects the outcome would have on the revolutionary party and its cause.

Nieuwenhuis, who advocated the general strike against war, maintained that distinctions between defensive wars and wars of aggression were irrelevant and impossible to make; a combination of diplomacy and propaganda could make any war appear defensive.[12] This was not the view of the international socialist leadership or of Engels who, after the Brussels congress, engaged in a somewhat acrimonious controversy on socialist policy in the event of war between Germany and a Franco-Russian coalition.

Engels visualized an attack on Germany by such a coalition. The rapprochement between Germany's eastern and western neighbours had found ostentatious expression at the visit of a French naval squadron to Kronstadt earlier that year. The squadron was enthusiastically received, and the tsar stood bareheaded, listening to the 'Marseillaise'. Engels mentioned the 'fraternization of Kronstadt' and wrote:

> Those (French) people must realize that a war against Germany in alliance with Russia is primarily also a war against the strongest and most efficacious (*schlagfertigste*) party in Europe, and that we would have no option but to hit back, with all our strength, at any aggressor who helps Russia. For either we are beaten, and then the socialist movement in Europe is finished (*kaputt*) for twenty years, or else we ourselves shall seize power... The present system in Germany could on no account survive the war. [13]

If it came to war, the Social Democrats should demand general arming of the people. They should also proclaim to the French people, *inter alia*, that, as soon as the socialists came to power in Germany the people of Alsace-Lorraine would determine their own fate. But something else must be made clear in that proclamation: 'We must declare that... if war is forced upon us — that is to say war by France in alliance with Russia — we should have to regard this as an attack on our existence and to defend ourselves with all possible means, making use of all positions at our disposal including, in that case, Metz and Strasbourg.'

Engels could not resist dwelling on the military problems for Germany in a future war on two fronts. As Austria and Italy could not be counted on as reliable allies, the German army would have to bear the brunt of the fighting. Engels sketched a plan of campaign which anticipated the basic idea of the famous *Schlieffen* plan: defensive holding operations in the east, and an offensive in the west designed to knock out France; that would be the first phase of the war. He then turned to the political aspects:

> Once France's offensive strength has been broken, but hardly before that, the conquest of Poland... can be undertaken. It must be carried out with *revolutionary* methods, combined if necessary

with the cession to a resurrected Poland of part of Prussia's Polish provinces and the whole of Galicia.[14] If that works out well there will probably be a radical upset in France. At the same time we must insist that the French are offered at least Metz and Lorraine as part of a peace settlement.

It appears from this letter that Poland was still, for Engels, the one Slav nation (apart from Russia) with an historical claim to national independence. As for the frontier changes he thought appropriate, it is interesting to note that he was far less generous to Poland (at Germany's expense) than Stalin who, after the Second World War, gave the Poles not only *all* of Germany's Polish provinces (that is, the territories which had belonged to Poland before the eighteenth-century partitions) but large slices of eastern Germany as well.

Towards the end of the letter, Engels recapitulates his main thesis:

If we (i.e. the Germans) are beaten, the flood-gates will be open, for years to come, for chauvinism and clamouring for a war of revenge. If we win our party will come to power. *Thus Germany's victory is the victory of revolution, and if war comes we must not only hope for a German victory but must do all we can to bring it about.* (Emphasis added.)

This emphasis on the desirability of a German victory, in a just war against a Franco-Russian alliance, seemed to justify the position of the German 'social-patriots' (to use Lenin's term which was meant to be abusive) of the First World War.

In a later letter to Bebel, Engels raised the question which led to a split in the party in 1915 – the vote of the SPD Reichstag group on the war credits. He thought it possible that a war would start in the spring of 1892, in which case the government, led by Chancellor Count Caprivi, would ask the Reichstag to approve the war budget. This is how Engels assessed the situation:

If we are convinced that the balloon will go up next spring we can hardly be opposed *on principle* to these requests for money. And then we should be in a pretty awkward position. All the sycophantic parties would shout with joy, saying that they had been right and that we now had to trample our twenty-year-old policies underfoot. And such an about-turn, without preparation, would also lead to tremendous friction within the party – as well as internationally.[15]

He suggested that the SPD should vote for the credits on certain conditions, which would include reforms in army organization in the direction of a people's militia. If the authorities made provision for the military training of the masses of fit but untrained men, to be disposed in *cadres* for real fighting, not parades and square-bashing, the party could agree to the war credits. But there would also have to be political conditions:

> We could tell the Government that...we should be prepared to support them against the external enemy, provided they pursue the war with utter determination, using all available means, including revolutionary ones. If Germany is attacked from both east and west, all defensive means are good. What will be at stake is the nation's existence and, as far as we are concerned, the position and the prospects for the future, which we have fought for and won and intend to hold on to. The more revolutionary the warfare, the closer will it be to our own ideas. And it could happen that the bourgeois and the gentry turn out to be cowards, bent only on saving their property, so that *we* would then appear to be the only resolute war party. Of course, it could also happen that we must take power and act the way the French did in 1794 in order to expel the Russians and their allies from our country.

This is exactly the policy of 'revolutionary *defencism*': the Socialist Party's rise to power would be the result, not of their own government's defeat but of victory obtained with the socialists' superior determination.

In the autumn of 1891, when these letters were written, Engels accepted an invitation from Guesde's Workers party *(Parti Ouvrier)* to contribute to the Party's *Almanach* for 1892. He welcomed the chance to expound his ideas about socialist policy in the event of war, in an article which would be read by all active French socialists. He gave Bebel a *précis* of what he intended to write, reiterating some of the points made in his previous letters, and adding further considerations and arguments. He would tell the French that there could be no possible reason for a Franco-German war over Alsace-Lorraine, and continued:

> But if nevertheless the French bourgeois go to war and in so doing place themselves at the service of the tsar...then they would be

betraying France's revolutionary mission. It is the duty of us German socialists...to maintain our position in the vanguard of the labour movement, not only against the internal enemy but also against the foreign foe. *If the Russians win we shall be crushed* (emphasis added). Therefore, if Russia starts a war, we'll hit them hard, we'll hit the Russians and their allies, *whoever they may be* (Engels's emphasis)....We have not forgotten the glorious example the French gave us in 1793, and if we are forced we shall, maybe, celebrate the centenary of 1793, by proving that the German workers of 1893 are not unworthy of the *sansculottes* of the past: if then French troops cross our frontiers they will be received with the defiant words of the 'Marseillaise': Quoi, ces cohortes étrangères feraient la loi dans nos foyers? (Should we let these foreign cohorts lay down the law in our land?)[16]

Again we have a complete rejection by Engels of defeatist tactics: 'If the Russians win we shall be crushed.' He was convinced that a Russian defeat of Germany, a comparatively liberal state, with the rule of law and a legal labour movement, would mean the end of German socialism. Engels was probably wrong in his belief that a German victory achieved with socialist participation would lead to the seizure of power by German Social Democracy, but he was right in thinking that a victorious Russia would make a clear sweep of the achievements of the German labour movement and of libertarian and democratic features of imperial Germany.[17]

Engels's article was published in the *Almanach* for 1892 under the heading 'Socialism in Germany'. The chapter dealing with the problems of socialist policy in a war between capitalist countries, and specifically between imperial Germany and a Franco-Russian alliance follows the general plan outlined in Engels's letter to Bebel. Paraphrasing his and Marx's previous statements, Engels asserted that the annexation of Alsace-Lorraine had made German reconciliation with France impossible for years and had made Russia the arbiter of Europe without gaining any real advantage for Germany. As against the existing German empire, the French republic represented the revolution, albeit bourgeois, but only so long as it did not take orders from the tsar.

In a war against a Franco-Russian coalition, Germany would be fighting for her existence. If she won she would have nothing to annex: there were no German-speaking territories to east or west, and she already had too many foreign-speaking provinces. If Germany lost, Russia would annex East Prussia and the Polish provinces, Denmark would get the whole of Schleswig, France the entire left bank of the Rhine:

> Should France refuse this conquest, Russia would force it upon her. For Russia needs a perpetual bone of contention, a cause of never-ending discord between France and Germany. Reconciliation between these two great countries would end Russia's hegemony in Europe. Germany, thus dismembered, could keep alive only by preparing for another war for the restoration of the conditions of her national existence. [18,19]

In the circumstances, socialists could not want war: 'The socialists of all countries are in favour of peace....'

Engels then modified, to some extent, his mental picture of events if the great European war broke out after all. Masses of armed men (he now put the figure at fifteen to twenty million) would 'slaughter each other', and there would be unprecedented devastation. The war would lead either to the immediate triumph of socialism or leave behind such ruin that capitalist society would no longer be viable. In that case, the social revolution might be delayed for ten or fifteen years but would then 'all the more rapidly and thoroughly' achieve victory.

Bebel and the other leaders of German Social Democracy agreed with Engels on the desirability of peace and the need to defend Germany against a Russian attack. On the latter issue there had never been much doubt amongst the German party's leadership. When Engels wrote to Bebel in 1885 that, if war proved unavoidable, he hoped to mount a horse again, he knew he would not be misunderstood. Bebel, who had refused to vote for the credits in the war against France in 1870, repeatedly expressed in later years his party's willingness to defend Germany against Russia. In 1891 he told the SPD Congress at Erfurt — the first congress of the reconstituted Social Democratic Party after the expiry of the Anti-Socialist Law: 'If Russia, the refuge of cruelty and barbarism, the enemy of all human culture, attacks Germany in order to dismember and destroy her... then we are as much or even more concerned than those who lead Germany today, and we shall fight to repel the attack.' [20]

If Engels's article in the *Almanach* encountered no criticism from the German socialist leadership, reaction in France was by no means uniformly favourable. Guesde and Lafargue had approved it beforehand, but several leading members of the Workers' Party, in particular Vaillant and Bonnier, violently disputed Engels's contention that German Social Democrats should defend their country against Russia and her allies.

In the ensuing discussion within the French leadership, Jules Guesde pointed out that French socialists would also take part in a war of defence if France were attacked. Engels agreed, but a critical letter from Bonnier contrasted the respective positions of the French and the German socialists: while the French had protested against the alliance with Russia and would not hear of war against Germany, Engels and Bebel visualized the possibility of a defensive war which German socialists would support. Engels replied that all German socialists had always taken it for granted that, if Germany attacked France, French socialists would take up arms in defence of their country. This was so obvious that there had been no need for the French comrades to state it explicitly. Engels added that his whole *Almanach* article would have been absurd but for the implicit assumption that the French socialists would act that way in a defensive war. 'All I must insist on is that the same principle is applied to the German socialists in the event of a Russian attack, even if that attack has the backing of official France.'[21] In a further letter, Engels reminded Bonnier of Guesde's statement that the Workers' Party would take part in armed resistance if Germany attacked France. 'Thus Guesde and I are entirely of the same opinion, and you will have to argue it out with him.'[22]

He then turned to the problem of preventing war by socialist action. Bonnier had mentioned that at the 1891 Brussels International Congress he had voted for the 'general-strike-against-war' resolution of Domela Nieuwenhuis. Engels commented: 'With his plan you would ruin all socialist parties in Europe.' It was an illusion to think that socialists could hinder the kaiser, the French president or the tsar in provoking war: 'If war breaks out then those who are on the losing side will have the possibility and the duty to carry out the revolution – that is all.'

This is perhaps the nearest Engels ever got to a revolutionary-defeatist formula; but he was still far from embracing the doctrine Lenin later proclaimed as 'axiomatic'. Engels merely stated the obvious fact that the defeat of one's government tends to facilitate revolution. There is no reason to think he no longer believed that 'if the Russians win we (German socialism, not the German imperial establishment) shall be crushed', which meant that socialists and workers of a Russian-occupied or Russian-dominated Germany would be unable to make a revolution.

Engels did not say, or imply that because of this connection between defeat and revolution a socialist party should either want the defeat of its own government or work for it. Such an interpretation is precluded by what he had said about the French socialists' right and duty to repel German aggression. If the French republic waged a defensive war against Germany, with socialist support, and suffered defeat, the French socialists would have 'the possibility and the duty', according to Engels, to exploit their bourgeois government's plight by carrying out a revolution to replace the bourgeois republic by a proletarian dictatorship. This is what the *Communards* tried to do in 1871, when Engels and Marx approved their policy of combining resistance to the Germans with the attempt to overthrow the defeated French government. In the opinion of Engels in 1892, and of both Marx and Engels in 1871, a defencist policy was fully compatible with revolutionary exploitation of defeat.

The Workers' Party in France was a Marxist party, and those of its members critical of the *Almanach* article were still using moderate terms when speaking of a German nationalist bias in the speeches and writings of Engels or Bebel. Some non-Marxist French socialists, anarchists and syndicalists were more outspoken. They renewed the charges previously levelled at Marx and Engels by prominent anarchists, branding the two friends as 'Prussian socialists' who had always stood for German supremacy on the continent and supremacy of their own theory in the international field.

No less harsh were the complaints voiced at the International Socialist Congress in Zurich in 1893 against the Germans, and more specifically against August Bebel and his anti-Russian stance. One of the chief critics was the Dutchman Nieuwenhuis who again moved a resolution calling for general strikes as a response to war. Nieuwenhuis had written a pamphlet entitled *Currents in German Social Democracy* in which he argued that Engels and Bebel had advocated joint action against Russia by the bourgeoisie and the proletariat of Germany, and that this amounted to an abandonment of the class struggle.[23] Bebel had also been guilty of jingoism and of betraying the principles of internationalism. At the Zurich congress, Nieuwenhuis again accused the German Social Democrats of chauvinism.

He was rebuked by the foremost Russian Marxist, G.V. Plekhanov, who in turn accused Nieuwenhuis of kindling hatred between the French and the Germans. Plekhanov denied that Bebel had preached national hatred; Bebel's denunciation of tsarism and the tsar had the full approval of the Russian Social Democrats who believed that tsarism must fall if liberty and the Russian people were to prevail. He continued, 'If the German army crossed our borders, its soldiers would come as liberators, just as a hundred years ago the French troops of the National Convention entered Germany...to bring the people freedom.'[24]

It appears that in 1893 Plekhanov was defeatist for his country, in that he hoped for the victory of a comparatively progressive Germany over reactionary Russia. He believed that the defeat of tsarism would bring about the régime's revolutionary overthrow, and he therefore sided with his country's enemy, as Lenin did in the Russo-Japanese war of 1904–5. Plekhanov was not an all-round defeatist, as Lenin was from 1914 to 1917. By the time that hypothetical war between Germany and Russia became a reality, Plekhanov had made a complete about-turn. In 1914 he was what Lenin called a 'social-patriot'; he maintained that as Russia had now acquired the rudiments of parliamentary institutions and of freedom of the press, she was no longer the bulwark of reaction and despotism she had been before the 1905 Revolution; in comparison with the Central Powers, the Entente camp comprising Russia and her democratic West European allies was more progressive and deserved support.

At the Zurich Congress, Domela Nieuwenhuis moved a more incisive version of the anti-war resolution defeated at Brussels two years earlier. This said that socialist workers in the countries concerned should react to a declaration of war by general strike, by refusing to serve in the armed forces, and by an appeal to women to keep their husbands and sons at home. The resolution suffered the same fate as its predecessor. Congress carried instead a resolution tabled, with Engels's approval, by the German party; it called upon socialists everywhere to combat the chauvinistic designs of the ruling classes, to strengthen the bonds of international working class solidarity, and to strive relentlessly for the abolition of capitalist class rule: its overthrow would mean the end of war, the achievement of world peace.[25] The Dutch delegate's attacks on Bebel (and by implication Engels) were also rejected, and Engels received a standing ovation when he arrived to deliver the closing address. Plekhanov was by no means the only delegate to speak up in defence of the Germans.

Engels and Bebel had, of course, a cogent defence. They could refute the charge of being German nationalists by pointing out that they would support France against an aggressive war launched by Germany as they had made clear. But for Engels it was not only Germany's independence but her unity as a state that was worth preserving and defending, by force if need be. In a letter to Paul Lafargue, written in June 1893, he took the French socialists to task for declaring, in an appeal to French workers, that their party was at one with the German Social Democrats *'contre l'empire d'Allemagne'*. Engels pointed out that the French word *empire* could mean either a monarchy under an emperor ('imperial Germany' corresponding to the German *'Kaisertum'*), in which case the phrase used by the French comrades would be correct, or else it could be the equivalent of the German word *'Reich'*, with the stress on central power as the representative of *national unity*. The French phrase would then denote opposition to German unity. In other words, the formula was ambiguous and therefore objectionable; in fact, the German bourgeois press, Engels said, had rendered the phrase as 'against the *German Reich*', thus giving the impression that the *Parti Ouvrier* thought the achievement of German national unity was to be nullified. Engels added: 'For this unity, as the political basis of their existence, the German socialists would fight to the last. *Never* would we allow Germany to be reduced to the state of fragmentation and impotence that existed before 1866.'[26]

So Engels, while intensely disliking Bismarck and his policy, was adamant about the need to defend Bismarck's main achievement, the unification of Germany (minus Austria). As for his predictions of what would happen to Germany if she were defeated in a two-front war, they have largely come true, in a small way after the First, more fully after the Second World War. Germany lost much territory − less than Engels thought she would lose in the west, but much more than he expected in the east; the country was partitioned, albeit not to the extent of pre-1866 conditions; on the other hand, one of the German states emerging from the partition no longer enjoys independence. It is a supreme irony of history that nearly all these disasters (as Engels would have termed them) were inflicted upon Germany by a great power whose rulers claim that their guiding principles derive from the teachings of Marx and Engels.

2 The Sino-Japanese War 1894—5 and its Aftermath

The last international conflict Engels commented on was the war between China and Japan which broke out in 1894. It arose from rivalry about supremacy in Korea, one of China's 'tributary kingdoms'. In the 1880s Japan, who had rid herself of her antiquated institutions and embarked upon a modern capitalist development, challenged the influence which decrepit imperial China still wielded in Korea, a country having strategic importance as well as valuable natural resources (especially coal and iron).

Growing tension led to naval clashes, and in August 1894 Japan declared war. In addition to the fighting at sea, there were land battles in Korea. Japan was victorious on all fronts, and China sued for peace in March 1895. By the treaty of Shimonoseki, China ceded Formosa (Taiwan), some other islands, and the Liaotung peninsula to Japan, and also made some economic concessions. A few months later Japan, under pressure from Russia, France and Germany, returned Liaotung to China, but her victory gained her international prestige and set her on the road to great power status.

Engels was alive and active when all this happened. (He died of cancer on 5 August 1895.) His published writings contain two mentions of the Far Eastern conflict and the problems it engendered. He believed that the war heralded a profound economic transformation in China: the emergence of large-scale industry, a modern railway system, and so on, would lead to the emigration of masses of Chinese coolies to Europe, and this would speed the final crisis of European capitalism. China, Engels added, was the only backward country still to be conquered for capitalist production: it was 'the splendid irony of history...that while the conquest is being completed, capitalism is becoming impossible in its own home'.[1] Engels was obviously still convinced that the end of European capitalism was at hand.

He assessed more closely what he thought would be the results of the war in a letter to Laura Lafargue, written at about the same time. He predicted, correctly, that China would be beaten at sea and on land, and again spoke of the inevitable collapse of old China and her traditional economy.

The Chinese...will have to Europeanize themselves, to open their ports to general trade, to build railways and factories, thus wholly destroying the old system which enabled them to feed so many millions. There will suddenly be a steadily rising excess population...Millions will want to emigrate. And then the Chinese coolies will be everywhere, in Europe, America and Australia, and they will try to lower the wages and depress the living standards of our workers to the level of Chinese standards...The English (workers) will be the first to suffer from this invasion...I confidently expect that this Japanese-Chinese war will hasten our victory in Europe by at least five years and facilitate it immensely, because it will bring all non-capitalist classes over to our side. [2]

In the 1850s, when China was involved in hopeless wars against Britain and France, Engels had also spoken of the impending death agony of 'the oldest empire in the world', and of the beginning of 'a new era for all Asia'. He had regarded the war then in progress as a catalyst for fundamental changes and that vast country's evolution towards modern capitalism. His view was unchanged nearly forty years later. But in the 1850s Marx and Engels had denounced the European powers as aggressors against international law and humanitarian standards. Engels made no such condemnation of Japan in 1894, although her interference in Korea was clearly the beginning of long-term territorial conquest and expansion on the mainland of Asia — a project which kept Japan's military machine busy for the ensuing half-century. Engels seemed to welcome Japan's actions because he believed and hoped that China's defeat would bring about social — though not yet socialist — revolution in China and set off a chain reaction which would hasten proletarian revolution in the whole of the advanced West.

An *obiter dictum* on the Sino-Japanese war is to be found in the article, written ten years later, where Lenin expressed joy at the Japanese capture of Port Arthur in January 1905. He recalled that Russia, France and Germany had forced Japan to modify the terms of the treaty of Shimonoseki, and return the Liaotung peninsula to China. 'Ten years ago...reactionary Europe was upset by the breaking-up of China by Japan, and united to deprive her of the best fruits of her victory.'[3] These 'best fruits' included the outright annexation of Chinese territory after a war of aggression. As Bertram

D. Wolfe remarks, the fact that the territory in question (of which Port Arthur formed part) belonged to China and not to either Russia or Japan does not seem to have bothered Lenin at all. [4]

The European powers were not slow to take advantage of China's defeat: they demanded, and obtained, commercial concessions, special privileges, leases of territory. Germany grabbed Tsingtao in 1897, and Russia Port Arthur the following year; other powers prepared to share in what seemed to be incipient partition of the huge empire. Xenophobic outbursts by the Chinese people were a natural reaction. Unrest and anti-foreign riots intensified during 1898 and 1899, and in 1900 the Boxer rising, partly abetted by the authorities, proclaimed as its aim the elimination of the foreign presence in China.

Thousands of foreigners, including missionaries, were killed, and so were many Chinese Christians. The German minister in Peking was assassinated, and the legation quarter was besieged by rebels. An international force of British, French, Germans, Russians, Japanese and Americans entered the country. Peking was taken, and looted, and the rising was quelled. The interventionist powers extorted indemnities and imposed sanctions. The upshot was the opposite of what the rebellion had hoped to achieve: enhanced foreign influence and more concessions.

The fighting that followed the Boxer rising, and especially Russia's part in the suppression of the rising, was the subject of Lenin's first comment on a contemporary war. It appeared under the title 'The War in China' in the first issue of *Iskra*, in December 1900. [5] The article is a fierce attack on the tsarist government, and dwells at length on Russian army atrocities and the sufferings Russia and the other powers were inflicting on the Chinese people. The government was claiming that it was on a 'civilizing mission' by crushing a revolt and helping the legitimate Chinese government to restore law and order. The revolt, according to the official version, stemmed from 'Chinese hatred for European culture and civilization'. In truth, Lenin wrote, the Chinese did not hate the European peoples with whom they had never had any quarrel:

They hate the European capitalists and the European governments...How can the Chinese not hate those who have come to China solely for the sake of gain...for the purpose of deception, plunder and violence; who have waged wars against China in order to win the right to trade in opium . . . and who hypocritically pursued their policy of plunder under the guise of spreading Christianity?[6]

This was, Lenin continued, the policy of colonialism, based on the need the industrialized capitalist countries felt to acquire under-developed territories 'as markets for manufactured goods and sources of high profits'. To enable a handful of capitalists to reap profits, bourgeois governments were waging endless wars, sending soldiers to die, and driving colonial peoples to desperate revolts or death from starvation: 'We need only recall the rebellion of the native peoples against the British in India and the famine that prevailed there, or think of the war the English are now waging against the Boers. And now the European capitalists have placed their rapacious paws upon China.'

Beneficiaries of the Russian government's policy of conquest in China would be capitalists making goods for the Asian market, contractors piling up profits on urgent war orders, and a few nobles in the civil and military services. No benefits would accrue to the Russian working classes, quite the reverse:

Thousands of ruined families, whose breadwinners have been sent to the war; an enormous increase in the national debt and the national expenditure; mounting taxation; greater power for the capitalists, the exploiters of the workers; worse conditions for the workers; still greater mortality among the peasantry; famine in Siberia — this is what the Chinese war promises and is already bringing.

The Russian press was conducting a hate campaign against the Chinese, against 'the savage yellow race', and Russian workers should not fall for that kind of propaganda: 'The duty of all class-conscious workers is to rise with all their might against those who are stirring up national hatred and diverting the attention of the working people from their real enemies. The policy of the tsarist government in China is a criminal policy which impoverishes, corrupts, and oppresses the people more than ever.'

Yet Lenin issued no defeatist slogan and no call to the workers and peasants in uniform to turn their weapons around and wage war against their commanders and the country's rulers. 'There is only one

116

way in which the new burden the war is thrusting upon the working people can be removed, and that is the convening of an assembly of representatives of the people, which would put an end to the autocracy of the government and compel it to have regard for interests other than those solely of a gang of courtiers.'

Thus Lenin's only solution was the summoning of a constituent assembly, a demand already made by socialists, bourgeois liberals and nearly all groups and tendencies opposed to the tsarist establishment. A constituent assembly did meet in Russia seventeen years later, a few months after the Bolshevik seizure of power. After just over twelve hours of debate, Lenin ordered its dissolution. It was never reconvened.

3 Colonial Wars of the United States 1898–1901: Cuba and the Philippines

A revolt against Spanish rule began in Cuba in 1895. American opinion was inflamed when the Spaniards reacted with harsh repression. Tension between Spain and the USA grew, and the blowing up of an American battleship in Santiago harbour led to war. In June 1898 American troops landed in Cuba, and Spain was soon defeated. By the peace treaty of Paris, in December, Spain relinquished Cuba and agreed to US occupation of the island.

Another Spanish colony, the archipelago of the Philippines, was in revolt during the closing years of the nineteenth century. On the outbreak of the Spanish-American war the rebels proclaimed an independent republic, but the United States purchased the archipelago from Spain and refused to recognize its independence. It took nearly three years for the Americans to put down what they called the 'insurrection', and the territory was annexed.

From the Marxist point of view the wars in Cuba and the Philippines were typical colonial wars: wars waged by a colonial power for colonial conquest, or for the defence of colonial possessions. The conventional Marxist view of colonialism is that it was the outright plunder of colonial wealth in the sixteenth, seventeenth and eighteenth centuries, while in the twentieth-century age of 'imperialism' colonial expansion is the acquisition of new markets for the export of capital, and of sources of raw material, to be tapped profitably with the help of cheap native labour.[1]

The question of colonialism and imperialist war was on the agenda of the Paris congress of the Second Socialist International in 1900. When that congress met, the Spanish-American war was over, but that in the Philippines was still in progress, as was that between Britain and the two Boer republics in South Africa.[2] The Socialist World Congress unanimously carried a resolution (moved by the Dutch delegate Van Kol) stating that capitalist development was leading to colonial expansion and international disputes, to growing chauvinism in all countries and to ever-increasing military expenditure. The resolution urged the working classes 'to combat, with all means at their disposal, the colonial expansion of capital; to condemn the colonial policies of the bourgeoisie; and everywhere emphatically to castigate the innumerable acts of injustice and cruelty to which the natives are unavoidable subjected in all colonies...'[3]

The wars with Spain and with the Filipinos were not universally popular in the USA. The Cuban campaign was too short to produce lasting controversy; besides, it ended Spanish colonial rule and gave the islanders some independence, which pleased American liberal opinion. The long war in the Philippines, waged not against a European colonial power but against natives struggling for freedom, aroused more hostility. People from all walks of life felt that conquering colonial territory and subjugating the inhabitants violated American principles and traditions.[4]

The socialist movement in the United States was too weak to play a significant part in the anti-war campaign. In 1900 the Social Democratic Party had nominated Eugene V. Debs as its candidate for the presidency. The Social Democrats sometimes denounced the Philippine war, but generally regarded the question of imperialism as secondary to their objective of victory for socialism at home. Their approach to the war was not unlike that of some British Fabians who considered the question of the South African war to be outside the society's province, since 'Socialism is an economic issue and has nothing to do with other questions.'[5]

Some American socialists, however, came forward as champions of anti-imperialism. In Chicago in 1900 several party members announced their support for President McKinley's Democratic opponent, William J. Bryan, who demanded immediate Philippine independence. Samuel Jones, the socialist mayor of Toledo, also backed Bryan, and some members of the SDP in Boston signed an Open Letter to Eugene Debs, urging him to stand down in favour of Bryan. They declared:

> The actual issue...in this campaign is monopoly versus the people. Imperialism itself is simply monopoly showing its teeth on foreign soil. The war of conquest in the Philippines is merely to give the trusts more markets...A vote for Bryan is a vote for the first practicable step toward the cooperative commonwealth, though neither Bryan nor the Democratic party may realize that fact.

The Democrats, according to the signatories, represented mainly 'the farmers and artisan classes, the small merchants and the masses of the common people', while 'the Republican party is owned and controlled by the monopolies.' The signatories, all personal friends of Debs and middle-class members of the party, emphasized that by continuing his candidature Debs would draw votes from Bryan and help to elect McKinley, 'the tool of the trusts'.

Debs had been reluctant to accept nomination, but now he refused to withdraw. The Philippine issue does not seem to have figured prominently in his campaign. In 1917, he would fiercely oppose United States participation in the First World War, but in 1900 he did not agitate for the end of the war and independence for the Filipinos. His party's manifesto demanded, *inter alia*, the 'abolition of war as far as the United States are concerned, and introduction of international arbitration', but did not mention the Philippine war in which the USA was engaged at the time.

4 The South African (Boer) War 1899–1902

The twentieth century opened with two colonial wars in progress, one in the Philippines and the other in South Africa, between Britain and the two Boer republics of Transvaal (the 'South African Republic') and the Orange Free State.

The Boer War was preceded by protracted wrangling about the

British imperial claim to paramountcy and the degree of self-government to be granted to the Boers. In 1877 Britain, already the possessor of two crown colonies in Southern Africa – the Cape and Natal – had annexed the Transvaal; in 1881 she annexed the diamond-rich region of the Orange Free State. A Boer uprising and the defeat of a British force in 1881 regained a measure of independence for the Transvaal, subject to British supervision in foreign affairs.

Britain's policy changed radically when gold was found in the Transvaal in 1886. The government championed the claims to political rights of the *uitlanders*: immigrants, mainly from Britain, whom the discovery of gold had attracted to the Transvaal. Negotiations between the British high commissioner Milner and President Kruger of the Transvaal were fruitless, and war began in October 1899. The Orange Free State joined the Transvaal.

Initially, the campaign went badly for Britain, but during 1900 she reconquered and annexed most of the Boer territories. Guerilla warfare continued throughout 1901 and the beginning of 1902; in May 1902 the Boers had to agree to a peace treaty making their territories crown colonies, with the promise of future self-government within the empire. Self-government was granted within a few years, and was followed by federation with the other British colonies and the establishment, in 1910, of the 'Union of South Africa'.

From the socialist point of view, the Boer War was unquestionably an 'imperialist' war of conquest and colonial expansion on Britain's part. The discovery of gold played a crucial part in Britain's determination to regain possession of the Transvaal. In a contemporary pamphlet, George Bernard Shaw had this to say: 'A troublesome and poor territory, which the empire cast off into the hands of a little community of farmer emigrants, had unexpectedly turned out to be a gold-reef; and the Empire accordingly takes it back again from the farmers.'[1] This was not intended as a denunciation of the British government's war aims; Shaw thought it right that the British empire, rather than the Boer republic, should control the gold mines.[2]

The war found Britain's socialists, and indeed the whole of the country, in a state of profound disunity. The Conservative Party, then in office, was solidly behind the war policy of Lord Salisbury's government. The bulk of the Liberal Party supported the war; but their radical wing opposed it. Most of the people were pro-war, many fanatically so, and critics of government policies encountered violent hostility. Hatred of the 'pro-Boers', as all opponents of the war were commonly called, was so strong that speakers at anti-war meetings were often howled down and sometimes physically assaulted. Lloyd George, one of the prominent Liberal radicals, escaped from a raging mob after a speech in Birmingham only by putting on a policeman's uniform. Keir Hardie and Fred Jowett – pro-Boer like all ILP leaders – faced angry crowds in Scotland, Yorkshire and Lancashire.

At the outbreak of war the British labour movement, with its long-standing trade union traditions, was on the point of branching out into independent politics. The Labour Representation Committee was founded in 1900, forerunner of the Labour Party which emerged a few years later as a political force. The movement was deeply divided over the war. The Independent Labour Party, founded in 1893, was un-equivocally opposed. Fred Jowett, one of its leaders, declared the war an imperialist venture in the interest of capitalist exploiters who coveted the Boer gold mines. It was the duty of socialists to denounce the war and everything connected with it. But other socialists, such as Robert Blatchford of the *Clarion*, supported it.

The Fabian Society, with a membership of less than 1000, was split three ways. A few of its leading members considered the war to be justified and acquiesced in the government's policies. The majority took the view, expressed in a postal ballot, that the society need not commit itself on the war question which was 'outside its province'. Edward R. Pease, for many years general secretary of the society, devoted many pages of his *History of the Fabian Society* to this episode of the South African war. From his account, the non-committal majority took refuge in such formulae as 'Socialism is an economic issue and has nothing to do with other questions,' or the question of the war was one 'which Socialism cannot solve and does not touch'.[3] But a substantial minority of Fabians were pro-Boer, and some were active members of the (anti-war) ILP. Some of these accepted the majority decision without approving it; but fifteen die-hard opponents resigned; they included Ramsay MacDonald, (Britain's first Labour prime minister in 1924), and the suffragette leader Emmeline Pankhurst.

Bernard Shaw and Sidney and Beatrice Webb belonged to the non-committal majority, but Shaw came very near to justifying the war. He undertook to draft a lengthy statement on behalf of the executive, setting out the society's view and taking into account the criticisms and conflicting views of socialists generally. The result was his 100-page pamphlet *Fabianism and the Empire*; after being approved by the majority, it was adopted as the society's manifesto for the impending general election. The pamphlet stresses the responsibility of the great powers for administering the world's resources 'in the interests of civilization as a whole'. As regards South Africa the pamphlet declared:

It is not to those interests that such mighty forces as goldfields, and the formidable armaments that can be built upon them, should be wielded irresponsibly by small communities of frontiersmen. Theoretically they should be internationalized, not British-imperialized; but until the Federation of the World becomes an accomplished fact we must accept the most responsible imperial federations available as a substitute for it...This was the best answer, for the purpose of excusing the war, to Kruger.[4]

Shaw's pamphlet has been praised by some British socialists and bitterly attacked by others, both at the time of publication and in after years, when the controversies about the Boer War were recalled. Margaret Cole called Shaw's reasoning an example of 'dangerous special pleading'.[5] Ramsay MacDonald was more outspoken:

The society stated its views on imperialism in a tract which ranks among the worst ever published by any democratic body...Mr. Shaw must have written it as a perverse joke, but the Fabian Society took it as philosophy and common sense. Never has a militarist and exploiting international capitalism received such a brilliant defence. When the thing was published those of us who had resigned were filled with gladness that our Fabian days had ended.[6]

On the society's refusal to condemn the Boer War, MacDonald said, 'A socialist society which...condones the South African War might be admirable for drafting gas and water programmes, but it was evidently quite useless for educating people into the independence of thought and strength of judgement without which gas and water are of no importance.'[7]

Beatrice Webb took a completely different view. She gave as her opinion that Shaw had done his job 'with incomparable skill', and that his tract could be regarded as 'the most prescient and permanently instructive public document of its date, notably as regards the relative rights and duties of the white and the coloured citizens of the empire'.[8]

One has the impression that Beatrice Webb cannot have had a clear recollection of the pamphlet's contents, and especially of what it said about the rights and duties of different ethnic groups.

Shaw did refer to the coloured inhabitants of South Africa: he spoke of 'the native races who must be protected despotically by the empire or abandoned to slavery or extermination'.[9] When discussing the settlement which should follow the British empire's victory, Shaw advocated the early establishment of self-government: 'What we have to do in South Africa...is to guarantee a free constitution of responsible government within the empire to the *white inhabitants* of these vast territories.' (Emphasis added.)[10] The implied exclusion of the non-whites in a socialist document, even one written in 1900, makes strange reading. While few people would have advocated at that time what is now called African majority rule, it is a fact that native suffrage already existed in both Natal and the Cape colony. Property qualifications excluded the non-Europeans (Africans and Indians) from representation corresponding to their numbers, but race or colour were not specified in the statutes as relevant to the right to vote. Shaw's insistence that 'a free constitution of responsible government' should be guaranteed to the 'white inhabitants' of South Africa is thus a suggestion to disenfranchise those Africans who possessed a vote – which is exactly what happened.

It is therefore extraordinary that Beatrice Webb should have praised Shaw's tract for what it said about the 'relative right and duties' of white and coloured South Africans, but this was not the only example of her memory letting her down about what people said or did during the Boer War. In respect of the controversies raging at the time, she says, 'No one in Great Britain or South Africa seems to have remembered that these various claimants to power, whether Boer or British ...were only a minority...amid a vast majority of Kaffirs...amid whom this variegated white minority had intruded itself.'[11]

It is probably true that Beatrice and Sidney Webb and many other Fabians, including Bernard Shaw, gave little thought to the position and problems of the black majority in the disputed territories, but other British socialists paid great attention to the effect the war was likely to have on their interests.

Justice, organ of the (Marxist) Social Democratic Federation (SDF), dealt with this in detail. The issue of 20 July 1901 carried a letter from H.M. Hyndman, the SDF leader, in which he explained his decision to stop agitating against the war and for the independence of the Boer republics. After paying tribute to 'Boer pluck and Boer persistence in resisting our attempts to conquer them', Hyndman wrote:

> I hold...that this is a struggle between two burglars...The country belongs neither to Boer nor to Briton...Some of our eager members of the SDF...disregard the fact that the independence of the Boers, for which they clamour, necessarily involves the complete submission of the natives...The future of South Africa is, I believe, to the black man; and if I am going to agitate for the independence of anybody, it is for the independence of the splendid native tribes who are being crushed by the Boers and ourselves together that I propose to go to work.

Hyndman, who had previously denounced the reconquest of the Sudan (concluded by the battle of Omdurman where about 10,000 of the enemy were killed), was a pro-Boer when the South African war started. At the International Socialist Congress in 1900 he endorsed the criticisms some continental socialists levelled against those British comrades who found excuses for Britain's war. Hyndman later realized that the empire was bound to win and dropped his opposition. He also believed that a British victory would be in the interests of the Africans. He eventually came to support the war − for more respectable reasons, as a socialist, than for instance Blatchford who felt that as a former regular soldier it was his duty to support the British army in action. Hyndman succeeded in converting the SDF Executive, which adopted a resolution that further anti-war propaganda was 'a waste of time and money'.[12]

Not all pro-Boers within the organization were silenced, however, and there were several replies highly critical of Hyndman. A letter from another social democrat, H. Dalchow, reflects the way some socialists at the turn of the century viewed the prospects of what is now called African majority rule: 'Comrade Hyndman is probably right that the future of Africa is for the black. Unfortunately, however, that future is anywhere between one thousand and three thousand years to come, the nearest approach to their happiness being, therefore, good laws to guard their standard of comfort...'[13]

Some other SDF members, such as Theodore Rothstein and Ernest Belfort Bax, who had maintained their anti-war position, advanced more cogent arguments against Hyndman's change of front. Belfort Bax claimed that the Boers had a better record in their treatment of the natives than the British; and that Boer legislation to protect the kaffirs from excessive exploitation had been one of the grievances of the capitalist *uitlanders* and had thus, indirectly, been one of the causes of the South African War.[14] As for Hyndman's point about Boer independence involving submission of the natives, would not British domination have exactly the same effect? Bax unashamedly voiced his hope that Britain's enemies would be victorious and achieve their aspirations: he confessed that he was looking forward to 'a United Africander Republic from Zoutpansberg to Capetown. And that may come yet.'[15]

Other British politicians, socialists as well as Liberal radicals, were pro-Boer in the sense that they wanted the Boers to drive the British army to the sea. Even some Fabians took that line.[16] They were not 'revolutionary defeatists', since they neither expected nor wanted a revolution in Britain to result from the British defeat; revolution was plainly not on the cards. They wanted the Boers to win because they felt that Britain should not have gone to war and because they believed that defeat would mean the fall of the Tory government and its replacement by a Liberal administration.

5 The Russo-Japanese War 1904–5 and the Russian Revolution of 1905

The setback Japan sustained when she was compelled to disgorge some important gains after defeating China[1] did not end her colonialist and expansionist aspirations. In the short term, Russia seemed to be the main beneficiary of Japan's victory. By posing as China's protector, Russia strengthened her influence in that moribund empire; she gained the Liaotung peninsula and the ice-free harbour of Port Arthur; and when several European powers intervened in China against the Boxer rebellion of 1900, she sent troops into Manchuria and did not withdraw them after the rebellion.

Negotiations took place between Japan and Russia in 1903. Japan's objectives were Russian withdrawal from Manchuria and recognition of Japanese supremacy in Korea. When no progress was made, Japan resolved upon war. She struck in February 1904 without a formal declaration (just as in 1941). Japanese warships attacked the Russian fleet in Port Arthur and inflicted losses. The ensuing war was fought mainly on territory which, strictly speaking, belonged to China. After long periods of trench warfare, interspersed with pitched battles, Japan emerged victorious on land and at sea. Outstanding events, which provoked Lenin's comments, were the Japanese capture of Port Arthur in January 1905 and the destruction of Russia's Baltic fleet (which had sailed to the battle area) in the Tsushima Straits in May. In the peace treaty of August 1905, Russia recognized Japan's influence in Korea, agreed to transfer the lease of Liaotung to Japan, and ceded the southern part of the island of Sakhalin. Both sides agreed to withdraw their troops from Manchuria.

The war with Japan was unpopular with the whole of progressive Russia — socialists, liberals and nationalists among the ethnic minorities. Lenin, who openly rejoiced at Japan's victories, was not the only opponent of tsarism within Russia to sympathize with the Japanese. 'Defeatist' moods could be discerned in the ranks of bourgeois liberals, and some of the non-Russian activists favoured direct support for Japan. The leading Finnish radical Konni Zilliacus[2] made contact with Japanese agents to obtain money and arms for the internal fight against tsarism; at his instigation, several members of national revolutionary and minority socialist parties (for example, in Poland and in Georgia) did the same. Zilliacus also approached Plekhanov and other social democrats, suggesting they enlist Japanese aid; he was rebuffed and told that social democrats would not get involved with imperialist adversaries of the tsar's government.[3]

Lenin openly sympathized with Japan, and expressed the hope that the mikado would win the war against the tsar. In January 1905 he explained why Russian socialists must welcome a Japanese victory: by defeating the Russian autocracy the Japanese bourgeoisie was carrying out a 'revolutionary task'. The proletariat, while hostile to all manifestations of the bourgeois system, had to distinguish between 'the historically progressive and the reactionary representatives of the bourgeoisie'. Success of the worldwide struggle for socialism depended largely on the defeat of tsarist Russia. Guesde and Hyndman had rightly observed that the progressive nature of 'Japan's free-trade bourgeoisie' should earn that capitalist country the sympathies and the support of socialists the world over.[4] It seems to follow from these comments that had he been a Japanese socialist in 1904–5, Lenin would have been a 'defencist': a 'social-patriot' or 'social-chauvinist', to use the terms he coined in the First World War.

Lenin rejoiced at all Japanese victories. He wrote that the Baltic fleet had been despatched to the Far East because 'the autocracy' knew that ultimate defeat in the war with Japan 'would be tantamount to a victory of the "internal enemy", namely, of the revolution'. The débâcle in the Tsushima Straits meant that 'the war has been lost irretrievably.' The Japanese would now expel the Russian army from Manchuria and seize Sakhalin and Vladivostok. The inevitable consequence would be 'the collapse of the entire political system of tsarism'. European bourgeoisie was alarmed 'at the growing power of young and fresh Japan', and at the impact of the Russian revolution upon the European proletariat, which might result in 'a revolutionary conflagration on a world scale'. [5] Lenin seems to be pointing to an additional reason why socialists should want a Japanese victory: the possibility or probability of revolution in Russia spreading to Central or even Western Europe.

He was a little over-sanguine in expecting, and hoping for, the Japanese capture of Vladivostok and the ejection of the Russian army from Manchuria, but the war did end in a resounding Japanese victory and tremendous increase in her international prestige. Lenin was also right in expecting Russia's defeats to lead to revolution, but again over-optimistic in his prediction of the immediate downfall of tsarist autocracy. Tsarism survived to fight, and lose, another war.

The Mensheviks' reaction to the war differed fundamentally from Lenin's. The journal *Iskra*, originally Lenin's mouthpiece but now under Menshevik control, protested against Russia's foreign policy and declared that the war was an adventurous move made from domestic political motives and not in keeping with the requirements of capitalist development. An article by Trotsky rejected the view that the war was part of the Russian bourgeoisie's struggle for foreign markets: Trotsky tried to demonstrate that the war, not being waged for capitalist economic interests, would inevitably lead to an aggravation of the antagonism between tsarist reaction and Russia's bourgeois society. [6] Trotsky's article, like many of his writings at the time, met with Plekhanov's disapproval but was apparently endorsed by Martov, who then edited *Iskra*.

The main demands of the Mensheviks and of *Iskra* after the outbreak of the war were the earliest possible return to peace, and the calling of a constituent assembly as a step towards peace. *Iskra* did not share the 'defeatest' pro-Japanese approach of certain bourgeois liberals and Bolsheviks; it refused to make excuses for Japan's annexationist policies, and said it was in the interest of the Russian people and the revolutionary cause that a post-war settlement should not place heavy burdens upon the Russian nation. Freedom could not be brought to the Russian people on the bayonets of the Japanese army. The Mensheviks – as indeed most socialists – stressed that the war was between the Russian and Japanese rulers and not the people.

This attitude was reflected in a remarkable episode at the Amsterdam International Socialist Congress in August 1904. The Dutchman Van Kol, who was in the chair, and flanked on the platform by Plekhanov and the Japanese delegate Katayama, extended a special welcome to the Japanese and Russian socialists. They had the courage, while their countries were at war with each other, 'to profess their faith...in the international solidarity of the workers of all lands'. Thereupon Plekhanov and Katayama rose and shook hands, amid the prolonged thunderous applause of the congress delegates. Both then made speeches; Plekhanov, still in the defeatist mood he had displayed in 1893,[7] said that Russia's defeats in the war foretokened 'the well-deserved end of despotism' in his country.

Writing some thirty years later about these events, Karl Kautsky called the incident 'an inspiring moment' which, however, had misled socialists into reaching wrong conclusions about the international movement's reaction to a future war: in their belief that the solidarity of the workers and the socialists would never be affected by war, they tended to ignore the peculiarities of the Russo-Japanese war then in progress. That war was unique in that it was fought largely on a third country's territory, hardly affected the vital interests of the masses in either belligerent state, and neither side had to fear the invasion of its heartland in the event of the enemy's victory.[8]

Events in Russia in 1905 did not bear out the expectations of Lenin and other socialists that tsarist autocracy would collapse immediately, but they did confirm the view of nearly all Marxists that there is a distinct link between war and revolution. Pressure for change was exerted on the Russian establishment before the main military disasters. In the autumn of 1904 liberal organizations petitioned the tsar (unsuccessfully) for the grant of constitutional civil rights. The revolution began in earnest after the massacre of 'Bloody Sunday', 22 January 1905 (9 January according to the old Russian calendar), when cossacks opened fire on a peaceful mass demonstration for human rights outside the Winter Palace in St Petersburg, the imperial residence; several hundred people were killed and many more wounded.

Strikes, student unrest, mutinous acts by soldiers and street riots continued throughout the year. In August, spurious concessions – including a purely consultative assembly – provoked general indignation and led to more upheavals. The movement culminated in what was virtually a general strike in October, after peace with Japan had been concluded. There was peasant unrest in the countryside where landlords' estates were often seized. In the major towns revolutionary workers' councils ('soviets') sprang up spontaneously; the one in St Petersburg, the imperial capital, soon came under the influence of a young social democrat, Leon Trotsky, and thanks to his energy and drive soon became the virtual government of the city.[9]

At last the tsar was persuaded, by his liberal prime minister Count Witte, to issue a manifesto which promised a genuine constitution, with a parliament (the *Duma*) and civil liberties. The manifesto was published on 30 October, and at the same time the tsar declared a political amnesty. In November 1905 Count Witte prepared legislation for land reform, involving the expropriation of large estates; his programme predictably incurred the hostility of much of the nobility.

After reaching its climax in October and November 1905 the revolution lost its impetus. The working masses grew weary of the struggle, and the strikes petered out. By early December the government felt strong enough to hit back. The members of the Petersburg soviet, including its vice-chairman Trotsky, were arrested, and the tsar regained control of his capital. An armed uprising in Moscow in the same month was crushed with ruthless brutality. In 1906 there were still terrorist acts, unrest, naval mutinies and calls for strike action, but the government gradually regained mastery of the situation. Yet there was not complete return to the *status quo ante*. The *Duma*, the parliament established by the October manifesto, met in April 1906. It did not wield much power: the proclamation of the 'Fundamental Laws of the Empire', just before parliament's first meeting, severely limited its legislative authority. Yet the very existence of parliamentary institutions, and the periodical (albeit often rigged) elections guaranteed the continuance of a rudimentary constitutional set-up.[10]

Thus while a disastrous war did not topple tsarism, as Lenin and others of its opponents had hoped, events in Russia in 1905 confirmed an essential tenet of the doctrine of revolutionary defeatism: the propensity of defeat in a modern war to engender revolution or at least revolutionary commotion.

6   Socialists Debate the Threat of War 1906–13

When Frederick Engels warned his contemporaries and, in particular, his fellow socialists a few years before his death, of the foreseeable horrors of a European war, the possible causes of war he had in mind were Austrian-Russian tension over the Balkans, and France's desire for the recovery of Alsace-Lorraine. Balkan tensions were indeed one of the initial issues in the First World War, but the question of Alsace-Lorraine did not play a major part in the preceding crisis. Other sources of potential conflict between France and Germany had emerged, and an antagonism which was to play an ominous part in the pre-war era: the growing strain in British-German relations in the first decade of this century.

Hostility between the Triple *Entente* and the Central Powers

British-German tension was due largely to Germany's increasing military strength, and more specifically to the decision of the kaiser's government to build a powerful navy. This was widely regarded in Britain as a challenge to her naval supremacy, and indeed as indicative of Germany's aggressive intentions, especially as Germany was unwilling to conclude an agreement limiting the sizes of the two navies. The *Entente* with France, and soon after with Russia, was the British response to the German challenge.[1]

Tension between the Anglo-French *Entente* and the Central Powers soured the relations between the socialists of the countries concerned. The German Social Democratic Party, the leading party in the Second International, was accused of nationalist and imperialist heresies by some French and British socialists. Charles Andler, Professor of German at the Sorbonne and a right-wing member of the French

Socialist Party, fiercely attacked the Social Democratic leaders in a radical monthly (November/December 1912) for adhering to a 'teutomanical colonialist and predatory type of socialism'.[2] Andler had the backing of some prominent French socialists but was strongly criticized by others and also in *L'Humanité*, the French party's official organ. The quarrel did not affect top-level solidarity between the two parties in their opposition to the military and armaments policies of their governments. When France reintroduced three-year military service at the beginning of 1913, and Germany increased her arms budget, the French and German parties issued a joint manifesto protesting against these measures; it was published on 1 March 1913 in French and German in both *L'Humanité* and *Vorwärts*.

Tension resulting from the Anglo-German naval rivalry produced even stronger ill-feeling between the socialists of the two countries. Some of the harshest critics of Germany's Social Democracy were the British socialists who shared the German party's name and basically Marxist creed. H. M. Hyndman, leader of the Social Democratic Federation, was so worried about the increase in Germany's war potential that he constantly advocated British rearmament including, in 1910, the building of 'an aerial fleet'.[3] He attacked the German Social Democrats for not resisting the expansionist designs of the imperial government. In 1905, Hyndman said that he was getting sick of the German social democrats, 'Kautsky included': 'What is the use of talking of internationalism, when the party is becoming more nationalist each year since [Wilhelm] Liebknecht's death, and Bebel himself delivers more or less jingo speeches?'[4]

Kautsky recalled much later a conversation he had 'about 1906' with Hyndman, whom he called 'the father of British Marxism'. German naval armaments had been one of the obvious subjects:

I explained to Hyndman that we Social Democrats in Germany were most energetically fighting against these armaments but were greatly hampered in this by the propaganda for British armaments, which Hyndman and his friends were conducting. Hyndman asked whether I could guarantee that the German Social Democrats would prevent an invasion of England by German troops. I felt constrained to reply that it would be very rash for me to give such an undertaking. We would do all we could to prevent the outbreak of war; whether or not we succeeded would depend on as yet unforeseeable circumstances. 'Well then,'

Hyndman replied, 'as soon as you German Social Democrats are strong enough to prevent the naval armaments, or for that matter to prevent war being waged against us, we in England shall fight against any kind of rearmament. But so long as we can't rely on you in this respect, we shall have to rely on other factors nearer home.' There was, alas, not much to be said against this, at least not from my point of view, since I did not share the illusions of Keir Hardie, Hyndman's great antagonist, that wars could be prevented by strikes.[5]

Hyndman became more outspoken as time went on. When Germany's new and enlarged navy held manoeuvres in the summer of 1908, Hyndman and Blatchford saw it as an occasion to agitate against the 'German menace'.[6] On 31 July 1908 Blatchford's *Clarion* carried an article by Hyndman entitled 'The Coming German War against Great Britain'. It said *inter alia* that 'the success of the German pan-Teutonic, anti-English, anti-French scheme of aggression would throw back socialism in Europe for fully two generations.' Tirades of this kind met with contradiction from within the British labour movement. The ILP leaders with their pacifist tradition denounced what they regarded as Hyndman's anti-Germanism; Keir Hardie did so in somewhat abusive terms, which caused Hyndman to refuse to share a platform with Hardie at a proposed 'socialist unity' rally. Hyndman's British critics, incidentally, were not all from the socialist camp; some Liberal politicians denounced him as a 'warmonger'.

Nor were the British social democrats solidly behind Hyndman on the issues of the German danger and of British rearmament. Hyndman had the qualified support of Harry Quelch but was denounced as a 'bourgeois nationalist' by J.B. Askew, and attacked for his anti-Germanism by Theodore Rothstein and Zelda Kahan, a prominent social democrat of Russian-Jewish origin.

At the 1910 Conference of the Social Democratic Party (SDP), as the SDF had decided to call itself in October 1907,[7] Hyndman again urged delegates to support 'the provision of an adequate navy for the defence of our commerce and our coasts', and once more overcame the opposition within the party. But the Labour Party in the House of Commons generally took the ILP's line on defence, and opposed the strengthening of the navy. Hyndman protested against this semi-pacifism of the parliamentary Labour Party; in a letter to the Conservative *Morning Post* he again stressed the need for rearmament, and suggested that the requisite amount of about £100 million be raised by a special tax on all incomes above £300 a year, so as 'to secure a permanent superiority in the narrow seas'.[8] A section of the SDP rank-and-file again demurred: several branches passed resolutions against Hyndman's letter. There were renewed attacks from foreign socialists, including (as might have been expected) from the German party; its central organ, *Vorwärts*, said there was no place in any socialist party for people holding Hyndman's views.

The SDP met again at Coventry in April 1911, and for the first time Hyndman and his friends faced a concerted challenge from the anti-rearmers. The latter tabled a resolution calling upon Social Democrats to combat the demand for additional armaments, but the conference adopted an executive amendment, moved by Harry Quelch, which endorsed the Second International's resolution for peace and arbitration[9] but insisted on the maintenance by Britain of 'an adequate navy'.

The passing of this amendment led to the resignation from the party of two senior members, and once again, there was adverse comment from abroad. One of the foreign critics was Lenin. In reporting on the Coventry conference Lenin approved the statement by Zelda Kahan that the SDP's advocacy of naval rearmament amounted to 'identifying the party with the jingoist warmongers', and that 'the British Social Democrats have placed themselves outside the international movement'. He attacked Hyndman, whose pro-Japanese stance he had applauded six years previously, for having been frightened 'by the screams of the British bourgeois press about the "German menace"', and berated Quelch for resorting to 'miserable sophistry' (because he had called the British navy a champion of the liberty of small nations), and for 'going over to the chauvinists'. Lenin agreed with the London correspondent of *Vorwärts* who had 'justly remarked that the best criticism of the SDP's position was an article in the *extremely jingoist Daily Mail* which *praised* the wisdom of the social-democratic leaders.'[10]

A few months after the SDP's Coventry conference the British Socialist Party (BSP) was founded, made up of the membership of the SDP and other socialist groups, as well as pacifist defectors from the ILP. The new party contained a stronger anti-militarist element than had existed in the SDF or the SDP. When the BSP executive adopted by five votes to three a resolution in favour of disarmament in December 1912, Hyndman threatened to resign as party chairman; he then changed his mind and managed to get the executive to suspend the anti-militarist resolution some months later. The quarrel was patched up at the BSP conference at Blackpool in May 1913, when Hyndman promised not to raise the armament question 'in a way that would prejudicially affect the party'. The party did not split, at least not until 1916; then the pro-war minority, which included Hyndman and Belfort Bax, broke away to found the (ominously named) National Socialist Party (NSP).[11]

Lenin also commented on the Blackpool conference. He again singled Hyndman out for his strictures. For several years, he wrote, Hyndman had acted against the party on the important question of armament and war:

> Hyndman has got it into his head that Germany is threatening to crush and enslave Britain and that socialists should, therefore, support the demand for a 'proper' (i.e. strong) navy for the defence of Britain! Socialists in the role of supporters of a 'strong' navy — and this in a country whose navy helps enslave and plunder in the most shameless, feudal manner the *three hundred millions* of India's population, tens of millions of people in Egypt and other colonies.[12]

In the same article, Lenin welcomed the general trend of the Blackpool conference, reflected on the departure of Hyndman from the party executive and the passing of a resolution congratulating the socialists of France and Germany on their opposition to rearmament in their respective countries, and endorsing the anti-war resolutions adopted by the International Socialist Congresses at Stuttgart in 1907 and Basle in 1912.[13]

The charges levelled by some French and British socialists against German Social Democracy — for example, condonation of the kaiser's aggressive policies, — were not devoid of substance, although it was often a case of the pot calling the kettle black. Imperialistic attitudes were indeed to be found in the German socialist and trade-union movements. Gustav Noske was frequently criticized for his ultra-patriotic speeches. The naval armament programme was genuinely popular in Germany, and an enthusiastic response came from some sections of the working class. Max Schippel, Südekum, Ludwig Quessel were the best-known Social Democrats with colonialist tendencies; their mouth-piece was the monthly *Sozialistische Monatshefte*.[14] Yet there was no real equivalent in Germany, or for that matter in France, to Britain's SDF or SDP under Hyndman's leadership. The bulk of the stronger and more unified socialist movements in the two great continental countries was staunchly opposed to any arms race; no specific group or faction existed with a platform demanding increased arms expenditure on the grounds that the country had to prepare for war against another European power.

Socialist World Congresses 1907, 1910 and 1912

The parties of the Socialist International naturally devoted much time, and many strenuous debates, to the danger of a European war. Between 1905 and 1914 the main subject of national and international socialist congresses was what could and should be done to prevent the catastrophe, and how socialists should act if war broke out. This was the principal issue at three congresses of the International – Stuttgart in 1907, Copenhagen in 1910, and Basle in 1912. The last of these met while war was in progress in the Balkans. A further congress was to be held in Vienna on 23 August 1914: by that date, the First World War had to all intents and purposes caused the demise of the Second International.

At Stuttgart, August Bebel submitted a resolution on behalf of the German delegation declaring that the fight against militarism and war was an integral part of the socialist class struggle. Wars were inherent in capitalism and would not cease until it had been abolished. Meantime the working classes and their parliamentary representatives had to oppose armaments, 'to refuse to supply the means therefor', and to educate working-class youth 'in the spirit of the brotherhood of nations and of socialism'. Workers should exert pressure on their governments for disarmament and a system of arbitration for the settlement of international disputes. If war threatened, the working classes should try to prevent its outbreak 'by applying the means which seem to them most effective; if war should start nevertheless the workers should strive for its speedy termination.'[15]

The French delegation, led by Vaillant and Jaurès, wanted congress to be more specific about the means to be used to avert war, and to state, 'The task of averting and preventing war is to be performed by national and international socialist actions of the working class with all available means, from parliamentary intervention and public agitation to mass strikes and insurrection.' This was not inconsistent with Bebel's text which did not, directly or by implication, exclude mass strikes and insurrection as means of combating the threat of war. The Vaillant-Jaurès amendment did, however, contradict the position Engels and many leading socialists took — including, incidentally, Vaillant — in the early 1890s, when they opposed Domela Nieuwenhuis's attempt to commit the International to a 'strike against war' policy. Vaillant and Jaurès did not go as far as Nieuwenhuis had gone: they did not include a call to workers to refuse military service, nor did they reject the distinction between aggressive and defensive wars, as Nieuwenhuis and his friends had done. Mass strikes and insurrection were permitted weapons only against a guilty government, one which refused to submit its case to a court of arbitration. [16] Even so, this motion was not acceptable to the majority of delegates in Stuttgart.

The majority which opposed commitment to mass strikes and insurrection included a minority of the French delegation, led by Jules Guesde. Guesde argued that the methods proposed by the extreme anti-militarists — desertion, military strike and insurrection — would hamper propaganda and recruitment for socialism and postpone the victory of the proletariat which would end the era of militarism and war. The clash between the majority of the French delegation and the more flexible Bebel-Guesde position threatened the unity of the International; surprisingly, some delegates mediated who generally stood far to the left of both tendencies. Lenin, Rosa Luxemburg and the left-wing Menshevik, Martov, proposed a compromise formula, an amendment to Bebel's resolution which made no mention of mass strikes or uprisings and put more emphasis on the need for revolutionary action in the event of war.

The amendment and the amended resolution were carried unanimously by the delegates. The resolution accordingly ended with a passage exhorting the workers to do their utmost to prevent war, and declaring:

> Should the war nevertheless break out, they (the working classes and their parliamentary representatives in the countries concerned) must strive for its speedy termination and must make every effort to exploit the economic and political crisis resulting from the war in order to arouse the masses and thus hasten the downfall of capitalist class domination.

The unanimous adoption of this resolution by nearly 900 delegates from all over the world – moderates and extremists, pacifists and advocates of national defence, believers in revolutionary violence and champions of peaceful gradual evolution – tends to indicate that this paragraph was not a new departure, a total commitment to extra-parliamentary methods and an abandonment of peaceful reforms. Nor is it incompatible with support for national defence in a war where one's country is the victim of unprovoked aggression. The Luxemburg-Lenin-Martov amendment does no more than restate a generally accepted tenet of socialism in the strategy for gaining power, one shared by all tendencies, groups and factions within the movement. As Kautsky put it some thirty years after the event:

> Arousing the people, that is an object we are pledged to pursue not only in wartime but also in peacetime, indeed under all circumstances. Our tasks during a war differ in this case from our peacetime tasks only in so far as one assumes that war, because it is prone to cause an economic and political crisis, creates highly favourable conditions for arousing the people.[17]

It may seem strange that a compromise endorsed by all delegates originated among the revolutionary Left wing of the Socialist International. There is a simple explanation. Luxemburg, Lenin and Martov were orthodox Marxists; while not objecting in principle to such revolutionary weapons as mass strikes and armed risings, they knew that Marxist doctrine did not believe such methods effective in forestalling or instantly terminating a war. Apart from being inclined to follow the Marx-Engels line on revolutionary tactics, they saw no reason to doubt Engels's view that a plan to call mass strikes in the event of war would not only be impracticable but would spell disaster for the international socialist movement.

On Lenin's part at least, there was probably a further motive for inserting a passage about exploiting a war-conditioned crisis for hastening the downfall of capitalism. It seems likely that Lenin discerned an indirect logical link between the wording of the amendment and his own, as yet unexpounded, concept of revolutionary defeatism. If it was accepted that war must engender an economic and political crisis which in turn would create favourable conditions for socialist revolution, it could be argued that defeat was most apt to bring about such a crisis, and that socialists must therefore wish and work for their own government's defeat. This is not what the amended Stuttgart resolution said or meant, and it is certainly not what the majority of delegates, many of whom believed strongly in national defence, had in mind when they voted for the amendment.

In any case Lenin did not interpret the Stuttgart resolution as Kautsky did: that the definitive text merely re-defined accepted strategy in the specific context of war. In several articles Lenin reported on the congress and especially on the anti-war debate. He criticized Bebel's draft rather harshly as 'dead' and 'dogmatically one-sided', more mildly in another article where he said only that Bebel's resolution 'had one shortcoming − it failed to indicate the active tasks of the proletariat.' Lenin added that this had enabled some opportunist delegates, such as the German revisionist von Vollmar, 'to read Bebel's orthodox propositions through opportunist spectacles'. To clarify the position, Rosa Luxemburg, with the support of Lenin and Martov ('who here spoke in full harmony') had moved the amendments stressing that social democrats should exploit the crisis to hasten the downfall of the bourgeoisie. The amendments had transformed Bebel's draft 'into an altogether different resolution'. The amended version was 'rich in thought' and clearly formulated the tasks of the proletariat: 'It combines the stringency of orthodox − that is, the only scientific Marxist − analysis with recommendations for the most resolute and revolutionary action by the workers' parties. This resolution cannot be interpreted *à la* Vollmar, nor can it be fitted into the narrow framework of naive Hervéism.'[18] Yet neither von Vollmar nor the French extreme anti-militarist Hervé, an admirer of Nieuwenhuis, hesitated to vote for a resolution which Lenin considered an example of Marxist revolutionary orthodoxy.

Some of the die-hard extremists at the Stuttgart congress made about-turns and became 'social chauvinists' (Lenin's phrase) a few years later. An outstanding example is Gustave Hervé. At Stuttgart he asked congress to declare that socialists should bear arms only to achieve or defend 'the collectivist or communist system', and that military strikes and uprisings were the only possible answer to a declaration of war, 'from whichever side it may come'.[19] Congress rejected these motions virtually unanimously. Lenin wrote:

Hervé's plan of 'answering' any war by a strike or an uprising betrayed a complete failure to understand that the employment of one or other means of struggle depends on the objective conditions of the particular crisis, economic or political, precipitated by the war, and not on any previous decisions that revolutionaries may have made.[20]

Gustave Hervé suddenly turned moderate and reformist in 1912 and became an ardent French patriot in 1914.

A German social democrat who also espoused the Nieuwenhuis approach and who moved from left to right was Paul Lensch. At the Essen congress of the German Social Democratic Party, held in 1907, Lensch maintained that no war was imaginable which could deserve socialist support.[21] He became a fierce nationalist during the First World War, and soon left the socialist camp.[22]

In 1907 Lensch was almost isolated on the left of the SPD. It was generally accepted by the leaders, including Bebel and the majority of the rank-and-file, that the SPD would back national defence if Germany was attacked. Even Clara Zetkin, a staunch left-wing internationalist during the First World War and later one of the leaders of the German Communist Party, did not reject defencism on principle. At the Essen congress she said: 'We cannot, regardless of circumstances, give an assurance as a matter of course that we shall shoulder the rifle for the bourgeois nation-state, for the interests of the exploiting classes. . . What we do and omit to do in the event of war will depend on the actual historic conditions obtaining at the time.'[23]

Kautsky, too, raised doubts about this issue at the Essen congress. He did not challenge the principle of socialist support for a war of defence, but argued that it was sometimes impossible to establish which side had committed aggression. The part should not pledge itself in advance to support the war if the government asserted that Germany had been attacked. He explained:

> The German government might one day fool the German workers into believing that they were the victims of aggression; the French government could bamboozle the French people in the same way, and we would then have a war in which German and French proletarians, with equal enthusiasm. . . cut each other's throats. This can be avoided if the criterion we apply is not that of aggression but that of proletarian interests which are, at the same time, international interests.[24]

This was basically the criterion Marx and Engels applied to the wars of the nineteenth century. Bebel disagreed with Kautsky, saying that it had been possible in the past, and would no doubt be possible in the future, to identify and name the aggressor. This was one of the rare occasions when the two friends differed.

At the Socialist World Congress in Stuttgart the German Social Democrats, like all other delegates, voted for the resolution which included the Luxemburg-Lenin-Martov amendment. Yet at the subsequent Essen congress of the German party no one appeared to think that the clause about exploiting the crisis to hasten revolution precluded socialist support for a war of defence, a view emphatically expressed by Lenin and Rosa Luxemburg.

The Stuttgart formula does not in fact bear out the accusations which Lenin, Luxemburg and other 'internationalists' levelled at the socialist parties of Germany, France, and so on, that by voting for the war credits they had broken the pledge given at the pre-war world congresses. The resolution does not say, or imply, that a war cannot be just and defensive, or that socialists should try to aggravate the crisis caused by the war. The French *communards* tried in 1871 to exploit a war-induced crisis, but they supported the war and demanded its vigorous prosecution. When the German Social Democrats supported the kaiser's war in 1914 and voted for the credits, they did not consciously break the commitment in the 1907 resolution. Where they, and possibly other socialists, went wrong was to accept the government's denial of war guilt and of aggressive intentions.

The unanimous adoption of the compromise resolution at Stuttgart did not end the debate about the socialist answer to the threat of war. The next International Congress at Copenhagen in 1910, was to consider a lengthy resolution denouncing secret diplomacy and the arms race, and advocating international arbitration and respect for the principle of self-determination. The text had been agreed in committee; but in the plenary session an amendment was moved jointly by Vaillant and Keir Hardie. It called for proletarian action to avert or prevent war, not necessarily by a general strike but by massive strike action, especially in the industries supplying war materials and in transport.[25]

This amendment was rejected by the congress majority. The entire German delegation opposed it. The SPD's spokesman was George Ledebour, who stood on the extreme Left of the German party and who had endorsed the all-out anti-war position of Paul Lensch at the Essen congress.[26]

No compromise permitting a show of unity was possible on this occasion. The sponsors of the amendment, Edouard Vaillant and Keir

Hardie, stuck to their guns and would not accept mediation. Keir Hardie took an extreme pacifist line, putting forward a 'unilateralist' argument frequently heard some seventy years later in the context of nuclear disarmament. He said that the first nation to disarm completely, to discard all its weapons, would open a new and glorious chapter in world history: no other power, not even despotic Russia, would dare to attack an unarmed country and defy mankind's sense of justice and liberty.[27] This reasoning failed to convince the majority of delegates.

As unity could not be achieved, it was decided not to put the amendment to the vote. This was suggested by the Belgians who were inclined in principle to support the Vaillant-Hardie Amendment, but not unless its unanimous adoption was assured. They proposed that the question be re-examined, and submitted for decision to the next congress, to be held in Vienna in 1913. The Belgian motion was carried unanimously.

7 Curtain-raisers to World War: the the Italo-Turkish and Balkan Wars

Before the date for the scheduled congress arrived, an extraordinary meeting of the Socialist International was convoked because of the international situation – the outbreak of the Balkan War in October 1912. The Copenhagen congress had instructed the International Socialist Bureau in Brussels to take steps towards concerted action by the socialist parties to ward off the danger if war should threaten. The bureau accordingly arranged for a congress to be held at Basle at the end of November 1912.

Italy's war against Turkey was undoubtedly a war of aggression and colonial conquest. The object was the annexation of Tripolitania and Cyrenaica, (which became the Kingdom of Libya after the Second World War and is now a republic). In 1911 it was the only part of the North African seaboard which had not already been snapped up by a European power; Britain had established herself in Egypt and France in Morocco, Algeria and Tunisia, which Italy had also coveted.

The Ottoman empire had put up no resistance when Britain and France helped themselves to some of the nominally Turkish possessions in North Africa; but when Italy declared war in September 1911 on a feeble pretext, and invaded Tripolitania, the Turks made a determined stand. Power had recently passed to the 'Young Turks', and a more warlike spirit prevailed. Turkish resistance, and the hostility of the native Arab and Berber population, slowed down the Italian campaign. But in the autumn of 1912 Turkey realized that she was about to be attacked by the Balkan kingdoms of Montenegro, Bulgaria, Serbia and Greece, so she made peace with Italy and permitted her a north African colony, which she then held for three decades.

In Italy the war against Turkey was popular with some of the middle classes, but the bulk of the working class was solidly opposed.[1] Italian socialism was deeply divided but, except for some right-wing members of parliament and individuals, all socialist factions and tendencies, all leading figures (including Benito Mussolini) and the trade unions united in opposing the government's war policy. (Bissolati and some other right-wing, pro-war socialists were expelled from the party in July 1912.)

If ever there was an opportunity to demonstrate the practicability of the Nieuwenhuis-Vaillant-Keir Hardie concept of preventing war by massive strike action, Italy in 1911–12 was the place for it, but no serious attempt was made. The trade unions and the parliamentary Socialist party did call a twenty-four-hour general strike, and in all parts of the country where the socialist movement was strong, the strike was total and impressive. But that limited action did not shake the government's determination to continue the war. The Syndicalists called for the prolongation and extension of the strike, to the point where it would hamper the prosecution of the war; but their appeal went unheeded.[2]

The Italo-Turkish War was a colonial war fought outside Europe. The International Socialist Bureau evidently did not regard the conflict as likely to spread and assume major dimensions; it did not see the need for emergency action, such as the convening of an extraordinary congress. But when the Balkan War broke out the following autumn a new and delicate situation arose. Throughout the nineteenth century, the Balkans had been a hotbed of tribal and ethnic disputes. it was also a region where the spheres of influence of the tsarist and the Habsburg empires met, and so an area of potential collision between two great powers.

The situation which led to the war in 1914 began to emerge: Austria feared the growing strength of Serbia, especially its psychological effects on the Slavs in the Habsburg empire. The International Bureau felt that this was precisely the international crisis the delegates at Copenhagen had in mind when they instructed the bureau to initiate and co-ordinate international working class action to counter the threat of war.

The agenda of the Basle congress consisted of a single item: 'The international situation and the joint action against war'. The debate was a remarkable demonstration of harmony and unity, which had been absent both at Stuttgart and at Copenhagen. A plausible explanation of this was given later by Karl Kautsky:

> The International was divided as long as it was faced with war as such, war in the abstract, which could be imagined in different ways by different people. . . But as soon as the issue was a specific, concrete war, full unanimity was possible – albeit only where the international situation concrning the war was easy to grasp, which means that there could be no differences of opinion where the basic approach was the same.
>
> It is also significant that in the face of a concrete, specific war situation no serious politician within the International thought of preventing war by any form of direct action. . . Not a word was spoken at Basle about the kind of actions that had caused such heated debates at Stuttgart and Copenhagen. [3]

A further possible reason why no one at Basle was urging extra-parliamentary proletarian action was the weakness or absence of a socialist labour movement in the countries concerned. Very few socialists were sitting in the parliaments of two of the Balkan states – two in Serbia, one in Bulgaria. All three denounced the war with Turkey, arousing the indignation of the other deputies.

During the early part of 1912, Serbia, Bulgaria and Greece had negotiated a military alliance for a showdown with Turkey. The ostensible issue was alleged repression in Macedonia, then still under Turkish rule. Montenegro, not formally a member of the alliance, declared war early in October; by 18 October the three states of the 'Balkan League' had joined in.

The war went badly for the Turks from the start. Within weeks they were defeated in battles against the Serb and Bulgar armies. By the beginning of December the Turkish collapse seemed complete, and an armistice was concluded, but in January 1913 the 'Young Turks' staged another coup and fighting was resumed. The great powers took a hand in peace talks, and a treaty was concluded on 30 March. Under the treaty Turkey lost nearly all her European possessions; but the victorious allies began to quarrel about the distribution of the spoils. The Second Balkan War started at the end of June 1913, with an isolated Bulgaria fighting her former allies – Greece, Serbia and Montenegro – and, after a few weeks, a new belligerent – Rumania. After about a month, Bulgaria sued for peace; in the peace treaty of Bucharest, where frontiers were again settled under the sponsorship of the great powers, she had to cede territory to her Balkan neighbours.

Socialists from all over Europe who met in Basle in November 1912 knew that no decision of theirs would halt the war in south-eastern Europe. Their concern was to stop the war spreading. They were anxious to prevent – by agitation and political influence, not by strikes or other subversive actions – the very thing that came to pass within two years of the holding of the International congress, partly because of the Balkan upheaval.

The spirit of unity and co-operation at Basle led to the unanimous adoption of the 'Basle manifesto', a comprehensive document on the international situation and the socialists' struggle for world peace. It reiterated and re-affirmed important parts of the Stuttgart resolution, including the exhortation to exploit the economic and political crisis resulting from war to stir up the masses and hasten the downfall of capitalist class domination.[4] Dealing with the tense international situation after the outbreak of the Balkan war, the manifesto advocated a democratic federation of the Balkan peoples. The socialists of the peninsula were told to assert the brotherhood of all Balkan nations, including Albanians, Rumanians and Turks. The socialists of Austria-Hungary were urged to ward off the threat of Habsburg aggression against Serbia, and to go on fighting for the right of the southern Slavs to democratic self-government within the Habsburg monarchy. The Russian and Polish socialists were alerted against tsarist intrigues in the Balkans and against Turkey. The manifesto called on the working classes of Germany, France and Britain to press their governments to remain neutral in the Balkan conflict.

The greatest threat to peace, according to the Basle manifesto, stemmed from British-German enmity. 'The congress therefore welcomes the efforts of the working classes of both countries to bridge the existing gulf.' The socialists of Britain and Germany should work for agreement between their countries on naval armaments. Congress evidently had a good grasp of the crucial aspects of the world situation. The manifesto drew attention to the delicate problems which finally produced the cataclysm of 1914:

> The elimination of the antagonism between Germany on the one hand and Britain and France on the other would remove the greatest threat to world peace; it would shatter the power position of tsarism which exploits that antagonism; it would render an attack by Austria-Hungary on Serbia impossible.... Hence the efforts of the International should be directed above all towards that aim.

In conclusion the manifesto proclaimed that the entire Socialist International was agreed 'on these principles of international politics'. In his closing speech – his last public speech ever – August Bebel contrasted the unity and harmony of socialist workers with the divisions in the bourgeois world, where 'triple and quadruple alliances are confronting each other.' Karl Kautsky later recalled the united resolve and the spirit of confidence in the strength of the world proletariat which had marked the Basle congress. All socialists had been convinced that even world war would not affect this great unity of the workers who would stand together and act together throughout and after the war. 'Before long,' Kautsky added, 'our confidence was put to a severe test.'[5]

The chief concerns of the Socialist International at the time were the containment of the Balkan conflict, the lessening of international tension and the preservation of world peace. The International criticized Habsburg aggressiveness and tsarist intrigues, but did not generally apportion praise or blame between the powers concerned. Socialist parties and individuals were more inclined to take sides and voice critical opinions about the regional wars which preceded the First World War. The Italian socialists condemned their government's aggression against Turkey and the conquest of Libya. This was the consistent position of socialists the world over.

In one of his despatches on the First Balkan War, Leon Trotsky spoke of the historic significance of that war in connection with the Italo-Turkish war which preceded it, and said that 'Italy's onslaught on Tripolitania was an act of crude capitalist banditry.'[6] Karl Kautsky also denounced the 'policy of banditry' pursued by Italy's rulers.[7] He later called the war a predatory venture, 'definitely a war of aggression..., the brutal assault on a peaceful citizen, carried out by a fully armed robber'.[8] Lenin was no less outspoken! This was a 'typical colonial war', caused by the greed of the Italian money-bags and capitalists, 'who need new markets and new achievements for Italian imperialism'.[9] Thousands of Arabs were being massacred with the most up-to-date weapons; yet Italy was neither better nor worse than the other capitalist countries. Lenin did not mention the Italian socialists' strong opposition to the war.

When the First Balkan War broke out in October 1912, Lenin expressed his sympathy with the Balkan peoples who fought against Turkey. Yet he disliked the expression of similar feelings by the Russian bourgeoisie and the capitalist press; and he objected to intervention by Russia or any other European power: 'For the Balkan peasants and workers, any intervention by the European powers, whether hostile or would-be friendly, means only adding all sorts of fetters and hindrances to free progress...It is "Europe" that is hindering the establishment of a federal republic.'[10,11]

A few days later Lenin hailed the first victories of the Balkan League as a new chapter in world history:

> The defeat of Turkey is beyond question. The victories won by the Balkan states...are tremendous...Although the alliance which has come into being in the Balkans is an alliance of monarchies and not of republics, and although this alliance has come about through war and not through revolution, a great step has nevertheless been taken towards removing the remnants of medievalism in Eastern Europe.[12]

Quoting, and endorsing, a statement by the Austrian Marxist Otto Bauer, Lenin explained why the conquest of Macedonia by the Serbs and Bulgars could be described as progressive: in that province the feudal oppression of the peasants (Christian Slavs) by the landlords (Moslems and Turks) would end and give way to 'the formation of a more or less free class of peasant landowners'.[13] Thus Turkey's defeat would bring the people of Macedonia economic and not just national liberation, as the Russian bourgeois press would have it.

While never faltering in his support for the allied Balkan states, Lenin was intensely annoyed and indeed abusive when he found that his feelings were shared by Russian 'reactionaries'. A few days after the outbreak of the war, the St Petersburg City Council, consisting of liberals and conservatives, unanimously adopted a resolution saying to the Balkan powers (according to Lenin): 'St. Petersburg shares your hope of a bright future of independent liberty for the oppressed peoples, a liberty in whose name you are shedding your blood.'

This apparently innocuous resolution aroused Lenin's fury. In an article signed 'T' and headed 'A Disgraceful Resolution', he described the resolution as 'a specimen of bourgeois chauvinism'[14] and went on to assert:

> Never and nowhere has 'liberty' been won by the oppressed peoples through one people waging *war* against another. Wars between peoples merely increase the enslavement of peoples. Real *liberty* for the Slav peasant in the Balkans, as well as for the Turkish peasant, can be ensured *only* by complete liberty inside *every* country and by a federation of thoroughly democratic states...The reactionary and liberal chauvinists...in the St. Petersburg City Council...advocate turning the peoples into cannon fodder![15]

It is difficult to discern any 'chauvinism' in the city council's resolution quoted by Lenin. The charge he levelled against the 'reactionaries and liberals' could apply to him for claiming, about the same time, that the Serbo-Bulgarian victories in Macedonia were achieving the 'national and economic liberation' of the native peasants, an assertion scarcely consistent with the statement that 'wars between peoples' could lead only to increased enslavement.

Lenin used the phrase 'war between peoples' advisedly: he meant to imply that this condemnation of war did not extend to the kind of war he constantly advocated, civil war, war between classes. Yet another article on the Balkan War dwelt on 'the horrors of war' without any such qualification; it reads like pacifist propaganda. Lenin quoted the correspondent of the British *Daily Chronicle* reporting on a battle in which 40,000 Turks were killed: a 'wholesale massacre of starving, exhausted, tormented, helpless peasants from Anatolia'; the survivors in their disorderly flight a 'stupefied...and maddened mob', and there had been no adequate provision for attending to the wounded.[16] For once Lenin's article was purely descriptive, devoid of political argument or conclusions. He could not have claimed that such horrors were typical only of 'wars between peoples' and could not occur in a civil war.

When Adrianople fell to the Bulgars in March 1913, Lenin rediscovered the potentially progressive aspects of a 'war between peoples'. He wrote that thanks to the conclusive victories of the Balkan allies the war had become 'one link in the chain of world events marking the collapse of the medieval state of affairs in Asia and Eastern Europe'. The Balkan peoples could have solved their historic tasks of ending feudal oppression and liberating the peasants in the Balkans more easily, and with far fewer sacrifices, if they had formed a Federative Balkan Republic; this would also have assured them 'of truly rapid, extensive and free development'.[17]

The inconsistencies and *non-sequiturs* in Lenin's treatment of the First Balkan War apparently stem from the fact that he found himself on the horns of a dilemma. The last three pre-war congresses of the Socialist International, at Stuttgart, Copenhagen and Basle, had emphasized the need to preserve peace by negotiation, agreement or arbitration, and had urged socialist parties to demand that their respective (bourgeois) governments counter the threat of war. Lenin had made a contribution to the definitive wording of the Stuttgart resolution, and like all socialists, of whatever persuasion, he had approved all those non-controversial appeals for peace. Yet privately he wished for war: war between the great powers, not some minor Balkan states. A letter to Maxim Gorky, written in January 1913, illustrates his belief in the revolutionary potentialities of a major conflagration. 'A war between Austria and Russia would be a very useful thing for the revolution (thoughout Eastern Europe), but it is not very likely that Franz-Josef and Nicky will give us this pleasure.'[18] The incompatibility of official international policy of fighting for peace – a policy Lenin felt duty-bound to uphold in public – with his secret hope for a major war accounts for the incongruities and internal contradictions in his writings immediately prior to the First World War.

From his point of view, Lenin was right that a war between great European powers would be 'a very useful thing' for the revolution he hoped would break out soon. The following year Francis-Joseph and Nicholas did given Lenin and his friends the pleasure of a war which dragged in all other great European powers. Three years and three months after its outbreak Lenin became the head of a revolutionary Russian government.

A more comprehensive picture of the Balkan wars – their background, the issues involved, and the immediate and the long-term consequences – came from Leon Trotsky, who was in the Balkans most of the time and able to watch events at close quarters. In the autumn of 1912, Trotsky accepted an offer from the leftish (but non-partisan) Kiev paper *Kievskaya Mysl* to work as its correspondent on the impending war. The reports Trotsky sent from Serbia, Bulgaria and Rumania were largely descriptive; apart from dealing with military operations and developments, they conveyed the author's impressions of social and political conditions, but they also reflected Trotsky's view on the significance of the conflict, its rights and wrongs, and the consequences for the peoples concerned and for the world at large.

Trotsky was not at that time a Bolshevik, and he was by no means close to Lenin in the continual factional struggles in the Russian Social Democratic camp. His explanations and judgements on the Balkan wars differ considerably from Lenin's sketchy comments; and his evaluations are no more consistent. But in one respect he agreed with Lenin, and with the consensus within the International: he was even more explicit than Lenin, or the Basle manifesto, on the need for a multi-national Balkan federation. In an article for the Kiev paper in October 1912, when war had been declared, Trotsky explained the war as a reflection of the historic urge for unification:

> The present war in the Balkans gives expression to the striving of the broken fragments of Balkan Slavdom to draw closer together...and to create a broader basis for their economic and political development. At bottom this striving is irresistible, historically progressive, and cannot but evoke sympathy from the masses of the people in both Western and Eastern Europe...The mixed composition of the populations undoubtedly constitutes in itself a very great hindrance to the creation of political conditions for co-existence, co-operation and development. Nevertheless, it is possible to create such conditions...The United States of America and the Swiss Confederation provide in this respect the best refutation of all pseudo-realistic scepticism.[19]

The reference to the mixed populations and to (multi-national) Switzerland seems to indicate that the phrase 'broken fragments of Balkan Slavdom' does not imply the exclusion from the proposed Balkan federation of such non-Slav nations as Greeks, Rumanians and Albanians. The purport of the passage is that the member states of the Balkan League were prompted to go to war with Turkey by the (possibly subconscious) desire to overcome the political fragmentation of the peninsula, an objective which could not be achieved without forcible elimination of 'Turkey-in-Europe'.

As time went on, Trotsky's dispatches became more and more critical of the war policies of the Balkan states, and more doubtful about the progressive character of the war. He contradicts himself regarding the people's attitude to the war. Writing from Sofia in October 1912 he said, 'the war is now undoubtedly very popular here: the army — and here the mobilized army really is the people — wants war.'[20] A few days later he explained why both Serbia and Bulgaria were bound to favour war:

> Serbia needs an outlet to the sea. The creation of normal living conditions in Macedonia is an elementary requirement for steady and calm development in Bulgaria...A warlike mood has arisen not only among the political leaders but also among the broad masses of the people...Thus, although the socialist parties of Serbia and Bulgaria have resolutely protested against the war, I have encountered a rather large number of socialists who have been seized by the general movement of national patriotism...It would, therefore, be a mistake to suppose that the war has been produced artificially from above. No, the government's initiative was undoubtedly met halfway by a certain wave of feeling from below.[21]

That sounds quite unambiguous. Yet, barely six weeks later, Trotsky conveys an entirely different picture:

> It has been written that the Bulgarian people wanted war. Especially insistent on this were certain Russian journalists who obtained their information from the general staff...The people did not want war and could not have wanted it...They would have been glad if there had been a peaceful settlement of the issue. But the ruling classes proved incapable of finding any way out of the situation but a mutual extermination of Bulgarian and Turkish peasants.[22]

Trotsky was apparently one of the journalists who had been misleadingly briefed by the Bulgarian general staff.

In March 1913, when Lenin hailed the victories of the Balkan allies as marking 'the collapse of the medieval state of affairs in Asia and Eastern Europe', Trotsky waxed more critical still of the war against

Turkey. He praised the Bulgarian social democrat, 'our friend Sakazov', and the Serb social democrat, 'our friend Lapcevic', for speaking out against the war in the parliaments of the two countries. [23] And when it was all over, after the Bulgarian débâcle in the Second Balkan War and the signing of the peace of Bucharest, Trotsky summed up, in July 1913, the results of the fighting:

> The war...swallowed up, in killed, wounded and dead from disease, not less than half a million men. Not one of the basic problems of Balkan development has been solved...We see the enmity of each toward all and all toward each. The Balkan states breathe mutual hatred...The material resources of the peninsula have been exhausted for a long time to come.... [24]

In his dispatches on the first war, when Bulgaria bore the brunt of the fighting against Turkey, Trotsky kept reporting and denouncing atrocities by the Serbs and Bulgars against Turks and Moslem Albanians. When the Bulgarian censors stopped his visiting the front and sending back articles, he accused them of acting not in the interests of military security but of propaganda to conceal the excesses of the military. In an Open Letter to the Chief Censor – a radical Bulgarian poet – he wrote in December 1912:

> Your censorship...has not been concerned to safeguard military secrets, but rather to conceal...all the cruelties and crimes, all the infamies that accompany every war, and your war in particular...You defined your war as a crusade for civilization against barbarism...But now Europe will learn that the path of the crusading army was marked by crimes that must provoke shudders and nausea in every cultured person, in everyone capable of feeling and thinking. [25]

He went on to give details of the wholesale slaughter by Bulgarian soldiery of defenceless civilians, including women and children, and of the censorship's methods of suppressing the relevant facts. He made himself unpopular not only with the censors and with Bulgarian public opinion, but with Russian Pan-Slavists like the 'Cadet' leader Miliukov who dismissed Trotsky's assertions as distortion or fabrication.

History had an ironic twist in store for Trotsky. Not many years later, as Commissar of War, he directed military operations in the Russian

Civil War. Reports abounded in the press of many countries of atrocities and acts of inhumanity by Bolshevik troops and civilian officials. Some were true, others untrue or exaggerated: probably the same as the reports he had received and passed on during the Balkan wars.

Now in the dock, Trotsky reacted in much the same way as the men he had accused, in 1912 and 1913, of responsibility for similar crimes, or of hushing up such crimes: he either denied the accuracy of the stories or explained why certain actions during the Civil War had been necessary and justified. Replying to Kautsky's denunciation of Bolshevik cruelties, he wrote that 'destruction and cruelty are inevitable in any war.'[26] In a revolutionary period there had to be 'widespread recourse to shooting', that is, to killing active opponents, because 'the party which has been thrown from power...cannot be deterred by the threat of imprisonment, as it does not believe in its duration.' Kautsky had censured the Bolshevik régime for abolishing freedom of the press and suppressing newspapers. Trotsky retorted, 'During war all institutions and organs of the State and of public opinion become, directly or indirectly, weapons of warfare. This is particularly true of the press. No government carrying on a serious war will allow publications to exist on its territory which, openly or indirectly, support the enemy.'[27]

The Bulgarian censors could have said the same in 1912–13. No doubt Trotsky would have treated any press reports of Bolshevik atrocities between 1918 and 1921 as supporting, at least indirectly, the enemy in the Civil War. With equal justice, the Bulgarian censors could have claimed that Trotsky was at least indirectly supporting the Turks in his despatches from Bulgaria.

Trotsky reacted with derision to Kautsky's complaint that the victorious Bolsheviks had even banned the newspapers of the other socialist parties, Mensheviks and Social Revolutionaries, and arrested their leaders. According to Trotsky, it was 'scholastic pedantry' on Kautsky's part to regard Mensheviks and Social Revolutionaries as socialists of a different hue, whereas 'in the course of the revolution they have been transformed into an organization which works in active co-operation with counter-revolution and carries on against us open war.'[28] Trotsky went on to list the counter-revolutionary misdeeds of these parties: their active support for White generals, the killing of Bolsheviks and other reactionary crimes committed in alliance with foreign interventionists, with the last German kaiser and later with

Lloyd George. Here again, history took a cruel revenge on Trotsky. In the 1930s, his Stalinist enemies charged him with similar counter-revolutionary actions, with being in league with foreign imperialists and working for the dismemberment of the Soviet Union.

The debate on Bolshevik inhumanity during the Civil War came to life again some twenty years later, at the time of the Moscow purge trials. Trotsky's critics – who included some erstwhile adherents – recalled some of the reports published during the Civil War. In this controversy it was said that in 1919 Trotsky had signed a decree providing that the relatives of active 'counter-revolutionaries' could be taken and held as hostages. [29] In his polemical reply, Trotsky admitted responsibility for the measure and defended it unreservedly:

> We will not insist here upon the fact that the Decree of 1919 led scarcely to even one execution of relatives of those commanders whose perfidy not only caused the loss of innumerable lives but threatened the revolution itself with direct annihilation...If the revolution had displayed less superfluous generosity from the very beginning, hundreds of thousands of lives would have been saved. However that may be, I carry full responsibility for the Decree of 1919. It was a necessary measure in the struggle against the oppressors. [30]

The propagandists of Bulgaria and Serbia during the First Balkan War might also have argued that harsh methods would shorten the war and save far more lives than they destroyed. [31]

In their comments on the Balkan wars both Lenin and Trotsky were inconsistent in endorsing the aim of ending Turkish rule in the Peninsula but sometimes deploring the war without which the aim could not have been attained. Neither ever suggested that the Ottoman empire would have relinquished the remainder of its European possessions without armed struggle. But in another respect Trotsky's approach differed from Lenin's. It was free of the hypocrisy of Lenin's written statements: the publicly professed wish for peace and the private hope for an early war between Russia and Austria-Hungary. There is no reason to believe Trotsky was insincere when he painted his vivid picture of the war, and warned the peoples of Europe that the unresolved Balkan problems might provoke a more terrible conflict.

PART III
The First World War

1 International Socialism at the Outbreak of the First World War

The First World War had a more profound and more divisive effect upon the international socialist movement than any previous armed conflict. The Second International was one of its first casualties. Mortal enmity between socialists in opposite camps replaced the solidarity of the last world congress. Enmity, often more intense, divided pro-war and anti-war socialists within the belligerent nations.

The international crisis which led to war was sparked off by the assassination of Francis Ferdinand, heir to the Habsburg throne, at Sarajevo in Bosnia on 28 June 1914. Bosnia was Habsburg territory, annexed in 1908, and the assassin was a young Bosnian Serb.[1] The Austrians had watched the growth of Serbia's influence after her successes in two Balkan wars, and were worried about the attraction that country might have for the many Slavs under Habsburg rule. The outrage at Sarajevo seemed a godsent opportunity to remove the threat of Slav *irredentism* by humbling or destroying Serbia.

Austria accused the Serb authorities of complicity in, or at least fore-knowledge of, the murder plot, and sent an ultimatum on 23 July. The harshness of its terms showed that the Vienna government did not expect or want it to be accepted, but intended to use its rejection as the pretext for war. Serbia was anxious to avoid war. She accepted the substance of the Austrian demands and offered to submit the outstanding points to the Hague Tribunal or to arbitration by the great powers. Austria dismissed the reply as unsatisfactory, broke off relations and declared war on 28 July.

The crisis swiftly reached a climax. On 31 July Russia proclaimed general mobilization, to demonstrate her resolve to stand by Serbia. Germany demanded, in a twelve-hour ultimatum, that the order for mobilization be revoked, and after its expiry declared war. When France declined to pledge her neutrality, Germany declared war on her on 3 August, alleging some fictitious violation of German territory and air space. The following day German forces invaded Belgium, whose government had rejected a German request for free passage. The same day, 4 August, Britain, one of the guarantors of Belgian neutrality, declared war on Germany.

Socialist opinion everywhere had denounced Austria's patent desire for at least a localized war. Perhaps the strongest condemnation came from the German Social Democratic Party (SPD) a few days before the war started. As soon as the unreasonable terms of the Austrian ultimatum became known on 25 July, the SPD executive issued an appeal to the party membership. It denounced the intrigues of some Serb nationalist circles but protested emphatically 'against the frivolous war provocations of the Austrian-Hungarian Government': demands of such brutality had never before been addressed to an independent state; they were designed to provoke war. The appeal continued:

> In the name of humanity and of civilization the class-conscious proletariat of Germany protests fervently against these criminal machinations of the warmongers. It insists peremptorily that the German government exert its influence upon the Austrian government in favour of the preservation of peace, and that, if the shameful war cannot be prevented, the German government refrains from military intervention in any shape or form. Not a drop of a German soldier's blood must be sacrificed to the lust for power of the Austrian rulers, and in the interests of imperialist profits.
>
> Comrades, we urge you to demonstrate forthwith, in mass rallies, the unshakeable desire of the class-conscious proletariat for peace. The hour is grave...World war threatens. The ruling classes, which in times of peace gag you, despise you and exploit you, now want to misuse you as cannon-fodder. Our cry must ring in the ears of the rulers everywhere: We want no war! Down with the war! Long live the international brotherhood of the peoples![2]

In those last days of July 1914, Germany was indeed the country where anti-war rallies and demonstrations, organized by the SPD and the trade unions, were particularly impressive. The kaiser was worried by the mounting peace propaganda; in a marginal note to a telegram from the tsar he declared, 'Those socialists are staging anti-militarist agitation in the streets; this must not be tolerated, definitely not *now*. If that continues I shall proclaim martial law and have the leaders, the whole damned lot of them, locked up in gaol.'[3]

He was dissuaded from such action by the imperial chancellor Bethmann-Hollweg, who had read the minds of the Social Democratic leaders more correctly. He realized that in order to wage war with any chance of success the government would need the support of the working class, and that repressive action against the SPD, the strongest group in the Reichstag, would jeopardize that support. Bethmann-Hollweg also felt sure that official propaganda, adroitly handled, could convince the bulk of the socialist leadership that the country was waging a just war of defence, against the perennial threat of tsarist aggressive barbarism. Thus, when war had been declared no action was taken against any leading Social Democrat − not even Karl Liebknecht, Rosa Luxemburg or others on the extreme Left whose anti-militarist stance was well known. Within a few days the chancellor could claim that his calculation had been correct.

During the first half of July, while the international crisis was building up, preparations were still going on for the congress of the Socialist International in Vienna on 23 August. But it soon became obvious that the holding of the congress, in the Austrian capital of all places, was now not possible. Faced with the steadily growing danger of war, the International Socialist Bureau decided to call an augmented meeting at its seat in Brussels from 28 to 30 July, with three or four additional delegates from each country.

A fortnight earlier the French Socialist Party had held an extraordinary congress in Paris. Its debates were almost solely about the old problem of preventing war by a general strike, as proposed by Vaillant and Keir Hardie at the Copenhagen congress in 1910. In 1914, in Paris, a bare majority, including Jean Jaurès and Marcel Sembat, was in favour of a simultaneous and internationally concerted general strike.[4] But when the International Bureau met on 28 July no one even mentioned a general strike, nor did anyone suggest other anti-war measures such as those advocated at previous meetings of the International: insurrection or refusal to serve in the armed forces. At the end of July 1914, war hysteria had gripped the masses, and it was obvious that there was no chance of organizing strikes or other proletarian mass action against the war.

Those who addressed the Brussels meeting agreed that Austria should be condemned. All voiced suspicions about the attitudes of Russia and of Germany, but nobody challenged Jaurès's assertion that the French and British governments were sincere in striving for peace.[5] The general atmosphere was one of harmony, and there was no hostility between socialists from soon-to-be-enemy countries. When Hugo Haase, chairman of the German Social Democratic Party, told the meeting of his party's anti-war propaganda and of the peace rallies in German towns, he received stormy applause. What Haase and the other delegates did not know was that these demonstrations were on the point of being swamped by counter-demonstrations of hysterical mobs clamouring for war.[6]

Austria and Serbia were already at war when the International Socialist Bureau held its Brussels meeting. Vienna was out of the question as a venue for the International congress, but delegates thought it would be possible to meet in Paris on 9 August. On 29 July the bureau issued a communiqué, agreed unanimously, which announced the change of venue and time and added that the congress in Paris would 'give decisive expression to the will for peace of the entire world proletariat'. It enjoined the workers of all countries concerned 'not only to continue but to intensify the demonstrations against war, for peace and for the settlement by arbitration of the dispute between Austria and Serbia', and continued:

> The working classes of Germany and France will bring yet stronger pressure to bear on their respective governments, so as to make Germany exert a restraining influence upon Austria, and to make France induce Russia not to intervene in the conflict. The proletarians of Great Britain and Italy on their part will lend their most energetic support to these efforts.[7]

The following day, the SPD executive and the Reichstag group held a meeting to decide how the parliamentary party was to vote on the war budget if war should come.[8] The general feeling was that the group would not vote for the credits. It was decided that Hermann Müller,[9] a member of the executive (but not of the Reichstag), should go to Paris forthwith to try to co-ordinate the policies of the French and German parties, especially regarding the vote on war credits.[10] Müller went to Brussels and thence to Paris, with the Belgian socialists Camille Huysmans (secretary of the International Bureau) and Henri de Man. He was received with extreme cordiality by his French comrades, still shocked by the assassination on the previous day (31 July) of Jean Jaurès. Müller, the two Belgians, the French parliamentary party and members of the Socialist Party executive, held two meetings on 1 August.

Huysmans, the French deputy Renaudel, de Man, and Müller later published reports of these discussions; they tell substantially the same story, except for minor discrepancies. Hermann Müller told the French that the Social Democrats in the Reichstag would reject the war budget or abstain but would certainly not vote for it.[11] Marcel Sembat, who was in the chair, recalled the joint manifesto of the French and German parties of 1 March 1913,[12] and expressed the hope that the socialists both in the Reichstag and in the Chambre des Députés would abstain, thus demonstrating their continued unity. But Renaudel and other Frenchmen declared themselves convinced that the French government led by Viviani (a centre-left coalition) was doing its utmost to maintain peace: if war broke out, France would be the victim of an attack, and the French party would feel obliged to vote for the credits. Müller replied that he was sure the German government, and especially the kaiser and Bethmann-Hollweg, were striving for peace; the danger of war emanated from Russia, and it was up to France to exert pressure upon her Russian ally.[13]

When Müller left Paris that evening to return to Germany, no conclusion had been reached on how the two socialist parties would vote. But Müller felt sure that the French parliamentary party would vote 'yes'. He said that the French socialists, both right-wing and 'the Marxist left-wing', believed war could result only from German aggression, and that the French republic would have to fight for its existence and for the defence of the nation's freedom.

In France, as in Germany, mass rallies for peace had been held at the end of July, organized by the Socialist Party and the CGT, the socialist trade union. When the danger of war became more stark and immediate after the Austrian ultimatum to Serbia, the CGT's paper *La Bataille Syndicaliste* called for extreme anti-war action by the working class.[14] On 25 July the paper insisted that a 'revolutionary general strike' must be the instant proletarian reaction to the outbreak of war. An article by Jouhaux, CGT general secretary, referred to the official visit President Poincaré was paying to Russia at a time when revolutionary unrest and political strikes were spreading in the tsar's domains; by making a determined stand against war, the French workers would act in the interests of the Russian people as well, who were 'in revolt both against the crimes of tsarism and against the threat of European war.'[15]

Massive anti-war demonstrations and 'patriotic' counter-demonstrations were staged in Paris and other French towns from 25 to 29 July. But an indoor mass rally, called by the CGT for the evening of 29 July, was banned by the government — ostensibly to avoid clashes with right-wing militarist demonstrators. On 31 July Jaurès was murdered, and masses of workers gathered in the streets of Paris when the news broke. The next day Germany declared war on Russia, and general mobilization was proclaimed in France. With war inevitable and imminent, there was a rapid change of mood within the French socialist movement; anti-war agitation subsided.

On 2 August *La Bataille Syndicaliste* announced mobilization under the heading 'Folly triumphs over reason'. The paper appealed for international proletarian solidarity but no longer for working-class action against the war. It pronounced a curse, not on war in general but on 'the name of the old emperor, Francis Joseph'. When war started, the paper reacted with a cry of grief and despair, culminating in the wish, 'May this blood. . .be on the head of William II and the Pan-Germanists.' And on the 4 August the paper said, 'May social war break out again on the Spree and the Danube!' In his funeral oration for Jaurès the same day Jouhaux said, 'It is not hatred of the German people but of German imperialism that drives us on to the battlefield.' And on 8 August *La Bataille Syndicaliste,* which two weeks before had urged French workers to strike in the event of war, told the working-class soldiers that they would be fighting for the revolution: 'If you should be killed in action, all those of your comrades who as yet remain behind. . .swear solemnly, while bidding you farewell: vanguard soldiers of the revolution, you will not have died in vain.'[16]

The French Socialist Party, which at its extraordinary Paris congress in mid-July had pronounced in favour of an 'internationally concerted general strike against war', moved towards unanimous defencism during the last days of peace.

On 28 July the party's executive issued a manifesto accusing the 'capitalist-imperialist system' of having produced 'a permanent state of tension and a constant and ever-growing danger of war' during the preceding ten years. Austria-Hungary, with its brutal ultimatum to Serbia, had made the threat of war more acute. The French government, which was striving to reduce the risk, should bring pressure to bear on Russia to stop 'using the need to defend Slav interests as a pretext for aggressive action'. The manifesto applauded the position of the German socialists who had called upon their government to exert a moderating influence on Austria. The parliamentary Socialist Party gave the manifesto 'complete and unanimous endorsement', and said that Russian intervention would not help Serbia but would 'play into the hands of the most aggressive kind of imperialist Germanism'. France should support the British attempts at mediation. France had 'subordinated her claims to Alsace-Lorraine to the supreme interests of peace' for over forty years; she should not allow herself to be dragged into a war for Serbia.[17]

On 2 August, the Seine department branch of the Socialist Party held a members' meeting in the Salle Wagram in Paris. Here it became obvious that the habitual differences between right and left, between advocates of national defence and diehard anti-militarists had disappeared in the crisis. A unanimous resolution condemned Austria's attack on Serbia and the German declaration of war on Russia, and declared:

We uphold all our reservations concerning obligations stemming from secret treaties which have not been made known to us and which our parliament has not ratified. But, as we have always made clear, if aggression is committed against peaceable, republican France — aggression which threatens civilization and humanity — we shall respond with all our strength and all our energies.

In other words, the socialists of Paris did not want France to go to war because of some secret Franco-Russian treaty clauses, but they were ready to defend their country if it was attacked by Germany, which happened within twenty-four hours.

All speakers at the Salle Wagram emphasized the need to resist aggression by force. They included Marcel Sembat who at the recent extraordinary party congress had voted for a general strike against war, but who now told his fellow-socialists that they must fight for the defence of French culture and the freedom of nations. Edouard Vaillant, the old socialist who had tried to commit the International to general strikes in the event of war, told his comrades that, if France were attacked, they must 'do their patriotic as well as their socialist duty...for the fatherland, for the republic, and for the revolution'. Jean Longuet, Marx's grandson and generally on the left of the French party, spoke in the same vein; if France were invaded, socialists 'could not fail to be in the forefront of the defenders of France, the country of the revolution and of democracy'.[18]

The trend towards 'social-patriotism' (to borrow Lenin's phrase) became more marked in France during the first few weeks of war, under the emotional impact of the German invasion of Belgium and northern France, and the German army's advance on Paris. On 26 August a French 'Government of National Defence' was formed; the Socialist Party agreed to join it, and Jules Guesde and the old anti-militarist Marcel Sembat became ministers. The socialist press, *L'Humanité* and *La Bataille Syndicaliste,* supported the government's war effort uncritically. One of the main contributors to the pro-war *L'Humanité* was Vaillant, that life-long fighter against nationalism and war; but in 1914, his seventy-fifth year, he wrote a number of ardently patriotic, almost chauvinistic articles. He accused critics from the party's ranks of 'concealed propaganda for German imperialism', and, contrary to French socialist tradition, inserted anti-German tirades in his articles, speaking, for example, of 'the complicity and responsibility of the emperor who gives orders and the people which slavishly obeys'.[19]

Vaillant's new-found patriotic fervour was not shared by a substantial portion of French socialists; at any rate, it did not reflect the official position of the party. Vaillant's ideological background was Blanquist rather than Marxist. It is perhaps significant that Jules Guesde, an orthodox Marxist who had always insisted that socialists had the right and duty to defend their country against aggression, did not give way to nationalist or anti-German sentiments after the war had begun.

Guesde's and the Socialist Party's attitude to the issues and aims of the war emerged from a conversation he had on 14 August − before the party's entry into the government − with President Poincaré and Premier Viviani. According to a report drawn up by the socialist group in the Chambre des Députés, Guesde suggested that after the first French victory the government should solemnly declare in a proclamation to the German people that apart from Alsace-Lorraine, which must be returned to its own people, 'not an inch of German territory would be annexed';[20] The proclamation should also say that the French republic was ready 'to hold out a fraternal hand to the German nation, once the latter had rid itself of its *empire,*[21] its militarism and its emperor.' The socialist group's report says that Viviani agreed completely, and Poincaré with certain qualifications, with the Socialist Party's position as expounded by Guesde.

2   Socialist Reaction to the War in 1914

The decision of the French Socialist Party to support the war and to enter the government is wholly understandable. The French government had made no bellicose move during the critical weeks of July. The German government, on the other hand, had made demands which the French could not be expected to accept. When Russia had mobilized, Germany not only insisted on a French assurance of neutrality but demanded the handing over for the duration of the fortresses of Toul and Verdun, as pledges of French neutrality.[1] As far as France was concerned, it was a war of defence resulting from German aggression.

The situation appeared to be exactly what Engels had in mind in 1892 when he agreed with Jules Guesde that French socialists should not hesitate to defend their country against a German attack.[2] Engels would not have liked the Russian alliance; neither did most French socialists in 1914. But after the way the crisis had developed and war had been unleashed, the French Socialist Party, which considered itself a Marxist party, was entitled to assume that Marx and Engels would have approved of the decision to vote for the war credits and back the war effort.[3]

The position of the German Social Democratic Party was similar in one way to that of the French party, inasmuch as the great majority of German socialists approached the question of supporting or opposing a war from the same ideological angle. The Germans, too, thought it right in principle to support a just war of defence, but to refuse cooperation and to attack the government if it waged aggressive war for expansionist aims. The French and the German socialist parties came to opposite conclusions in 1914, not because they applied different criteria but because they saw and interpreted the facts differently. Whether or not the French party's views were factually correct in every way, German Social Democracy was certainly misinformed and misled by its government. When the SPD executive and the parliamentary party decided to endorse the war budget, they – or at least most leading members – believed the government's assurances that its intentions had been peaceful all along. They probably believed that French and Russian forces had violated German territory, and may also have accepted the official German claim that the invasion of Belgium forestalled the execution of a French plan to march through neutral Belgium against Germany. In sum, each of the parties supported its government in the belief that it was fighting to repel aggression. This belief, if justified, would have rendered support for the war defensible from the point of view of established socialist theory and practice.

The methods applied by the bulk of the SPD and the other sections of the International in determining socialist wartime policies are characterized by Karl Kautsky:

> The overwhelming majority of the party, including the Reichstag group, applied the method used by Marx and Engels, by Bebel and also, on the eve of world war, by Jaurès. This method prevailed throughout the International. It meant that socialists were not committed to either supporting or opposing their own government under all circumstances; rather they had to examine the policy which had led to war and which was being pursued by means of war. If it was found that one's own government had provoked the war and was striving for war aims incompatible with our own goals, then we must refuse them any support, including a vote for war credits. Conversely, it was not only the right but the duty of socialists to support their own government, if the latter had not wanted war, if it had been the victim of attack, or if not its victory but that of the enemy would imperil the general advance of democracy and the proletariat.[4]

These were indeed the criteria Marx and Engels used when deciding whose victory to favour in a war. The two main considerations mentioned by Kautsky as decisive for the socialist attitude in a war between non-socialist governments – responsibility for the war and the interests of progress and the proletariat – need not, of course, point in the same direction. The victory of the aggressor country could be more likely to promote the socialist cause than that of the victim of aggression. Kautsky, following Marx and Engels, held that in that case the consequences of victory or defeat should be considered more important than the desirability of frustrating aggression, not least because of the difficulty in deciding which side had committed aggression. Kautsky made this point at the SPD congress in Essen,[5] and he made it again in the context of an actual, not merely hypothetical, war. His reasoning is brought to light in his account of the considerations which induced the German Social Democrats to support the war waged by the kaiser's government in 1914.[6]

The Social Democratic group in the Reichstag met on 3 August to decide its vote on the war budget, to be taken the following day. Kautsky, who was a member of the SPD executive but not of the parliamentary party, was asked to attend. He wanted the Reichstag group to do what Bebel and Wilhelm Liebknecht had done in 1870 and what, incidentally, the Social Democratic group in the Russian *Duma* was to do on 8 August: abstain from voting. This was rejected by the deputies for a reason which Kautsky thought unconvincing, namely, that the SPD as the largest party in the Reichstag (110 out of a total of 397 members) could not sit on the fence in a matter of such gravity. Kautsky, who felt that a majority would vote for the credits, then proposed that the party should vote 'Aye' on condition that the government pledged itself to fight a purely defensive war and would, after victory, refrain from violating any foreign nation. What he had in mind was the formula later embodied in the 'Zimmerwald manifesto',[7] a peace based on self-determination, without annexations or war indemnities.

As he explained in his book some twenty years later, Kautsky did not feel able, in August 1914, to arrive at a clear verdict on responsibility for the war. He remained highly critical of Germany's and especially Austria's policies during the last weeks of peace, but felt that the official German version — last-minute readiness by Austria to come to terms, frustrated by French and Russian hostility — could not be dismissed out of hand. Russia might have had a real motive for provoking war as a means of silencing revolutionary unrest. Guilt or innocence was therefore not a suitable criterion, so Kautsky asked himself whose victory would have the more beneficial social and political consequences. No simple decision seemed possible on this basis either. He recalled what Engels had said in 1891 about the threat which a Franco-Russian alliance could pose to Germany. But conditions in 1914 were not what they had been in the 1890s:

> It would have been impossible for me to take unconditionally the German side, as some friends, referring to Engels, insisted we must do. Germany's victory would have meant the omnipotence of the German general staff, not only within Germany but throughout Europe. Furthermore, Russia was no longer the despotic country she had been in 1891 . . . On the other hand, Russia's victory could be tantamount to a strengthening of the tsar's power *vis-à-vis* his own people; it could bring about, at least for the

immediate future, the paralysis of the Russian revolutionary movement. Hence, the victory of either side would gravely threaten the prospects of democracy and the proletariat in Europe.[8]

In this complex situation, Kautsky argued, the compromise proposal he put to the parliamentary Social Democratic Party seemed the best way out. Acceptance by the government of the SPD's demands could mean that the war would be short, and its results less nefarious from the socialist point of view. If, however, the kaiser's government rejected the party's conditions, the group would vote against the credits in the Reichstag; after the government's refusal to define moderate war aims, the party's rejection of the credits would have seemed more reasonable to the mass of patriotic German workers than if the SPD had in all circumstances opposed the government's war policy.

On 3 August, the day the parliamentary party debated the issue of the war credits, two of its leaders, Hugo Haase and Philipp Scheidemann, attended a meeting of parliamentary party leaders at the office of Chancellor Bethmann-Hollweg, who informed them of the contents of the speech he was going to make in the house on 4 August. The question of the war budget was broached, and the two social democrats noticed that all those present assumed that the credits would be passed unanimously. When Haase and Scheidemann pointed out that the SPD group had not yet decided on its vote, Erzberger,[9] a member of the Roman Catholic Centre Party, remarked ironically: 'Well, I think in this case you'll be clever enough to vote "Aye".'[10]

Erzberger was right. The Social Democratic deputies, with one exception, turned down Kautsky's idea of a conditional acceptance of the war credits, on the grounds that a clearcut decision was required. The group then decided by a large majority (18 to 14, with 18 members either absent or abstaining) to vote for the credits. All, including Karl Liebknecht, obeyed the majority decision.[11]

After taking the decision to pass the war budget the parliamentary group appointed a committee to draft the statement explaining the party's 'Yes' vote. As a member of the committee, Kautsky made another attempt to introduce a specific reservation concerning social-ist support for the war. At his suggestion a sentence was inserted in the statement, saying that the party would 'most energetically oppose the government if the latter allowed the war to assume the character of a war of conquest.'[12] However, on 5 August, when Kautsky read the text of the statement made by Hugo Haase in the Reichstag the previous day, he was dismayed to find that the sentence had been omitted. Haase, who had been against acceptance of the credits, explained that this had been done at Bethmann-Hollweg's request. The Reich chancellor had asked to be allowed to read the draft statement and had remarked that this particular sentence might be seen to indicate that the Social Democrats suspected the imperial government of intending to wage a war of aggression; the British government might interpret the passage that way and be induced to enter the war on the enemy side. Strangely, this tortuous reasoning impressed the SPD Reichstag group, which then decided to delete the reference to a war of aggression.

When this conversation between Haase and Kautsky took place, Britain was already at war with Germany. The British government had declared war, not because of anything in the SPD's statement but – at least officially – because of an event the German chancellor had mentioned in the Reichstag on 4 August: the violation of Belgian neutrality. Kautsky says that if this had been known on 3 August, when the SPD Group deliberated on their vote, he would have backed those deputies who wanted unconditional rejection of the war budget.[13] When the government asked for a further credit of 5,000 million marks in December 1914, Kautsky did counsel rejection. The parliamentary party again decided to pass the war credits; Karl Liebknecht alone defied party discipline and voted against the budget.[14]

The statement Hugo Haase read out in the Reichstag on 4 August was not, even without Kautsky's passage, a radical break with traditional socialist concepts and policies. If the party had been right in the belief that Germany was being attacked, and that victory for tsarist Russia was the greatest of all possible evils for world socialism, the statement could be judged as the application to the circumstances of established Marxist opinions and criteria.[15]

The party's statement is specific about the Russian threat: a victory 'for the Russian autocrat, whose hands are stained with the blood of the best of his compatriots' would put all achievements in jeopardy. 'It is of paramount importance to avert this danger and to assure our country's independence.' The statement implies but does not say in so many words that Germany was fighting a war of defence. This is what the SPD leaders believed at the time. As Scheidemann put it:

At the time we all believed that Germany had been attacked — that the French had poisoned German water supplies and French airmen had dropped bombs on Nuremberg and Fuerth. These were press reports — eventually they all turned out to be unsubstantiated rumours. We were all convinced that all those in responsible positions throughout Germany had done their best to prevent war. [16]

In its statement the SPD held 'the imperialist policy of an arms race and of intensifying national antagonisms' to be responsible for the war. Socialists had always opposed such disastrous policies and had striven to the very last moment for the maintenance of peace by powerful demonstrations in all countries, 'above all, in close harmony with our French brothers'. But war had come, and with it the threat of enemy invasion. The party was faced with a decision, not for or against war, but about the means needed for the country's defence. The final paragraph explains the national and international aspects of the party's policy:

We are carrying out what we have pledged ourselves to do: we do not desert the fatherland in its hour of peril. In this respect we are in complete accord with the International which has always recognized the right of every nation to independence and self-defence; in agreement with the International we condemn all wars of conquest. We demand that, as soon as our security has been achieved and the enemies are ready for peace, the war should end in a peace that will make friendship with our neighbours possible. We demand this not only in the interests of international solidarity for which we have always stood, but also in the interests of the German people. We trust that the hard experience of war will awaken in millions of people a horror of war, and will win them over for the ideals of socialism and of peace on earth. Guided by these principles we shall vote for the requisite credits.

France and Germany were the only major belligerent countries whose socialist parties managed an outward show of unity in support of the war, for some time at least. The bulk of Russian Social Democrats, Mensheviks and Bolsheviks, opposed the war from the start. Their deputies in the *Duma* abstained when the vote on the war budget was taken. But many Russian socialists in exile in Western Europe, including Plekhanov, espoused the cause of Russia and her allies. In France hundred of emigrés, both Mensheviks and Bolsheviks, volunteered for the French army. The same Plekhanov, who in 1893 had said that invading German soldiers would be greeted as liberators by the Russian people, now appealed to the Social Democrats in the *Duma* to vote for the war credits, and to the workers of Russia to refrain from strike action while the war lasted; the victory of the *Entente* alone could save Russia from being dominated, economically and politically, by a reactionary Germany.[17]

In Britain a large section of the labour movement, including the ILP, voiced its opposition, largely on pacifist rather than Marxist-revolutionary grounds, as soon as war was declared. The majority of Italian socialists were against joining the Central Powers (to whom Italy was still officially allied) at the outbreak of war, and against entering the war on the side of the *Entente,* as Italy did in May 1915 in the teeth of socialist opposition.

Two countries of the *Entente* coalition were undoubtedly fighting a war of defence: Serbia and Belgium. In backward Serbia the socialist movement was weak; only two socialists sat in the *Skupshtina,* the country's parliament. Both belonged to the radical militant school, to whom the notion of supporting a non-socialist government in war or peace was abhorrent. And although Serbia was plainly the victim of aggression and had not made any provocative move during the pre-war exchanges, the two socialist members spoke out against the war. Apart from refusing in principle to co-operate with the country's rulers, they declared that, in the circumstances of 1914, Serbia was in the war as a member of an alliance of capitalist-imperialist great powers, which included Russia, a stronghold of oppression and reaction.[18]

The Belgian socialists had no hesitation in supporting the cause of national defence. Their country was an innocent victim of unprovoked aggression. Belgium had not even, like Serbia, been involved in a dispute with the neighbour who attacked her; no one had accused her rulers of complicity in a terrorist crime. As Kautsky pointed out, there was no alternative to an all-out effort to repel the aggressor, and there was no basis for disagreement within the Socialist Party. The Belgian socialist were just as ready as their French comrades to enter government.[19] Vandervelde, chairman of the International Socialist Bureau, became minister of state.[20]

Austria was without a parliament when war broke out. Parliamentary approval for war credits was not required so the question of passing or rejecting them did not arise. But there is little doubt that they would have followed the example of their comrades in Germany had parliamentary sanction been sought. The crisis caught the Austrian Social Democrats in the middle of preparations for the International Socialist Congress, scheduled in the Austrian capital on 23 August. Like the fraternal German party, they held a number of anti-war protest rallies until the very day of the declaration of war but, as in Germany, its outbreak produced a complete change of mood. The Austrian Social Democratic leaders also found theoretical excuses for supporting the war — chiefly the reactionary character of tsarism — and some of them became extremely bellicose.[21]

In Britain a war credit of £100 million was passed on 6 August without a division. This did not mean unanimous support for the war. Ramsay MacDonald, leader of the parliamentary Labour Party, spoke in the House of Commons against the declaration of war; so did some 'radical' Liberal members. When the Labour Party, after lengthy deliberation, decided to support the government, MacDonald resigned from the leadership and was replaced by Arthur Henderson. Keir Hardie, Philip Snowden and some other Labour MPs, who like MacDonald had been elected under ILP auspices, also opposed the war or urged the earliest possible conclusion of a negotiated peace.[22] The possibility of voting against the war credits does not seem to have been considered, at any rate not at that stage. The ILP periodical the *Socialist Review* carried a number of articles against the war and against the Labour Party's support for the war; but only at the end of 1916 did a contributor suggest that approval of the war budget was scarcely consistent with an anti-war stance. In the November/December 1916 issue of the journal Lancelot Eden recalled that on 11 October that year the Commons had passed an additional amount of war credits, 'to cover the cost of war till Christmas', without a division. In all belligerent countries except Britain, Eden observed, the vote on the war credits was regarded 'as a test question between the pro-war and anti-war socialists'. The vote for war expenditure by the anti-war group in parliament had caused surprise in other countries. In the spring of 1915 Eden had asked an (unnamed) ILP member of parliament when he was going to vote against the credits; the MP had been startled and exclaimed: 'I couldn't do it, I couldn't refuse to vote the money for feeding and clothing our lads in the trenches.' Eden commented:

He who wills the means wills the end. Those who vote the sinews of war, and those who give their tacit assent, will not merely 'the feeding and clothing of our lads in the trenches'; they will to supply them with arms and ammunition; they will the slaughter...the continuance of the war. ....Among the Allies England stands alone, or almost alone, in having no parliamentary representatives to take a definite stand against the continuance of the war, with that definiteness that can, under existing conditions, be manifested in no other way than by a defiant 'No' in the House of Commons when more money is demanded for the war. [23]

The article mentions Karl Liebknecht's courageous opposition at an early stage of the war, the conduct of the socialist members of the Russian *Duma,* the anti-war stand of the Italian socialists, the vote of three socialist members of the French Chamber against the war credits, [24] and concludes:

Who in England will lead the way, who among the international socialists in our parliament will hold out a hand to the international socialists in other lands?...Granted that it (a vote against the war budget) would evoke a storm of execration from the warmongers, I am confident that it would give a marvellous impulse to the concretion in this country of the growing sentiment against the continuance of this foolish and futile war...

There was no positive response to this appeal. Not one of the thirty-nine Labour MPs ever voted against the credits in the House of Commons during the First World War.

When war started, Britain did not possess a socialist party of the kind that existed in most countries of Europe. [25] The Labour Party did not officially profess to stand for socialism, although most of its leaders and affiliated members (there were no individual members then) were socialists. The party had been affiliated to the Socialist International since 1904, when it was admitted (on a motion by Karl Kautsky) as a party which practised the class war even though it did not preach it. The Fabian Society and the Independent Labour Party, which were affiliated to the Labour Party, were also separately affiliated to the International. So was the (Marxist) British Socialist Party (BSP), whose request for affiliation to the Labour Party was granted in 1916.

In 1914 the total (affiliated) membership of the Labour Party was about 1,650,000; the great majority were trade unionists. During the last twelve months of peace the International Socialist Bureau had been urging the unification of Britain's socialist movement. This led to the formation of a United Socialist Council, comprising the Fabians, the ILP and the BSP and, at the end of 1913, of a Socialist Unity Demonstration Committee, which organized demonstrations in favour of unity. But the attainment of unity was prevented by disagreements between the BSP and the other two socialist societies. When war broke out, the unity project was shelved; it proved difficult enough to preserve a degree of unity within the existing organizations.

The Labour Party's decision to support the war did not amount to an uncritical endorsement of government policy. A circular issued by the party on 7 August 1914 took the foreign secretary, Sir Edward Grey, to task for pledging British support to France in the event of war 'without the knowledge of the people', and 'before the House of Commons had any chance of considering the matter'. The *Entente* with France and Russia had been bound to increase Russia's power in Europe and Asia, and to endanger good relations with Germany. The labour movement had 'opposed the policy which had produced the war'; it was now its duty 'to secure peace at the earliest possible moment and on such conditions as will provide the best opportunites for the establishment of amicable feelings between the workers of Europe'.[26]

In the *Socialist Review* for the last quarter of 1914, the editor, J. Bruce Glasier, claimed that 'the ILP alone of all organizations affiliated to the Labour Party and to the British section of the International has withstood the onrush of war passion that has overswept the nation.'[27] It was indeed a fact that, as well as the parliamentary Labour Party, the TUC parliamentary committee and the BSP had proclaimed their support for the war, while the Fabian Society had not defined its position at all.[28] Glasier also mentioned that the national council of the ILP had dissociated the party from the decision of the PLP and the Labour Party executive to be active, with the Liberal and Tory Parties, in a 'non-political' recruiting campaign. The same issue carried the ILP's manifesto of mid-August on 'The War in Europe';[29] The Manifesto, which according to Glasier had been endorsed 'virtually unanimously' by the branches of the ILP, laid responsibility for the war on both the British and the German governments:

Even had Belgian neutrality not been wrongfully infringed by Germany we should still have been drawn in. If France in defiance of treaty rights had invaded Belgium to get at Germany, who believes we should have begun hostilities against France? Behind the back of parliament and people, the British foreign office gave secret understandings to France, denying their existence when challenged...Britain has placed herself behind Russia, the most reactionary, corrupt, and oppressive power in Europe.

The Manifesto laid great emphasis on international proletarian solidarity:

To us who are socialist the workers of Germany and Austria, no less than the workers of France and Russia, are comrades and brothers...Our nationality and independence, which are dear to us, we are ready to defend; but we cannot rejoice in the organized murder of tens of thousands of workers of other lands...Across the roar of guns, we send sympathy and greeting to the German socialists. They have laboured unceasingly to promote good relations with Britain, as we with Germany. They are no enemies of ours but faithful friends.

The ILP thus denounced the *policies* of the great powers, especially secret diplomacy and the arms race, but not, as a Marxist party would have done (and as Karl Liebknecht did in explaining his vote in December 1914) the capitalist profit system and international rivalry in the struggle for markets. Capitalist interests are mentioned only in connection with the arms race: according to the manifesto, 'powerful armament interests have played their sinister part, for it is they who reap rich harvest out of havoc and death.'

Nor was the manifesto unequivocal on the question of national defence. Readiness to defend 'our nationality and independence' might mean that armed resistance is called for only if the country is in danger of being invaded. Noteworthy, and not easy to explain, is the message of fraternal greetings to the socialists of Germany, without any mention of the fact that German Social Democracy had yielded as completely to 'the onrush of war passion' as had the British socialists attacked on that score by the ILP's organ.

As an anti-war document the ILP manifesto is far less emphatic than the pronouncements during the first months of the war by continental and British left-wing socialists, such as Karl Liebknecht and Rosa Luxemburg in Germany or John Maclean in Britain. As for the 'anti-war' ILP members of parliament, at least MacDonald and Snowden, though widely berated for their alleged lack of patriotism, never said anything to suggest that they did not wish for a British victory. Early in the war MacDonald wrote to the mayor of Leicester, who had invited him to address a recruiting rally. He declined but said, 'Victory ...must be ours... History will, in due time, apportion the praise and the blame, but the young men of the country must, for the moment, settle the immediate issue of victory.'[30]

Nor did MacDonald or Snowden change their minds in later years, when war weariness had begun to spread. In the House of Commons on 23 December 1916 Philip Snowden did not make so much play with the word 'victory' but, according to Hansard, he stressed 'the righteousness and justice of our national cause'. He then urged the government 'to bring this war to an end on terms and conditions which will realize the objects for which we are fighting', and added that it was wrong to stake all on a 'crushing military victory'. He went on to prophesy, 'When Germany has been crushed and ruined...another great war will be only a matter of time.' Three months later, also in the Commons, MacDonald said that Britain was in honour bound to refuse any peace 'which means the sacrifice of Belgian sovereignty to any extent,...not merely of Belgian sovereignty but of any portion of it'. He added that 'the same is true regarding France, so far as France has been invaded.' And in Swansea, in May 1917, he was emphatic that 'this country must not be allowed to make peace on account of war weariness.'[31] On 20 June 1918, he proclaimed, 'Neither defeat nor surrender is in my vocabulary.'

MacDonald and Snowden were clearly not toeing the party line which was unambiguously defined in a resolution passed by an overwhelming majority at the ILP's Newcastle Conference in April 1916. The resolution reads:

> This conference is of opinion that the socialists of all nations should agree that henceforth the socialist parties should refuse support to every war entered into by any government, whatever the ostensible character of the war, and even if such a war be nominally of a defensive character, and instructs the ILP to bring forward this policy at the next International conference.

Lancelot Eden, who quoted this resolution when reviewing a book on *Socialism and War* by the American Marxist Louis B. Boudin, remarked that 'many of those voting for the resolution were doubtless influenced by Tolstoyan or Quaker considerations.'[32] There was indeed more Christian pacifism than proletarian revolutionism in the text adopted at the conference: wars of defence were included, and revolutionary and national wars not explicitly exempted. But no action was apparently taken against ILP members of parliament whose utterances, in and out of the House of Commons, were inconsistent with the Newcastle resolution.

The closing months of 1914 witnessed a hardening of the pro-war attitude of the bulk of the British labour movement. On 15 October a manifesto was published, bearing the signatures of most Labour MPs, of the members of the TUC parliamentary committee and other Labour leaders. It was apparently designed to dispel the impression of ambiguity and qualified opposition to the war which the two documents of August (the Labour Party executive's circular and the ILP manifesto) must have created. The October manifesto put the entire blame for the war on the German government, implicitly repudiating the two earlier documents, and described the war simply as a conflict between democracy and military despotism. The only passage in keeping with the previous attitude of conciliation and detachment was a reference to the Labour Party's consistent stand 'for an international agreement among all civilized nations that disputes and misunderstandings in the future shall be settled not by machine-guns but by arbitration'.[33]

Unqualified support for the war, and co-operation to this end with the other political parties, remained Labour's line until the fighting ceased some four years later. The industrial truce and Labour's participation in the government (in May 1915) were landmarks on this political road. But the bitter debate between pro-war and anti-war socialists continued unabated, in Britain as in most other countries involved in the great conflagration, until the unity of world socialism was damaged beyond recovery.

3 Discord over Issues of War and Peace – the Austrian Socialists

During the four years and three months of global conflict attitudes of socialists to the war and its issues underwent some changes. But by and large, the bulk of the socialist labour movement in France, Britain and Germany, supported their respective governments' policy from beginning to end. Two important sections of the International were, so to speak, at war with a third – the most important of all. This made it impossible for the International to function or to survive.

The war caused no organizational split in the Socialist Party of the country whose rulers had 'let slip the dogs of war', Austria.[1] On 25 July 1914 the leaders of Austrian Social Democracry denounced their government's ultimatum to Serbia, but made no pronouncement on the beginning of the war with Russia, France and Britain. However, they did not enter into any formal agreement for a party-political truce, as socialist parties had done in other belligerent countries. The Austrian parliament was not meeting at the time. It had been prorogued in the spring of 1914 and was not summoned until May 1917, which is one reason why there was no crisis over war credits in the Austrian party.[2] (This issue of war credits did not arise for the socialists of Hungary either: the parliament did meet in the summer of 1914, but owing to the peculiarities of the electoral law it did not contain any socialists.)

The war and its issues were of course debated by the leadership and the rank-and-file of the Austrian Social-Democratic Party (SPOe); but as no decision of importance was to be taken, the debate remained academic. Victor Adler, its outstanding leader, and most of his German Austrian colleagues, shared the views of the majority of the German Social Democratic Party – the Ebert-Scheidemann tendency. So did the Austrian party's official press. The Vienna *Arbeiter-Zeitung,* the SPOe's central organ, hailed the German socialists' vote for the war credits as a momentous event for the German nation: 4 August, the paper declared the next day, had been 'a day of the proudest and most powerful exaltation of the German spirit'.[3]

Not many months passed before critical voices were heard. Between March and September 1915 the Vienna socialist weekly *Volkstribüne* carried articles by protagonists and opponents of the pro-war position of the majority. The main critic was Robert Danneberg, who argued along the lines of the German anti-war group led by Haase and Kautsky. One of Danneberg's partisans was Friedrich Adler, Victor Adler's son, who on behalf of 'the internationalists of Austria' addressed an anti-war manifesto to the Zimmerwald conference.[4]

This division never became a challenge to party unity. Both sides displayed moderation in their mutual strictures, and the polarization of opinion never went as far as it did in Germany. There were no Austrian equivalents to left-wing extremists like Rosa Luxemburg and

Karl Liebknecht, no advocates of a party split. Nor was there an equivalent to the German 'Social-Imperialists' who toyed with annexationist ideas and sometimes made jingoist speeches — men like Südekum, Haenisch, W. Heine — in the Austrian party. One of the reasons is that the Austrian pro-war socialists, unlike their German comrades, felt no real allegiance towards their state, the multi-national Habsburg empire. They regarded themselves as German patriots, in favour of re-unification with their co-nationals in the Reich, but professed no patriotic loyalty towards the empire whose subjects they were.[5]

Their support for the war was thus unemotional and pragmatic. Victor Adler made it clear that his and his friends' backing for the war, and for the policies of the fraternal German party, had nothing to do with devotion to the Austrian state: 'We don't care very much for this state, but we are concerned for the people living in this state; . . . and we do not want to see Russia becoming all-powerful and bearing down brutally upon us. Austria is bad enough, but we do not wish to exchange it for an absolutist Russia.'[6] This reasoning was not acceptable to the anti-war faction of Friedrich Adler, Robert Danneberg and other left-wingers. When the party's national council met in March 1916, the Left tabled a resolution which reflected the internationalist message of the Zimmerwald manifesto; the resolution was overwhelmingly defeated.

In October 1916 Friedrich Adler demonstrated his hatred of the war and the government waging it by a dramatic terrorist gesture: he shot and killed the Austrian prime minister, Count Stürgkh. This act of self-sacrifice had the long-term effect of changing the mood of the working masses from passive apathy to resolute militancy. The main impact was not from the action itself but from Adler's speech at his murder trial. In the words of his friend and biographer Julius Braunthal:

It (the speech) was a mighty appeal to the workers to come to their senses and to fight against absolutism and war. In a moving oration he. . .exposed the misdeeds committed under Habsburg rule, and laid bare the imperialist nature of the war. At the same time he accused the Socialist Party leadership which, in denial of the basic principles of socialism, had given moral and political support to the war.[7]

Friedrich Adler was sentenced to death, but the sentence was commuted to eighteen years imprisonment; in reprieving him the government (and the new Emperor Charles) probably took the new fighting spirit of the working class into account. [8]

The socialists of Hungary (who had no seats in parliament) followed those of Austria in supporting the war effort without enthusiasm, or a great show of affection for the Habsburg dynasty. Much more emphatic was the pro-war policy of the socialists in the Polish provinces of the Habsburg empire. Many actually welcomed the war against the hated Russian oppressor. They proclaimed a political truce with the régime and organized legions of 'revolutionary Poles'; their commander was a Polish socialist, Joseph Pilsudski, who later became the (non-socialist) dictatorial ruler of the Polish republic. [9] These Polish-Austrian legions were armed and equipped by the Austrian government, and placed under the supreme command of the Austro-Hungarian army. The political aim of their Polish organizers was not a completely independent Poland but a greater, unified Poland, incorporating what was then Russian Poland and enjoying some form of home rule under the Habsburg crown.

Thus the Hungarian, German and Polish socialists of the dual monarchy rallied to the defence of the Habsburg state. Not so the other nationalities of Austria-Hungary. The Italian subjects of the empire, whatever their political persuasion, hoped that Italy would join the anti-Austrian alliance and sided with her when she did in May 1915. Cesare Battisti, socialist member for Trento in the Austrian parliament, left Austria and volunteered for the Italian army. He was taken prisoner by the Austrians in 1916 and hanged as a traitor; several less well-known Italians suffered the same fate.

All classes and parties of the Czech people also wished to be rid of Austrian domination. Czech conscripts deserted *en masse* from the Austrian army; many deserters and prisoners-of-war joined the Czech legions raised in Russia and, after the Italian declaration of war, in Italy. The Czech socialists, like the other parties, regarded the war as an opportunity to bring to fruition the fight for freedom from Habsburg rule. This led to a political truce between the socialist and the bourgeois parties, not for the joint prosecution of the war but for joint resistance. The Austrian authorities reacted with mass imprisonment, death sentences and executions. Only very few political leaders, including some socialists, banked on an Austrian victory. The most prominent socialist was Bohumir Šmeral, who later transferred his allegiance from imperial Austria to communism and the Soviet Union.

Austrian repression in the territories inhabited by the southern Slavs – Bosnia, Hercegovina, Croatia and Slovenia – was more brutal still. A memorandum from the socialist parties of Croatia and Bosnia in 1917 dealt in detail with judicial and police terror in these regions: massive incarceration and thousands of death sentences passed by military courts.

The bulk of the people – socialist and non-socialist, working and middle-class – of the Italian, Czech and southern Slav regions of the dual monarchy were 'defeatist' rather in the sense in which Lenin was a Russian defeatist in the war with Japan, or Marx and Engels were German defeatists in the Franco-German War after the fall of Napoleon III: they wanted the enemy of their state to win the war. As far as the Czechs and the Croats were concerned, their resolve to achieve independence marks a significant change from the position about the middle of the nineteenth century, when Marx and Engels pilloried these ethnic groups as stooges of Austria. During the First World War the leaders in exile of the Czech independence movement, Masaryk and Beneš, openly sided with the *Entente* powers. According to Masaryk, so did the entire Czech nation. In his book *World Revolution*,[10] which he wrote after the war, he asserted that without wholehearted support from the homeland the leaders in exile could not have succeeded: all important Czech parties had espoused the cause of anti-Habsburg resistance.[11] There had been no chance of and no need for an armed rising until the end of the war, but 'the whole nation was opposed to Austria', and practised passive resistance which would give way at the appropriate moment to active hostility.

4   The French Socialists and the War

Anti-war tendencies developed in the French socialist and trade-union movements from 1915 but they never reached the dimensions of pacifist and internationalist opposition in Germany. Debates were less acrimonious, and the Socialist Party was not in danger of a split while the war lasted. Nor was the anti-war stance of the French opposition as extreme as that of Karl Liebknecht or Rosa Luxemburg. There were good reasons for this. Few Frenchmen doubted that the country was fighting a war of defence, both in the political-diplomatic and in the military sense. War had been forced upon France; short of making humiliating concessions to Germany the government could have done nothing to avoid it. Besides, almost from the first day, French territory had been invaded, and for several weeks the German army advanced victoriously towards Paris. The threat to the French capital was so imminent after a month of fighting that the French government felt compelled to leave for Bordeaux. This danger of immediate defeat stifled the doubts some pacifists and revolutionary internationalists might have felt about participating in the nation's defence.

For some anti-war socialists this link between the military threat and the policy to be pursued was not sub-conscious or semi-conscious but based on rational consideration. At the Kienthal International Socialist Conference in April 1916[1] the French socialist deputy Pierre Brizon encountered astonishment and some derision when he said that he and his friends would vote against the war credits if the military situation improved but not while it was unfavourable.[2] With few exceptions the French anti-war socialists, while opposing their government's policies, did not want their country to be defeated by the German enemy. They were unwilling to resort to any action, parliamentary or revolutionary, which might have caused France to lose the war.

In this context it is worth repeating that in the First World War a socialist's answer to the question of supporting or opposing the war did not generally depend on his or her being on the Right, Centre or Left of the movement. Nor can it be said that support for the war was a betrayal of Marxist principles, as Lenin and Luxemburg insisted. As we have seen, Jules Guesde and his Marxist friends could convincingly argue in August 1914 that Marx and Engels would have approved of their readiness to defend France against German aggression. This was also the view of Karl Kautsky, the most orthodox of Marxists.[3] After some hesitation Kautsky came out strongly against his party's war policy, not because he considered national defence intrinsically incompatible with Marxism but because he had concluded that Germany's war was one of conquest.[4]

The original pro-war harmony in the French labour movement did not last. An early instance of dissension was a clash between leading officials of the trade union federation, the CGT, during the first winter of the war.[5] At the end of November the CGT was invited to attend a conference of socialists from neutral countries in Copenhagen on 6 and 7 December 1914 to discuss possiblities of ending the war. After prolonged debates the CGT executive adopted a resolution that talk of peace at that stage was 'inopportune', and that no reply should be sent to the Scandinavian socialist parties which had issued the invitation. Two leading trade unionists, Raoul Lenoir and Alfred Merrheim, protested; a third, Pierre Monatte, resigned from the executive, and sent copies of a long explanatory letter to all CGT branches and prominent officials. But Monatte's action did not shake the solidly pro-war mood of the trade union rank-and-file.

A few months later Merrheim, secretary of the Metal Workers' Union, had a far greater impact in trade-union circles, when he published a special May Day edition of his union's journal, *L'Union des Métaux,* containing strong criticism of the wartime policies of the CGT and general secretary Jouhaux. It also carried a declaration of international solidarity by the executive of the Metal Workers Union which included, 'On this day we feel bound to tell our brothers in Germany and Britain, in Austria and Belgium, and everywhere else, that this war is not our war.'[6] Merrheim had the support of his union, but the reaction of the CGT leadership was outrage, and the authorities were said to have contemplated the arrest of Merrheim.

The initial unanimity in support of the war lasted a little longer among the leaders of the Socialist Party. In July 1915 the party's national council met and unanimously passed a resolution that the defeat of German imperialism was essential to rid the world of the fear of war. The party's pro-war policy had already met with criticism in some regional branches, and at its twelfth Annual Congress in December 1915, Bourderon, an internationalist trade union militant, tabled a resolution attacking the policies of the party leadership and the parliamentary party, and demanding that a campaign for peace be organized.[7] The resolution was defeated overwhelmingly, but the opposition began to gather strength. Several branches in the *départements* declared their support for the opposition and for the anti-war tenets of the Zimmerwald manifesto.[8] There was also substantial support in the Seine *Département,* which included Paris. The change of mood was reflected in the falling circulation of the ultrapatriotic *L'Humanité.* A rival pacifist weekly, *Le Populaire,* found more response among the workers.[9]

Karl Marx's grandson, Jean Longuet, editor of *Le Populaire,* was one of the organizers of an opposition group in the parliamentary Socialist Party. When the party's national council met in April 1916, the opposition mustered over thirty per cent of the votes cast. Eight months later, at the annual congress in December, it had nearly achieved parity – 1,407 votes against 1,437.[10] Early in 1917 opposition pressure made the party terminate its participation in government: Guesde and Sembat resigned as ministers.

It is worth reiterating that the French anti-war socialists, pacifists as well as revolutionary internationalists, never wanted to split the party and never espoused the Leninist concepts of turning the imperialist war into a civil war and striving for their government's defeat. When the Germans broke through the allied front in spring 1918 and advanced to within fifty miles of Paris, Alfred Merrheim said that he and those who shared his views would not want France 'to be subjected to a peace treaty like that of Brest-Litovsk'. The Leninist 'axiom' of revolutionary defeatism had no followers among French revolutionary socialists during the First World War.

5 Socialist War Aims: The Alsace-Lorraine Question

The majority of both French and German socialists adhered to the cause of national defence throughout the war. Thus each party wished and strove for an outcome of the conflict which the other wished and strove to frustrate.

At the same time there was a near-identity of the war aims of the two parties as far as the official formulae were concerned: the French and the German socialists visualized roughly the same kind of post-war settlement. Both declared themselves in favour of a peace of reconciliation, preventing for ever a recurrence of the catastrophe of war; both were against annexations and indemnities and favoured a settlement based on national self-determination. Yet each inserted in its peace programme a reservation objectionable to the other side.

Most French socialists, all those who followed Jules Guesde's line, insisted that removal of the fear of a future war presupposed the destruction of 'Prussian militarism' and of 'German imperialism'. Imperialism in this context meant not only pursuing expansionist external policies, but referred also to the imperial constitutional structure of Germany. As Guesde told Poincaré on 14 August 1914, France's readiness for reconciliation and friendship must depend on Germany's getting rid of her militarism, her 'empire' and her emperor.[1] The German Social Democrats resented this attitude. They had little love for either militarism or the monarchy, but felt that constitutional changes within Germany were a matter for the German people and should not be a pre-condition for peaceful and friendly relations between France and Germany. And why, they argued, should Germany's imperialism and militarism be singled out for destruction? Why should French and British imperialism (in the conventional sense) be spared?[2]

The peace programme of the majority of German socialists contained no demands or conditions regarding constitutional or other internal matters of the countries of the *Entente* coalition, but their qualification on the territorial settlement was unacceptable to the French socialists – and for that matter to any other French party. In the SPD's view, the phrase 'no annexations' implied that Alsace-Lorraine must remain part of Germany.

The issue was first discussed among Social Democrats in August 1915, when the Reichstag group and the party committee (*Partei-Ausschuss,* consisting of representatives of local SPD organizations) held a joint meeting on the controversial question of war aims.[3] The agenda included (1) No cession of German territory: the resolution stated explicitly that this precluded the return of Alsace-Lorraine to France. (2) No annexation of non-German territories to the German Reich. The second resolution was not controversial, but the first was passed by 81 votes to 14 by the Reichstag group and 31 votes to 7 by the party committee.

In June 1917 the German majority socialists formulated their views on the Alsace-Lorraine issue more comprehensively in the 'Stockholm Memorandum'. The occasion was an abortive international socialist conference, scheduled for Stockholm in the summer of 1917. Following a suggestion made by the Petrograd Workers' and Soldiers' Soviet after the February Revolution, the secretariat of the Second International in Amsterdam and a Dutch-Scandinavian committee made plans for an international meeting devoted primarily to ways of ending the war and creating an international order which would make impossible another cataclysm of that kind. Too few delegations arrived in Stockholm for the conference to be held, mainly because the British, French, Italian and United States governments refused to issue passports to intending delegates.[4]

The German and Austrian delegations were handed questionnaires prepared by the neutral organizing committee. These documents were meant to establish the attitude of socialists from the belligerent countries to territorial and other problems of a peace settlement. The German majority delegation, which included Scheidemann, Ebert, Hermann Müller, Eduard David and the trade-union leader Carl Legien, was asked its views on Alsace-Lorraine, Belgium and North Schleswig. Philipp Scheidemann described how he and his friends tackled this problem in the preliminary discussions:

> As the questionnaires merely mentioned Belgium, Alsace-Lorraine, North Schleswig, etc., we raised searching questions about Ireland, Egypt, India, Morocco, Tripolitania, Malta, Gibraltar, etc. Either, we argued, the peace settlement will have to re-distribute the whole world, in which case the territories we mentioned must be included, or else the settlement will only be concerned with areas that have been 'activated' ('in Bewegung gesetzt') in the war or which have changed hands: in that case Alsace-Lorraine and North Schleswig are excluded from the start...No one could challenge the logic of our exposition.[5]

The German majority socialists drew up a memorandum detailing their ideas: they reiterated their advocacy of a peace of reconciliation, without imposed annexations and indemnities. Belgium should be restored as an independent state and should not become a vassal of any other power, but Alsace-Lorraine was 'ethnically and linguistically' German: nearly ninety per cent of the population spoke German as their mother tongue. It had originally belonged to Germany but had been forcibly annexed by France. The treaty of Frankfurt in 1871 restored its former status as part of Germany. There was thus no justification for speaking of France's historical claim to Alsace-Lorraine; its enforced return to France would be annexation and incompatible with the principle of peace without annexations.[6]

A curious feature of this reasoning is the omission of the will of the people of Alsace-Lorraine as a criterion for the future of the province. According to the principle of self-determination, this should carry more weight than race or language. The SPD's memorandum avoids the dilemma by defining 'self-determination' in an unusual and rather restrictive manner: 'By self-determination we understand the right of each nation to maintain or regain its political independence.' The memorandum adds that Alsace-Lorraine had never been an independent national state, nor had it possessed a separate national identity. In their view national self-determination apparently did not include the right of the people of a disputed region to choose which state's claim was just.

This restrictive interpretation is not only contrary to the accepted meaning of the term; it runs counter to the stance which Marx, Engels and their German socialist contemporaries took on Alsace-Lorraine. Marx and Engels were vehemently opposed to its annexation by Germany, regarding it, in Marx's words, as 'the greatest disaster that could befall Europe and Germany in particular'. Marx and Engels also predicted, correctly, that the annexation would 'force France into the arms of Russia'. At the time the German Social Democrats agreed: after the German victory at Sedan in September 1870, they called for an immediate peace without annexations.

Again in 1887, when the Marxian forecast of a Franco-Russian alliance seemed about to come true, Engels repeated that there could be no dispute about Alsace-Lorraine between the French and the German socialists since the latter had always protested against the annexations of 1871. And in 1891 – 2 he explained to the French socialists that there was no reason for a war over Alsace-Lorraine: the Social Democrats would certainly come to power in Germany within about ten years and would then let the people of Alsace-Lorraine decide their own future. Engels obviously assumed that a plebiscite in Alsace-Lorraine would mean the return of the provinces to France.

Twenty years later German Social Democracy, that is, the pre-war majority factor, had changed their minds. Whether the SPD leaders realized it or not, they disowned the founding fathers as well as their nineteenth-century political forebears, and repudiated the specific assurances Engels had given the French socialists. When they defined their position in Stockholm, they were only about seventeen months from obtaining power in Germany, but when that moment came the decision on Alsace-Lorraine was no longer theirs to take: Germany's defeat had settled the issue.

To no one's surprise the SPD's Stockholm memorandum, and especially the passage about Alsace-Lorraine, caused dismay in French socialist circles. Albert Thomas, French pro-war socialist and minister of munitions, was in Stockholm at the time, *en route* for Petrograd where he hoped to persuade the Kerensky government to continue the war with maximum energy. Thomas was not in touch with the German delegation but had seen the memorandum and discussed it with two Danish socialists who had been present, Stauning and Nina Bang. [7]

Scheidemann records that Thomas's reaction was wholly condemnatory: 'Then the war must go on,' he is reported to have said, 'we can do no other.' [8] The Germans were told that Thomas had dwelt particularly on the Alsace-Lorraine issue. He had brushed aside the arguments about the historical, ethnical and linguistic bases of the German claim, saying that what mattered was not the people's language but their wish to become part of France again: they should at least be allowed to vote on the issue. The German Social Democrats did not think much of this idea of a plebiscite but did not reject it outright: 'We thought, once the war is over no one will want to start it again because of Alsace-Lorraine.' [9]

Scheidemann and his colleagues were apparently not worried about the angry French response. More disconcerting were the laudatory comments in German government circles, and by the kaiser who praised what the Social Democrats had done. 'We felt this was unfortunate,' Scheidemann wrote, 'but thought that it could not diminish the value of the work we had done in Stockholm.' [10]

While the French and some neutral socialists were naturally and justly disappointed at the SPD's intransigence over Alsace-Lorraine, the German socialists could justifiably complain of the French party's insistence on changing conditions inside Germany. The SPD, though republican and anti-militarist in principle, felt that the overthrow of the imperial monarchy and of German militarism was in its field of political action and should not be the war aim of another socialist party.

Philipp Scheidemann gave voice to this feeling when he spoke in the Reichstag in December 1915 about the Western powers' declared aim of destroying Germany's militarism: 'The militarism we are up against is something to be tackled inside our own national frontiers, just as French militarism and British *navalism* [11] will have to be tackled on the other side of the Vosges mountains and the English channel.' [12]

Another obvious objection to 'the destruction of German imperialism and militarism' as war aims was the implication of a fight to the finish and total victory. This was indeed what the French socialists had in mind, although they did not want a French victory to mean the imposition of a harsh peace. Thus the Christmas message of the French Socialist Party, published in *L'Humanité* on 25 December

1914, stressed that genuine and lasting peace must be based on international disarmament, to which a militarist Germany would never agree; nor would imperial Germany grant self-determination to the people of Alsace-Lorraine. The war must therefore continue until German militarism was laid low; peace without this would be the prelude to renewed German aggression. [13]

A resolution which the French party's national council adopted on 15 July 1915 contained the same message. It re-emphasized the German government's responsibility for the war and paid tribute to Karl Liebknecht, Rosa Luxemburg, Clara Zetkin and other socialist opponents of the war; it then reiterated the need for relentless struggle until victory: 'The conflict which has been forced upon the allies by the German rulers must be carried to its logical conclusion, that is, the defeat of German militarism, so that the world will learn the great and important lesson that a bid for hegemony has been crushed by the resistance of the free peoples.' [14] Pronouncements of that kind enabled the German majority socialists (as the pre-war faction came to be known) to claim that they had demonstrated their devotion to peace more convincingly than the French; after all, they were not clamouring for victory or for continuing the war until the enemy's military power was crushed. Their solution was a return to the *status quo ante,* a negotiated peace settlement without victors or vanquished.

Peace without annexations and indemnities was also the answer the two delegations from the Habsburg empire, representing the socialist parties of Austria and of Hungary, gave to the Stockholm questionnaire. They said that Serbia and Belgium should be restored; the Austrians wanted the southern Slav territories belonging to the dual monarchy (Slovenia, Croatia, Bosnia, Hercegovina) to remain part of the empire, but with a measure of autonomy. They advocated independence for Finland and Poland, the latter to have part of Austrian Galicia; Germany's Polish provinces should not be ceded to Poland but given autonomy. [15]

The proposal of autonomy for Germany's Poles provoked the wrath of some Pan-German press organs. They accused the Austrian socialists of helping the *Entente* to achieve its war aims and demanded that the Austrians be arrested on their way home and tried for treason. [16] The Pan-Germans also criticized the Vienna government for sanctioning the attendance by socialists whose anti-German views the Austrian authorities should have known.

The Austrian delegates also referred to the question of war guilt. They thought that all governments had been responsible to some extent but that this subject should not figure in the negotiations or the peace settlement.

6 The German 'Peace Resolution'; Social Democracy Splits

The attitude of the French and the German socialist parties on war and peace roughly reflected the positions of the respective civil and military authorities. Total victory, and the destruction of German imperialism and militarism had been, and remained, the watchword of the *Entente* camp from the start. The German government avoided committing itself on the question of annexations; and in December 1916 declared itself ready to open negotiations to end the war – an offer the Allies rejected. During the initial period, when military prospects seemed bright for the Central Powers, German politicians of the Right and even the Centre formulated wild annexationist demands. But by the summer of 1917 the climate had changed: the USA had entered the war in April of that year.

As the chances of a German victory receded, realism gained ground. Readiness for a compromise was enhanced when the Russian provisional government, which had emerged from the February Revolution, declared itself in favour of peace without annexations. After three years of war and great domestic hardships the German people felt inclined to settle for a 'draw' in the war, for the *status quo* peace which the enemy in the east was prepared to offer. Besides, the overthrow of tsarism and the establishment of a democratic and liberal régime in Russia diminished the alleged threat of Cossack barbarity.

In July 1917 a peace of reconciliation became the official programme of a majority in the Reichstag. The initiative came from Matthias Erzberger, one of the leaders of the Roman Catholic Centre Party (*Zentrumspartei*). Earlier, Erzberger had backed the Pan-German 'need for more living space' but, after studying the military situation and visiting some sectors of the Eastern front in 1916-17, he concluded that it was advisable for Germany to seek an early peace. He advocated a declaration that Germany was fighting a defensive war and sought no territorial aggrandizement.

The conversion to moderation of Erzberger and other non-socialist German politicians led to the formation of a bloc in the Reichstag, comprising the majority Social Democrats, the *Zentrum* and some progressive-radical groups; they had a parliamentary majority, and on 19 July 1917 carried the so-called 'Peace Resolution'. After recalling with approval the statement in the 'Speech from the Throne' on 4 August 1914 that Germany was 'not motivated by desire for conquest', and adding that the country was still fighting to defend her freedom and territorial integrity, the resolution went on:

> The Reichstag strives for a peace of understanding, of lasting reconciliation of the nations. Forcible acquisitions of territory, or measures of political, economic or financial violation are incompatible with such a peace.
>
> The Reichstag also rejects all schemes which aim at erecting economic barriers and perpetuating hostility among the nations after the war. . . .
>
> Yet so long as the enemy governments will not agree to such a peace; so long as they threaten Germany and her allies with conquest and violation, the German people will stand united, hold on unshakeably and fight on, until its right, and that of its allies, to life and progress is assured. In its unity the German people is invincible. . . . [1]

The resolution was carried by 214 votes to 116. The Alsace-Lorraine deputies voted in favour, the Poles abstained. The adverse votes were cast by the Conservatives, the National Liberals, other right-wing deputies – and the Independent Social Democrats (*USPD),* members of the anti-war socialist party founded three months previously.

The Pan-Germans and right-wing politicians, like Count Westarp and Admiral Tirpitz, continued to rail at what they called a 'peace of renunciation' *(Verzichtfriede)* or 'Scheidemann peace', but the resolution was not repudiated by the supreme command and not explicitly rejected by the government. The new Reich Chancellor Michaelis, who had replaced Bethmann Hollweg, accepted the resolution with the ambiguous phrase 'as I understand it'. How he understood it was made clear in a letter he wrote to the German crown prince a few days later: he told the kaiser's eldest son that he had deprived the resolution of its gravest danger; any kind of peace was now possible on the basis of that resolution. The imperial government evidently proposed to ignore the peace resolution in its policy.[2]

The Independent Social Democrats naturally refused to vote for a declaration that Germany's war had always been one of defence, and that the German people must fight on in unison. The USPD group in the Reichstag moved a separate resolution saying in part:

> The Reichstag is striving for a peace without annexations of any kind whatever, and without a war indemnity, on the basis of the right of peoples to self-determination. It insists especially on the restoration of Belgium and on the reparation of the wrong done to her. The Reichstag demands the immediate opening of peace negotiations on the basis of this programme. It calls for an international agreement for general disarmament...; for obligatory international arbitration for the settlement of all disputes. The most urgent condition for the establishment of such a peace...is the immediate revocation of the state of siege. Further, the complete democratization of the whole constitution and government of the Reich and its component states is required – a democratization which will culminate in the creation of a socialist republic.[3]

The resolution was, of course, defeated, with only the Independent Socialists voting 'Aye'.

The schism in German Social Democracy, and the emergence of a separate socialist anti-war party, was the ultimate outcome of a process which began on 3 August 1914, when fourteen members of the SPD Reichstag group advocated rejection of the war credits. The opposition observed party discipline and voted for the credits on the following day. When the government again asked the Reichstag to pass a substantial war budget in December, opposition within the Social Democrat group had risen to seventeen.[4] But in the Reichstag the opposition again toed the official party line, except for Karl Liebknecht.

The Speaker would not allow Liebknecht to explain his position, and refused to have a written statement entered in parliamentary records. But his intended statement was published in the *Berner Tagwacht,* the Swiss socialist paper which subsequently printed a number of oppositional statements and articles. Liebknecht's document was also reproduced as a leaflet and widely disseminated in Germany. It described the conflict as an imperialist war 'for the capitalist domination of the world market'. The war was also a 'bonapartist venture', designed to demoralize and destroy the growing labour movement. The German slogan 'Against tsarism' was as mendacious and nefarious as the Anglo-French slogan 'Against militarism'. Germany, accomplice of reactionary tsarism, had no right to pose as the liberator of nations. 'The liberation of the Russian and the German peoples must be achieved by each people for itself.' The credits the government was asking for were not required for defence of the fatherland since this was not a German war of defence. Every effort should be made to bring about its early end, and a peace without conquests, not humiliating to any country, should be secured by 'the international solidarity of the working class'. Liebknecht's vote against the war credits, the statement said in conclusion, was cast 'in protest against the war, . . . against the capitalist policy which provoked it, against the capitalist war aims, against the plans for annexations, against the violation of Belgian and Luxemburg neutrality'.[5]

In February 1915 some members of the Social Democrat Reichstag group moved for Liebknecht's expulsion from the parliamentary party, but this was rejected by a large majority; Karl Liebknecht was censured but not expelled.

When the imperial government submitted a much larger war budget in March 1915, thirty Social Democrat members favoured rejection,[6] and the differences between the majority and the anti-war minority produced an open clash in the Reichstag. On 20 March, Georg Ledebour expounded the opposition view and was rebuked by Philipp Scheidemann. In the divison two Social Democrats voted 'No': Karl Liebknecht and Otto Rühle; the other minority members left the chamber before the vote was taken. The parliamentary party censured Liebknecht and Rühle; but while the censure on Liebknecht in December had been unanimous, this time sixty-seven SPD deputies voted for censure and seventeen against.

By 20 August the anti-credit minority had risen to thirty-six.Liebknecht alone voted 'No' in the division; Rühle was absent. Three of those who at the party group meeting had advocated rejection voted 'Aye', the others left the chamber to avoid voting — still reluctant, it appeared, to defy party discipline. But four months later twenty anti-credit Social Democrats abandoned this halfway house and voted against the war budget; a statement on their behalf was read in the Reichstag by Fritz Geyer.[7]

In March 1916 Hugo Haase, who had resigned as chairman of the Reichstag group, caused uproar in the house — and among majority

Social Democrats – with an anti-war speech. Eighteen members, including Liebknecht and Rühle, voted 'No', fourteen others absented themselves. The majority's patience was exhausted. The eighteen members who had voted 'No' were expelled from the parliamentary party and constituted themselves as a separate 'Social Democratic Working Group' (*Sozialdemokratische Arbeitsgemeinschaft)*, with Haase and Ledebour as joint chairmen.[8] Eduard Bernstein soon became a member of the group.

The SPD party committee immediately condemned the 'Working Group', but the split at national level did not materialize until April 1917. During the second half of 1916, opposition to the war spread among the Social Democrat rank-and-file. In January 1917 the anti-war minority held a conference in Berlin, which some majority socialists held to be incompatible with continued membership of the party. But while some of the minority, including Kautsky and Bernstein, wished to maintain party unity, most of the leaders set course for an organizational breakaway. At Gotha in April, 143 anti-war socialist delegates met and founded the 'Independent Social Democratic Party of Germany' (*Unabhaengige Sozialdemokratische Partei Deutschlands – USPD);* the Social Democratic Working Group became the new party's Reichstag group.[9]

The anti-war conference was attended by two extreme left- wing groups, the International Socialists of Germany (*Internationale Sozialisten Deutschlands)* and the Spartacus League (*Spartakusbund).* The former was led by Karl Radek and Julian Borchardt and took its political cue from Lenin, then in Switzerland. The leaders of the Spartacus League were Karl Liebknecht, Rosa Luxemburg, Franz Mehring and Leo Jogiches. Rosa Luxemburg was its leading theorist. While in prison in 1915, she wrote a pamphlet later published under the pen-name 'Junius': 'The Crisis of Social Democracy' vehemently denounced the war policy of the SPD leadership.[10] The Spartacus League (but not the International Socialists) was also represented at the USPD's foundation congress in Gotha but maintained its separate existence as a faction within the new party.

The rift within the German party was reflected in the SPD's publications at an early stage. In November 1914 the editors of Social Democratic newspapers met to lay down guidelines for the party press to report and comment on the events and issues of the war.[11] It was agreed that the papers should eschew jingoist patriotic statements and annexationist tendencies, and that restraint should be exercised in reports of enemy atrocities, the ill-treatment of German prisoners, and so on.

The editors could not formulate clear rules on controversial issues, such as the attitude to the war, but it soon became obvious that these issues could not be kept out of the party's publications. The editorial board of *Vorwaerts,* the SPD's central organ, was in substantial sympathy with the anti-war minority, and while the paper did not reject contributions from the pro-war majority, it often carried editorials severely critical of the party's official policy. Some provincial SPD papers were equally outspoken: *Leipziger Volkszeitung* and *Schwaebische Tagwacht,* which appeared in Stuttgart, capital of the kingdom of Wuerttemberg. The expression of extreme anti-war views was prevented by censorship, but some opposition socialists sent statements and articles to Swiss socialist papers – for instance the *Berner Tagwacht,* which had published Karl Liebknecht's statement on his vote against the war credits.

The opposition became more vocal in the summer of 1915, after Italy had entered the war on the side of the *Entente.* In June an 'Open Letter', addressed to the party leaders and the Reichstag group, was printed as a pamphlet and circulated in hundreds among the rank-and-file.

It was originally signed by eleven members of the Reichstag, including Karl Liebknecht, Otto Rühle and Georg Ledebour, and about a hundred other prominent Social Democrats. The signatures of some 1,400 lesser known comrades were appended, and more were invited. The open letter denounced 'the policy of 4 August' (the vote for war credits in the Reichstag) and accused the SPD leadership of a secret understanding with the government. It also asserted that the majority of the Reichstag group had ceased to oppose the 'imperialist policy of conquest'. The letter urged the termination of the political truce (*Burgfrieden)* and the resumption of active class warfare.[12]

A document which aroused an even greater stir in party circles and among the public was a joint statement by party chairman Hugo Haase and the two old adversaries of the 'revisionism' dispute, Eduard Bernstein and Karl Kautsky. It was published in the *Leipziger Volkszeitung* on 19 June 1915 under the title 'The Need of the Hour' (*Das Gebot der Stunde).* [13] The authors listed some wildly annexationist statements made by German Conservative and national Liberal politicians, by the 'Industrial League' and other capitalist bodies, and

by the king of Bavaria who had recently demanded territorial acquisitions to give southern and central Germany better access to the sea.
The document recalled the condemnation by the party of all wars of
conquest; now that plans for conquest were seen to exist it was the
SPD's duty 'to assert most strongly its opposing views' and to take
decisive action for an early peace. The declaration implied that the
party in the Reichstag should vote against war credits, but to avoid
action by the wartime censor this was not openly advocated, as
Kautsky later observed.[14] Caution proved futile, however; the *Leipziger Volkszeitung* was banned for a week for publishing the
statement.

The SPD Directorate replied with a manifesto published in
Vorwaerts on 26 June 1915. It criticized the French, British and
Belgian socialists who wished, 'together with their governments, to
continue the war until the complete destruction of Germany'. The
allegation that the German party was not doing enough 'to assert the
peace wishes of the working class' was a machination to disrupt party
unity. The leadership and the Reichstag group had always
'unanimously opposed the policies of conquest and annexations'. It
was true that the Industrial League and leading bourgeois politicians
had bandied expansionist slogans, which could damage the prospects
for a negotiated peace. 'We raise anew the sharpest protests against all
efforts and pronouncements in favour of annexing foreign territories
and oppressing other peoples...The people desire no annexations!
The people desire peace.' The reply did not discuss whether a vote
against the war budget was the right response to the annexationist
demands and the government's failure to repudiate them.[15]

Haase, Kautsky and Bernstein, authors of 'The Need of the Hour',
did not wish or work for a split in the party, but they became
prominent members of the USPD after its foundation.

As for the majority socialists, some party members did hold the view
that a German victory would and should mean territorial aggrandizement. But the bulk of the old Social Democratic Party, while supporting the war effort and voting for the credits, emphasized that the war
should retain the defensive character they believed it had at its
inception. The party stuck to its line of peace without enforced
annexations. In his *Memoirs* Philipp Scheidemann recalled that on
some thirty occasions the party and its leaders and Reichstag deputies
had publicly advocated the early conclusion of a peace of
conciliation.[16] Scheidemann certainly had a clean record on the issue

of annexations, if one disregards his refusal to contemplate the handing back of Alsace-Lorraine to France. For example, on 15 May 1917 he provoked the fury of the Pan-Germans in the Reichstag by accusing them of making the German people hated throughout the world. In their eyes the peace he and his party favoured was a shameful 'peace of renunciation' − Yes, Scheidemann stressed, there were things the Social Democrats were willing to renounce, to do without:

> We can do without the continuation of the war, without hundreds of thousands of killed and maimed, . . . without the further devastation of Europe; but we renounce not an inch of German territory, none of our possessions; we renounce the illusion that the war will bring us benefits to which we are not entitled; . . . we renounce all plans of violating and oppressing other nations; but we do not renounce the right of the German people to emerge from this terrible war as a free nation. . . And there is something else we are willing to renounce, to do without: the Pan-Germans and their foolish jabbering.

Scheidemann then caused uproar by invoking the threat of revolution. He referred to the Russian provisional government's disclaimer of all intentions of annexing territory: he added that if the British and French governments made similar declarations and the German government did not but continued the war for conquest, 'then, gentlemen, you may depend upon it, you will have a revolution in this country.' Scheidemann was called to order by the Speaker, and the man who supported the war from start to finish was attacked by the Pan-German press as a traitor.

Scheidemann explained in his *Memoirs* that one of the purposes of that speech had been to force the government to dissociate itself from the Pan-Germans. The majority socialists made other attempts to achieve this. They threatened to vote against the war budget unless the government was more specific about the peace it envisaged. The threat was not implemented; and the SPD and other pro-peace politicians achieved nothing more than the ambiguous and dishonest 'acceptance' of the Reichstag's 'peace resolution' by Chancellor Michaelis.

7   British Marxism and the War

The British Socialist Party (BSP), Marxist like German Social Democracy but much smaller and much less effective — only about 20,000 members and no parliamentary representation — also saw its unity destroyed by the dispute over wartime policy. The schism had similar significance in both countries: in Germany and in Britain the anti-war faction emerging from the rupture would contribute, directly or indirectly, to the formation of a national section of the Third (Communist) International.

Henry M. Hyndman, the most prominent leader of first the SDF/SDP and, after 1911, the BSP, was a 'Social Patriot' long before 1914. He anticipated war with Germany several years before and had made it clear that in his view Britain's socialists should support that war. He had urged more vigorous measures of re-armament, including the creation of an air force, than the government were willing to adopt at the time. When war broke out, Hyndman was still the dominant figure in the BSP leadership; and only one of the nine members of the party executive, E.C. Fairchild, was an outright opponent of Hyndman's outlook and policy. The executive adopted a manifesto supporting the war, but not as wholeheartedly as if Hyndman had been its sole author. It condemned secret diplomacy as chiefly responsible for the disaster but stressed that, though tens of thousands might fall, 'the power of Prussian militarism' must be broken.[1]

During the last pre-war weeks the BSP, like other British socialist and labour organizations and the continental parties of the Second International, conducted an energetic campaign against war. On 31 July, when news reached London that the tsar's government had ordered general mobilization, the British section of the International Socialist Bureau adopted a manifesto drafted by Hyndman and signed by Keir Hardie and Arthur Henderson. It called upon the British government to refrain from any action of support for Russia and declared, 'As we have no interest, direct or indirect, in the threatened quarrels which may result from the action of Austria in Serbia, the government of Great Britain should rigidly decline to engage in war, but should confine itself to efforts to bring about peace as speedily as possible.'[2]

On 2 August Hyndman, Keir Hardie and George Lansbury took

part in a huge 'Stop the War' demonstration in Trafalgar Square. Like the other parties of the International, the BSP were acting on the bureau's appeal of 29 July enjoining all workers to intensify the demonstrations for peace and to bring pressure on their governments to act against the war threat. Yet when Germany invaded Belgium and Britain declared war, Hyndman backed the government's decision to intervene. Throughout the war he campaigned staunchly for the Allied war effort, sometimes even attacking the government for not conducting the blockade of Germany with the required energy and determination.[3]

At the beginning of the war, Hyndman still dominated the BSP executive, but he soon had to realize that the party was divided on 'national defence'. On 15 September 1914 the executive issued another statement, which echoed to some extent the phraseology of the pre-war resolutions of the Socialist International, in that it declared the war to be 'largely the outcome of the rivalry... for the domination of the world market'. However, it went on to say, 'Recognizing that the national freedom and independence of this country are threatened by Prussian militarism, the party naturally desires to see the prosecution of the war to a successful issue.'[4] After listing a number of political demands, the executive's statement urged the BSP membership to support the government's recruiting campaign, but the reaction of the party's rank-and-file was one of emphatic protest.[5]

At a conference of the London BSP, fifteen of eighteen branches represented voted for the withdrawal of the statement supporting the recruitment drive. In Scotland John Maclean, assisted by Willie Gallacher, led an internationalist anti-war campaign in Clydeside. Like the ILP leaders, Maclean denied that the violation of Belgian neutrality had been the reason for Britain's participation in the war; he claimed that it had been known to all those interested, including Sir Edward Grey, the British foreign secretary, that if war broke out between France and Germany the latter would invade Belgium. Grey had only waited for this to happen to have a 'moral' excuse for Britain's declaration of war:

The real reason was, and is, that he and his class knew that war between British and German capitalism had to come sooner or later... The absurdity of the present situation is surely apparent when we see British socialists going out to murder German

socialists with the object of crushing Kaiserism and Prussian militarism. The only real enemy of Kaiserism and Prussian militarism
. . . was and is German Social Democracy. Let the propertied class
go out. . . and defend their blessed property. When they have been
disposed of, we of the working class will have something to
defend, and we shall do it.

Opposition to the war and to the executive's line gained ground among
party members throughout the country, but there were differences of
opinion within the anti-war faction. Not all opponents went as far as
Maclean who preached resistance by all means, including strikes and
insurrection. But Maclean's paper *Vanguard* was important in
winning the majority of BSP members over to an anti-war position,
and in breaking Hyndman's hold on the party leadership.

Hyndman and the old guard of the SDF wavered neither in their
support for the war nor in their loyalty to what they regarded as the
principles of international socialism. Hyndman and Belfort Bax had
not seen eye to eye over the issues of the Boer War, but they were at one
in their view of the Great War. They held that support for the Allied
cause was in line with what Marx and Engels would have advocated,
because it was a just war of defence, and because victory over
Germany would benefit the cause of progress and of socialism, despite
the reactionary character of tsarist Russia. As Hyndman put it in 1915:

> Victory for the Germanic powers would be infinitely worse for
> civilization and progress than the victory of the allies. This is
> why. . . the peoples of western and southern Europe now make
> common cause with Russia against the most formidable enemy of
> democracy and freedom which has burst upon the world since the
> Ottoman Turks captured Constantinople nearly five hundred
> years ago. . . [6]

Altogether Hyndman and Bax made a point of demonstrating that
their view of the war was truly Marxist. They did so jointly, for
example, in an argument with Austin Harrison, editor of the *English
Review*. In November 1914 the journal carried two rather muddled
and superficial articles by Harrison on Marxism and German Social
Democracy. The first of these, 'The Materialist Conception of
History', purported to show that the influence of Marxist ideology
partly accounted for Germany's resort to a war of aggression and
conquest. [7] The second, 'The Collapse of Socialism', contended that

the German Social Democrats had ceased to be a party of revolutionary opposition some years before the war, and had sold out to militarism and German imperialism. [8] The December issue of the *English Review* published a reply by Hyndman and Bax, under the heading 'Socialism, Materialism and the War'. The authors criticized Harrison for having classed Marx with Pan-Germans like Treitschke and Bernhardi, which was ludicrous. [9]

> Marx, and with him Engels, was the most powerful opponent in Europe of what German Prussianized militarism stands for. He loathed it and all its works...Marx and Engels were strongly opposed to any policy which aimed at giving Germany, as organized in their day, a dominant position in Europe. More than this, they attacked the influence of Prussia and Prussian methods as directly injurious to Germany itself, and as tending to crush down the real greatness of the German people. [10]

Harrison's strictures on the German party's policies might have struck some chord with Hyndman and Bax who had themselves made scathing remarks about the SPD leadership. But some urge of international solidarity seems to have induced them to defend foreign comrades against an attack by a non-socialist. There was no excuse, they declared, for the 'panic which seized the majority' of the Social Democrat Reichstag group, but more credit should be given to the previous considerable efforts of the German socialists for peace; 'and still more should we applaud those like Karl Liebknecht, Mehring, Ledebour, Clara Zetkin, Rosa Luxemburg, and Bernstein, who have remained true to the faith.' [11]

According to Bax and Hyndman, prevention of the war was quite beyond the SPD's power. Even if all Social Democrat members of the Reichstag had voted against the war credits, Hyndman said, 'this would not have checked the war for a day'; and to call for mass resistance or a general strike would have been 'costly and futile'. [12] On the other hand the steady growth of the socialist movement in Germany had frightened the reactionaries, and especially the Prussian Junker class which had then seen war as a means of countering the threat: 'The vast development of anti-militarist Marxism throughout Germany, in the form of Social Democracy, was one of the main causes of the present war; for it engendered in the minds of the Junkers the fear that it would prove still more threatening in the near future.' [13]

Years before the war Hyndman had been critical of the German

Social Democrat leaders and had even charged Bebel with indulging in jingoist oratory,[14] but he did not hesitate to defend Bebel when Harrison revealed his ignorance of Marxist teachings by arguing that Bebel's advocacy of a defensive militia was an un-Marxist concession to militarism.[15] 'Far from it', Hyndman retorted; Bebel had, on the contrary, re-affirmed an important part of the Marxist programme:

> At every International Socialist Congress, from 1900 onwards, Marxists, with socialists of all shades of opinion, have voted unanimously in favour of the establishment of such a citizen army, with officers...elected by the rank-and-file, as the only effective means of upholding national independence against aggression from without and militarism within.[16]

Hyndman remained optimistic about the prospects of an early socialist victory in Britain, despite or perhaps because of what happened in the course of the war. He believed that progress towards socialism might result not, as Lenin predicted, from the defeat but from the victory of the capitalist government. Several factors seemed to point in that direction; he felt that economic planning, as a requirement in wartime, might prove effective and acquire a degree of permanency. Then, after the war, the victorious proletarians in uniform were likely to wield strong anti-capitalist influence. In a speech in Sheffield in April 1915, Hyndman said that on their return home the soldiers of a victorious army would 'have capacities of persuasion at their command which will preserve them from grovelling in misery at the feet of a plundering minority.'[17] Lastly, inevitable contacts with foreign (including enemy) troops would enhance international consciousness. The passage in *The Future of Democracy* from which we quoted above continues:

> The victory of the Allies will mean, I am firmly convinced, a victory for democracy in Britain...(The British workers) are learning day in day out that there is a war at home as well as a war abroad, that the German troops, whom they met in comradely fashion before the trenches last Christmas, have no real quarrel with them, as compared with the bitterness that both must feel against their respective masters at home. That feeling will grow...A complete success for the Allies will be even more valuable for the Germans than for ourselves. We shall need the democracy of Germany in years to come in order to withstand that very same development of Russian power which now is

working with us to clear aggressive militarism out of the path of Western Europe.

Hyndman was clearly no Germanophobe, despite his occasional chauvinistic outbursts. 'I should advocate a thorough *entente* with the German republic tomorrow,' he said in 1915 when he refused to join the newly-founded Anti-German League,[18] and the concluding paragraph of his and Belfort Bax's reply to Austin Harrison expresses the authors' 'sincere desire' that 'a new and greater Germany may again take a leading place in the ranks of great nations striving for human progress.'[19]

The majority of BSP membership would have no truck with Hyndman's vision of socialism as a consequence of victorious war, and rank-and-file opposition to the war soon brought about a radical change within the leadership. E.C. Fairchild did not long remain the only anti-war member of the executive. In October 1914 Joseph Fineberg, a Russian Jew and an internationalist, was elected with a huge majority to fill a vacancy which arose when another member volunteered for the army, and a few months later the anti-war faction narrowly won control of the executive. This was one of the results of five regional conferences early in 1915.

The decision to hold separate simultaneous divisional conferences – in London, Glasgow, Manchester, Leeds and Bristol – was taken because the convening of a national conference in wartime conditions appeared too difficult. The aggregate result of the voting showed that while there was no clearcut swing to an anti-war line, the Hyndmanites no longer enjoyed majority support.[20] A resolution was carried rejecting socialist participation in the recruiting campaign, and one demanding continuation of the war 'to the point when the Central European autocracies will have been destroyed' was resoundingly defeated. But the delegates passed a vote of confidence in the pro-war editor of the party organ, *Justice*. The outcome was thus inconclusive, but of the nine members of the new executive five were internationalists and only four followed the Hyndman-Bax line.

Diatribes in the party press reflected the increasing bitterness and hostility between the two wings of the BSP.[21] In May 1915 H.W. Lee, the Hyndmanite editor of *Justice,* said in an article about the sinking of the *Lusitania* that people who campaigned for peace 'with such villainy' were incurring 'an indelible stain'. Bax was more direct:

writing in *Justice* of 27 May he asked the rhetorical question, 'Is it not time that the apologists for Prussian militarism and its inhuman and dastardly crimes were eliminated from the ranks of socialist bodies?' Maclean's *Vanguard* retaliated some months later by denouncing *Justice* for its 'active support of the British capitalist class in the attack on Germany'.

A split in the party could be only a matter of time. In July 1915, BSP members from opposite wings came to blows. The occasion was a public meeting in London, organized by the 'Socialist National Defence Committee' a body set up by Victor Fisher and other right-wing BSP members, whose avowed purpose was to 'resist the anti-British, pro-German pacifist elements in this country'. Speakers at the meeting were British and foreign pro-war socialists, including Hyndman, Will Thorne, and Ben Tillett; prominent foreign speakers were Emile Vandervelde, member of the International Socialist Bureau and of the Belgian government-in-exile, and Marcel Cachin. Anti-war BSP militants also attended, including Fairchild who tried but failed to move a resolution demanding that the British labour movement respond to the German Social Democrats' manifesto advocating 'peace without annexations'. Scuffles broke out, and some of the internationalists were beaten up. Similar incidents, for which the Defence Committee bore the responsibility, occurred in the provinces.

The publication of *Vanguard* in Glasgow had to be suspended in January 1916 after Maclean, Willie Gallacher and other contributors had been arrested. But another anti-war fortnightly, *The Call,* was published in London by Fairchild from February onwards; its masthead proclaimed that it was 'An Organ of International Socialism'. [22]

The conflict between supporters and opponents of the war came to a head at BSP annual conference in Salford on Easter Sunday and Monday, 23 and 24 April 1916. Ninety-one branches were represented by 106 delegates. [23] To prevent victimization and secure free discussion, the executive proposed that proceedings be held *in camera:* the press would be excluded, and press statements issued at the end of each session. Delegates supporting Hyndman and Bax objected. After a heated discussion, with a great deal of shouting, booing and bandying of insults, the motion was carried by seventy-six votes to twenty-eight. Hyndman and twenty-one other delegates, representing eighteen branches, left the conference in a body, and two more walked out later. The defeated pro-war minority met in a Manchester hotel and decided to set up a 'National Socialist Advisory Committee'.

After the departure of the Hyndmanites the Salford conference adopted a number of anti-war resolutions. The delegates who had walked out were not expelled, but no member of the pro-war faction was elected to the new executive. 'Peace by negotiation', and 'International working class struggle against the whole capitalist régime' now became the party's official watchwords, but the BSP did not turn into a Leninist party. It did not call for the transformation of the imperialist into a civil war, nor did it declare the defeat of the capitalist British government to be the 'lesser evil' and a factor facilitating the socialist revolution. Like Merrheim, Monatte and other French anti-war socialists, the anti-war militants of the British Socialist Party had refrained from preaching revolutionary activity which might benefit the enemy. In October 1915 E.C. Fairchild challenged a pro-war BSP member, F.H. Gorle, to debate with him a resolution urging united action by the international working class, under the auspices of a restored Socialist International, for the conclusion of a peace without enforced annexations. The resolution Fairchild had drafted also stated that 'all action should be rigorously avoided calculated to endanger national defence,'[24] something Lenin had declared impossible for revolutionary socialists. At the Salford conference Joseph Fineberg, Fairchild's close associate, denounced 'this capitalist war' but added, 'It would certainly be a disaster for Europe if Germany were victorious.' H.W. Alexander, BSP national treasurer, said that being an internationalist did not preclude his being 'a nationalist, prepared to defend his own country'.[25] A delegate nearer the Leninist position was Albert Ward, a miner from Lancashire, who said that the workers had no country and 'no concern in the present conflict worth the shedding of a single drop of blood'.[26]

Most leaders of the post-Salford BSP – Fairchild, Fineberg, Alexander, for instance – would be classed by Lenin as belonging to the 'centre' group of 'confused and vacillating people', who stood between the 'social-chauvinists' and the revolutionaries, and who would use Marxist phraseology to justify their unwillingness to break with the opportunists and social-chauvinists.[27] He was thinking of men like Monatte and Merrheim in France, Haase and Kautsky in Germany, who opposed the war but were not at all anxious to split the party. Actually the anti-war leaders of the British Socialist Party were not keen on maintaining unity with the Hyndman-Bax faction; nor did they, in principle, reject revolutionary action against war. What really distinguished them from Lenin and the Bolsheviks was their unequivocal rejection of 'revolutionary defeatism'. They insisted that mass action against the war be co-ordinated at international level, if possible by the International Socialist Bureau, since unilateral upheaval in one country or in one of the warring camps would facilitate the victory of the other side.

As already mentioned, Hyndman and his friends of the national Socialist Advisory Committee were not expelled from the BSP; but they severed all ties with the BSP in June 1916 and founded a new party, the National Socialist Party (NSP). The new body kept control of *Justice; The Call* became the organ of the BSP. [28]

Hyndman and his new party continued to give wholehearted support to the war, without abandoning their socialist creed and their propaganda for social change. This is borne out by Hyndman's contributions to the work of the National Workers (War Emergency) Committee, a body set up in August 1914 to protect working-class interests in wartime. The committee, on which Hyndman represented the BSP from the outset, comprised all shades of labour and socialist opinion, pro-war as well as anti-war. On a number of issues Hyndman collaborated closely with the much more moderate Sidney Webb. [29]

In 1917, after the formation of the NSP, Hyndman tabled a radical anti-capitalist motion in the National Workers' Committee. It invited the committee to demand that, from 1 January 1918, 'the entire riches of this island be conscripted and placed at the disposal of the community at large, in order to meet the enormous cost of the war and the expenses of thorough social reconstruction after the peace'. The 'riches' would include home and foreign bonds and all shares in public and private companies, 'thus giving the community entire control. . . over all mines, factories, workshops, railways. . .', as well as bank deposits, insurance companies, all real property and buildings. Furthermore, the whole adult population would be 'liable to conscription for productive and distributive labour, as may be decreed by a constituent assembly, elected under proportional representation, all adults having the right to vote.'

The measures proposed were meant to be permanent, not limited to the duration of the war; there was no provision saying that the conscription of riches and so on should end with the conclusion of peace. Whatever the merits and feasibility of the proposals, they demonstrate that Lenin was oversimplifying when he equated pro-war socialists with opportunists. In Lenin's eyes Hyndman was an out-and-out 'social-chauvinist' but there is no doubt that he was still, in 1917, an out-and-out socialist. Incidentally his motion was passed by the committee but ignored by the Lloyd George government (which on occasions had consulted the committee) and not discussed in the daily press.

The secession of the Hyndman faction after the April 1916 conference turned the BSP into a distinctly anti-war party, on the lines of the German Independent Social Democrats, who founded a new anti-war party a year later. Seeing that the Labour Party's policy was avowedly pro-war, and that of the ILP leadership ambiguous and inconsistent, it could be said that the BSP was the only British party opposed to the war, apart from such small fundamentalist sects as the Socialist Labour Party and the Socialist Party of Great Britain. But there was still no uniformity in the party's approach to the topical issues of war and peace. Most of the leaders were pacifist and 'centrist', but a minority around John Maclean followed a revolutionary line close to that of the Bolsheviks or the German Spartacists.[30] Maclean and his followers wanted a revolutionary end to the war, though they never expressed a wish for the defeat of the British government. The Bolsheviks regarded Maclean as the true champion of revolutionary socialism in Britain.[31] The less extreme leaders of the British Socialist Party − Fairchild, Fineberg, and so on, favoured a negotiated peace and rejected unilateral revolutionary action against the war. Thus while the party proclaimed its solidarity with the Bolshevik régime it did not follow Lenin in adopting the concept and pursuing the policies of revolutionary defeatism.

In the international field after Easter 1916, the BSP demanded the reactivation of the International Socialist Bureau, to enable it to coordinate a working-class campaign in all belligerent countries for an early peace. The party backed the 'Zimmerwald Movement',[32] and cultivated links with foreign socialists with views akin to its own. Several Russian-speaking members of the BSP contributed to *Nashe Slovo (Our Word),* which appeared in Paris under Trotsky's and Martov's editorship until its suppression by the French authorities in September 1916. One of the contributors was G.V. Chicherin, Soviet foreign minister from 1918 to 1930, who was an active member of the British Socialist Party during the war.

Socialists all over the world welcomed the Russian revolution of March 1917, the 'February Revolution' which ended tsarist rule and gave power to a liberal-democratic 'provisional government'. Its psychological impact was strong in Britain where war weariness and hardships led to social upheavals, such as an unofficial strike of 200,000 engineering workers in May 1917. The BSP and the ILP responded to the revolutionary mood by jointly organizing the Leeds Soviet Convention, an assembly of about 1300 workers' representatives. It lasted only one day – 3 June 1917 – and had no enduring results. Not all delegates came from the extreme Left or held strong anti-war views. Moderates like Ramsay MacDonald and Philip Snowden attended and moved resolutions in support of revolutionary (pre-Bolshevik) Russia and for an early peace. The most radical resolution was proposed by the ILP militant W.C. Anderson and seconded by Robert Williams of the BSP: it called for the election throughout Britain of 'Councils of Workers' and Soldiers' Delegates'; but the proposer stressed that the resolution was not meant to be subversive or unconstitutional. The convention elected a nine-man provisional committee to launch a nationwide campaign, but this soon fizzled out.

The Bolshevik seizure of power in Petrograd on 7 November 1917 (25 October old Russian style) had a diverse reception in Britain, as one would have expected. It was welcomed by the BSP journal, *The Call*. On 29 November the paper described the Bolshevik *coup* as the establishment in Russia of 'the dictatorship of the proletariat'. At the end of January 1918 the executive of the party proclaimed its whole-hearted support for the October Revolution and in July *The Call* published articles by Lenin[33] and other leading Bolsheviks.

Hyndman and his friends, whose overriding concern was the victory of Britain and her allies in the war, understandably regarded the post-October Russian régime with extreme hostility. Hyndman criticized the Labour Party leaders for allowing Litvinov ('the representative of these Petrograd butchers') to address the January conference. He feared that the Bolsheviks would harm the Allied cause by concluding a separate peace with Germany. But, like Kautsky and other orthodox Marxists, he also thought of the new régime as a perversion of the socialist ideal. On the other hand, in line with a substantial sector of the British labour movement, he objected to British intervention in Russia, especially after the armistice on the western front, and urged the Allies to support only those Russian politicians hostile to both the Bolsheviks and the monarchists.

8 International Conferences before Zimmerwald[1]

Attempts to re-establish international contacts and co-operation among socialists were made early in the war by a number of parties and individuals. Socialists in the neutral countries in particular felt that they had the duty and the opportunity to help restore such relations and so work for an early end to the war.

In September 1914 the Socialist Party of the USA suggested holding a conference of socialist delegates from both belligerent blocs to hammer out a joint policy for restoring peace. At the end of September, Italian and Swiss socialists met in Lugano to discuss the prospects of an international campaign to end the war. The Italian delegation included Turati, Serrati and Angelica Balabanov, a Russian socialist who had settled in Italy. One of the representatives of the Social Democratic Party of Switzerland was Robert Grimm, who was to play a crucial part in the launching of the 'Zimmerwald Movement'. The Lugano conference agreed on a manifesto which called on the socialists of the countries at war 'to uphold the established principles of the proletarian International', and on the 'neutral' socialists to prevent the war from spreading and to urge their governments to initiate diplomatic moves towards peace.

The socialists of Italy and Switzerland made further efforts to revive the International. In the spring of 1915 they decided to send Morgari, secretary of the parliamentary group of the Italian party, to France and Britain, to persuade the leaders of the French Socialist Party and the British Labour party, and Vandervelde, president of the International, to convene a plenary meeting of the International Socialist Bureau. (Two delegates from each affiliated party formed the ISB.) But Vandervelde, who at the time was a minister in the Belgian government, refused to act 'so long as German soldiers are billeted in the homes of Belgian workers'. Other West European socialists were also unwilling to have contacts with German pro-war Social Democrats. Ernest Belfort Bax of the BSP/NSP went further and declared such contacts unacceptable for all time. He wrote in 1918:

No one calling himself a socialist should consent again to meet in congress or to hold any intercourse whatsoever, either directly or

209

indirectly, with traitors to the principles of socialism, to the International Socialist Party, and to humanity, such as the 'majority' of the present representation of the Social Democratic Party in the German Reichstag.[2]

It is ironic that Bax should have attacked the SPD leaders in much the same abusive terms as Lenin used to characterize pro-war socialists in all countries: for Lenin, Bax and Hyndman, Guesde and Sembat, Scheidemann and Ebert, Vandervelde and Plekhanov were all equally guilty, they were all traitors to 'the principles of socialism', to the International, and to humanity.

Despite the initial lack of success, 'neutral' socialists continued their efforts to bring socialists from belligerent countries together for a war-time conference. The socialist parties of the Scandinavian countries and the Netherlands issued invitations to a conference to be held in Copenhagen in January 1915 but only the organizing parties and some members of the Russian-Jewish 'Bund' turned up. The only positive result was the transfer of the executive of the International Socialist Bureau from German-occupied Brussels to a neutral venue – The Hague.[3]

On 14 February 1915, leading socialists of the *Entente* countries met in London, with Keir Hardie in the chair.[4] The suggestion for the meeting had come from Vandervelde. He was one of the Belgian delegates, some of whom had managed to come from their German-occupied homeland.[5] All shades of socialist opinion were represented except the extreme Leninist pro-civil war stance. The British delegation included supporters of the war like Henderson, then leader of the Labour Party, pacifists-centrists like MacDonald and Keir Hardie, and Bruce Glasier, editor of the anti-war ILP journal *Socialist Review*. Sixteen Frenchmen attended, mostly pro-war like Vaillant, Renaudel, Compère-Morel, Sembat (then a minister) and Cachin, but also the 'centrist' Jean Longuet, and Bourderon and Merrheim, who were to appear in Zimmerwald later that year. Russia was represented *inter alia,* by the Social Revolutionaries Chernov and Rubanovich; Bolsheviks had not been invited.

No reports of the debates were published, but three resolutions are on record. The conference protested against the persecution of social-ists and minorities in Russia, and especially against the arrest and deportation of the (anti-war) Social Democrat members of the *Duma*. Another resolution called for the restoration of the International, compulsory arbitration in international disputes, and an end to secret diplomacy and the influence of militarists and arms manufacturers.

The main resolution concerned the socialist attitude to the war. The pro-war majority of the French and Belgian delegates had drafted a bellicose text: war to the finish and no peace talks until German imperialism was eradicated. The British insisted on milder wording, and Merrheim of the French Metal Workers' Union (opposed to the war) also spoke against the Franco-Belgian draft. A compromise text was eventually agreed and obtained near-unanimity. It still expressed 'firm resolve to fight until victory', and declared that a German victory would mean the end of democracy and freedom in Europe; but the emphasis was on the condemnation of capitalism and colonialism, and of imperialist aggression in general: all governments were said to share responsibility for the carnage. The resolution said that the socialists of France, Belgium, Britain and Russia were not aiming to crush Germany politically and economically. Belgium was to be restored to freedom and receive compensation. Poland should either have complete independence or be an autonomous part of another state if her people should prefer it. The peoples of all European territories which had been forcibly annexed, from 'Alsace to the Balkans', must have the right of self-determination.

Only one vote was cast against the resolution, that of the Russian Social Revolutionary Chernov. The Menshevik Martov and the Polish socialist Lapinski, who could not attend because they had not obtained a British visa in time, later issued a statement that they would have voted against the resolution. They felt that it ran counter 'both to the spirit of the decision of the International Socialist congresses and to the views of the majority of Russian and Polish socialists who have expressed their solidarity with the attitude of the socialist group in the *Duma*'.[6]

A Russian Bolshevik was resident in London at the time: Maxim Litvinov, who was his party's representative on the ISB.[7] Although his position as a delegate was not established, he was allowed to address the conference. He protested against the failure to extend an official invitation to the Bolsheviks and read out a memorandum (drafted by Lenin) which demanded the resignation of Vandervelde, Guesde and Sembat from their respective governments, the annulment of the wartime political truce. and the rejection of war credits by all socialist parliamentary parties.

More conciliatory in tone than the London conference resolution on the war was a joint declaration of the Social Democratic parties of Germany, Austria and Hungary, issued on 13 April 1915 after a conference in Vienna, at which Victor Adler presided. [8]

The declaration called for 'a peace which humiliates no nation', a peace that would 'guarantee the lasting co-operation of all civilized nations'. The three Social Democratic parties were 'taking their stand on the decisions of the International Socialist congresses'. They were in favour of a post-war settlement comprising obligatory arbitration; democratic parliamentary control over all treaties between states; agreed armaments limitation, with general disarmament as the ultimate aim; and acknowledgement of the right of all peoples to self-determination. There was no mention of Alsace-Lorraine, Belgium, Serbia or any other specific area, but unlike the French and Belgian socialist parties those of the Central Powers deemed it possible for socialists on opposite sides to maintain relations within the framework of the International. The joint declaration included, 'The fact that the Social Democratic parties of the belligerent countries are defending their country and their nation must not be an obstacle to the maintenance of international relations among all socialist parties, and to the continued activity of their international institutions.' [9]

The Vienna declaration differed from the London resolution in one important aspect. It did not stress that the war must go on until one side was victorious. The Social Democrats of Germany and Austria would apparently have welcomed a negotiated peace, without victors or vanquished. In this respect they were less inflexible and less combative than the majority of French and Belgian socialists, or the Hyndman-Bax section of the British Socialist Party.

An international conference of socialist women was held in Berne from 26 to 28 March 1915; it was convened by Clara Zetkin, secretary of the International Council of Socialist Women's Organizations, after the exchange of views among groups in Holland, Great Britain, Russia and France. [10] Twenty-nine delegates from Britain, Holland, Germany, Switzerland, Russia and Poland took part, and one Frenchwoman who attended in a personal capacity: she was Louise Saumoneau, later imprisoned in France for anti-war propaganda. The Russian delegation included Lenin's wife, N.K. Krupskaya, and his close friend Inessa Arman.

Clara Zetkin moved a resolution which was approved by all except the Russians. It denounced the watchword and the policy of national defence which resulted from capitalist imperialism and was bound to cause enormous bloodshed and economic ruin. It declared that the war would have disastrous consequences for the workers in both the belligerent and the neutral countries, called for an immediate peace on the basis of national self-determination, and urged socialist women and socialist parties everywhere to organize mass actions to end the war.

The dissentient vote of the Russian delegates was explained and defended by Lenin in an article in a Bolshevik émigré journal.[11] On the face of it, Lenin argued, this 'middle-of-the-road' resolution was correct in rejecting 'national defence' in this imperialist war and in calling for mass action to end the war; it was also in keeping with the Basle Manifesto of 1912. But that was not enough. In view of the 'violation', by the 'opportunists and centrists', of the anti-war resolutions passed in Stuttgart and Basle, the socialist women should have made 'an irrevocable break with social-chauvinism in the entire direction and character of Social Democratic work'. Instead, the conference had 'helped Scheidemann, Haase, Kautsky, Vandervelde, Hyndman, Guesde, Sembat, Plekhanov and others to blunt the vigilance of the working masses'.[12] As the Social Democratic parties of the day were incapable of changing their policies, the conference should not have refrained, for reasons of 'diplomacy', from condemning their chauvinism and opportunism; yet 'the majority resolution... does not contain a word of censure for the traitors.'[13]

Lenin was restating the case for a split in the world socialist movement and for the formation of new revolutionary parties and a new (Third) International. He pursued this policy for the rest of the war, and translated it into practice after the October Revolution.

Another meeting of socialists from countries at war with one another must have had an element of piquancy. It was on a small, personal level. In June 1915 Karl Kautsky and Eduard Bernstein, who had just published (together with Hugo Haase) the challenging article 'The Need of the Hour'[14] went to Switzerland to meet some leading French socialists. The arrangements were made by S. Grumbach, a contributor to L'Humanité, who lived in Berne. Grumbach hailed from Alsace and was a citizen of the German Reich, but he considered himself a patriotic Frenchman. The French comrades he persuaded to meet Kautsky and Bernstein were Renaudel and the trade-union leader Jouhaux, both confirmed 'social-patriots'. Longuet, who was closer

WAR AND THE MARXISTS

to the 'centrist' line of the two Germans, had intended to come but found himself unable to make the journey to Berne.

Kautsky, who later told the story of this encounter, described it as a cordial, unembarrassed get-together of four old friends. But friendliness was confined to the personal atmosphere. Renaudel and Jouhaux stuck to the French party's view that an early negotiated peace, without the crushing of German imperialism and militarism, would be 'a threat to democracy'. Kautsky and Bernstein argued 'that a negotiated peace without any aggrandizement would be, in the eyes of the German people, a great moral defeat for militarism, and would severely weaken the power positions of the Kaiser and his generals.' The two Frenchmen shook their heads in disbelief: 'Our French comrades,' Kautsky concluded, 'bade us farewell in most cordial fashion, without any rancour, but without any prospect of our differences being bridged.'[15]

9 Zimmerwald, September 1915

When all efforts to convene a congress of the Socialist International or at least a full meeting of the International Socialist Bureau had failed, the executive of the Italian Socialist Party decided – a few days before Italy entered the war in May 1915 – to take steps to organize a conference of at least those parties and labour organizations which had demonstrated their international socialist principles by calling for mass action against the war and by rejecting the wartime party-political truce.

The guidelines for the conference were worked out at a meeting in Berne, in July, of representatives of the Italian and Swiss socialist parties and other socialists who happened to live in Switzerland.[1] No invitations would be sent to the leading members of the pro-war socialist parties of France and Germany and of the British Labour Party. But the organizers had no intention of splitting the International and paving the way for a new one. The official report of the Zimmerwald conference mentioned the preliminary Berne meeting and stated explicitly that the task of the conference was not the creation of a new International but the launching of effective actions for peace by the international proletariat.

The conference met at Zimmerwald in the Bernese Oberland from 5 to 8 September 1915; there were thirty-eight delegates. Organization had been chiefly in the hands of Robert Grimm, a left-wing Swiss Social Democrat and editor of the *Berner Tagwacht*. Selection of invitees had been largely arbitrary, and some of the delegates merely represented small groups, the editorial office of a newspaper, or themselves. Pro-war socialists and labour leaders were not the only ones excluded. The three German authors of 'The Need of the Hour' – Haase, Kautsky and Bernstein – had not been invited; nor had most of the German anti-war minority, except the Spartacists and some others on the extreme Left, like Ledebour and Adolf Hoffmann. (Karl Liebknecht had been called up for a non-combatant army unit; he sent greetings to the conference.) Britain was not represented because F.W. Jowett and Bruce Glasier of the ILP, and E.C. Fairchild of the BSP mandated by their respective parties, were refused passports by the foreign office.

Socialists from opposite camps in the First World War had, as we have seen, met one another on several occasions. What was new about Zimmerwald was the scale and scope of the meeting, and the fact that political and trade-union leaders from both belligerent camps achieved a measure of agreement on the strategy and methods of a joint struggle for peace. The Zimmerwald conference was also a milestone on the road to the worldwide schism in the socialist labour movement and the emergence of a new 'Communist' International.

A remarkable early event, propitious from the point of view of socialist internationalism, was the adoption of a common platform on the war by the French and German delegations. There were resounding cheers when their joint declaration was read in plenary session.[2] It held 'the imperialist and colonial policies of all governments' responsible for 'unleashing the carnage'. It condemned the inter-party truce in the belligerent countries and re-affirmed the tasks which the three pre-war International congresses had deemed incumbent upon all socialists.

We German and French socialists and trade unionists proclaim that this war is not our war! We most emphatically denounce the violation of Belgian neutrality, which was solemnly guaranteed in international conventions to which all belligerent states had adhered. We demand, and shall go on demanding, the restoration of Belgium's full integrity and independence. . . We want this war to end with an early peace, on terms which preclude the oppression of any nation. . . The right of the peoples to determine their own destinies must be rigorously upheld. . .

The declaration was signed for the French by Merrheim and Bourderon, left-wing trade unionists who did not speak for the French Socialist Party to which they did not formally belong. Ledebour and Adolf Hoffmann signed for the German delegation. All four were what Lenin would call 'vacillating centrists'; it is not surprising that the declaration did not call for civil war and did not mention a connection between defeat and revolution. But these 'vacillating centrists' achieved a genuine consensus on relevant points. They were not divided by the issues that set the majorities of the French and German socialist parties at odds with each other. Although the joint declaration did not mention Alsace-Lorraine, emphasis on the rigorous observance of the principle of self-determination can only have meant that the German Zimmerwald delegates would permit the citizens of Alsace-Lorraine to opt for France. On the other hand, the declaration contained no reference to the destruction of 'Prussian militarism' and Germany's imperial constitution as a pre-condition for peace; it simply urged the early conclusion of peace without conquests, without oppressive terms, without victors or vanquished.

The centrist position reflected in this declaration was held by most Zimmerwald delegates. Although the most prominent German 'centrists' had been exluded, the majority of those invited and attending represented various shades of 'centrism'. The difference between them and the 'Zimmerwald Left' − the embryonic inception of the Communist International − was one of the main themes of the debates. This is how Trotsky, who played an important part in Zimmerwald, sketched the atmosphere and summarized the outcome:

The days of the conference. . . were stormy ones. The revolutionary wing, led by Lenin, and the pacifist wing, which comprised the majority of the delegates, agreed with difficulty on a common manifesto of which I had prepared the draft. . . Lenin was on the extreme left of the conference. In many questions he was in a minority of one, even within the Zimmerwald Left. . . He was laying the cornerstone of the revolutionary International. [3]

The 'Zimmerwald Left' sided with Lenin on most issues, but not invariably. Apart from Trotsky, there was Lenin's close collaborator Zinoviev, Karl Radek (then representing a Polish party), a Lithuanian, two Swedes, a Dutchwoman, and a representative of the 'International Socialists of Germany'.[4]

The resolutions tabled by Lenin reflected his conviction that a new International was essential, and that it must be based on a complete and definitive break with the 'social-chauvinists' and the 'centre group around Kautsky'. According to Lenin, the German Kautskyans pretended to oppose the majority's pro-war policy but had 'surrendered the Marxist stand to the chauvinists' and were really social-patriots themselves.[5]

The Zimmerwald conference rejected Lenin's draft by a huge majority; some delegates described its demands as 'childish' and 'dangerous nonsense'. Even left-of-centre delegates like Merrheim and Ledebour declared the 'civil war' proposals unacceptable and impractical. As an Italian delegate put it, the task of the conference was to find ways of ending the war then in progress, not to unleash other wars − civil wars. Lenin's insistence on the need for a new International was equally unpopular. The conference did elect an 'International Socialist Commission', consisting of two Swiss and two Italian delegates and charged with maintaining and developing contacts between pro-Zimmerwald parties and groups; but it was understood that the commission would be disbanded as soon as the International Socialist Bureau was able to resume its proper role.

The Zimmerwald manifesto, which according to Trotsky was endorsed in the end by both the revolutionary and the pacifist wing, was broadly in line with the 'centrist' position.[6] It asserted the war guilt of capitalism-imperialism and attacked the socialist and labour organizations which supported their governments in the war, had voted for war credits, had authorized their members to join bourgeois governments, and had abandoned the class struggle in the interests of 'victory'. These bodies shared the responsibility of the ruling classes for the war and its consequences. The International Socialist Bureau, too, had failed in its task, but the manifesto said nothing about splitting the International and nothing about a new International. While it exhorted the European proletariat to fight for socialism and a peace based on self-determination, without annexations or war indemnities, it contained no reference to the Leninist concept of transforming the imperialist war into civil war.

Lenin and his friends noted and criticized what they regarded as the shortcomings of the document, yet they all voted for the manifesto, making its adoption unanimous. Lenin was one of the nineteen delegates whose names appear under the document: he signed it on behalf of the Russian delegation, together with the Menshevik Paul Axelrod and the Social Revolutionary M. Bobrov. After the conference Lenin explained, in an article headed 'The First Step', why his party had decided to endorse the manifesto. He pointed out its inconsistency and timidity, its failure to denounce the treachery of the opportunist leaders and to specify the revolutionary methods of the struggle for socialism and peace, yet maintained that it was 'a step towards an ideological and practical break with opportunism and social-chauvinism':

> It would be sectarianism to refuse to take this step forward *together* with the minority of German, French, Swedish, Norwegian, and Swiss socialists, when we retain full freedom and full opportunity to criticise inconsistency... It would be poor war tactics to refuse to adhere to the mounting international protest movement against social-chauvinism just because this movement is slow... and because it is ready and willing to take a step backward tomorrow... [7]

Lenin added that the Bolsheviks were not deterred by the fact that Mensheviks and Social Revolutionaries had also signed the manifesto, without breaking their links with the social-patriots – links which would help to 'unmask' them.

10 Kienthal: the Second Zimmerwald Conference, April 1916

The Zimmerwald manifesto was published in socialist papers in Italy, Britain and a number of neutral countries. In Germany, France and Russia it was distributed clandestinely as an illegal pamphlet. There was no reaction, except for some flippant and desultory comments, from the International Socialist Bureau or the socialist parties which supported their governments. But it did have a great impact on the determination and morale of internationalists in the belligerent countries.

Before Zimmerwald, anti-war socialists were handicapped in their

propaganda and political action by a feeling of isolation, by the belief
– fostered in the media and by the majority socialists – that there was
no corresponding anti-war mood or activity among socialists of the
enemy countries. The Zimmerwald manifesto bearing the signatures
of prominent socialists from nearly all warring countries, disposed of
this myth by demonstrating the existence of internationalist militancy
throughout the world at war. The result was a rapid growth of what
became known as the 'Zimmerwald Movement'. Between the conference of September 1915 and the 'Second Zimmerwald Conference',
held in Kienthal in the Swiss Alps from 24 to 30 April 1916, a large
number of groups and parties of the Second International endorsed
the manifesto. They included the British Socialist Party and the ILP,
the socialist parties of Russia, Switzerland, Poland, Rumania,
Bulgaria, the USA, Argentina, and the socialist Youth of Sweden.[1]

By no means all affiliated parties were able to send representatives
to Kienthal. A total of forty-four delegates attended, from more or less
the same groups as had been in Zimmerwald. The Social-Democratic
Party of Switzerland took part officially, whereas some of its leading
members had attended at Zimmerwald in a personal capacity. Britain
was not represented because the members chosen by the ILP and BSP
were again refused passports. Seven Germans represented the 'centre'
(the future USPD) and left-wing extremists. The eight Russian
delegates included Lenin and Zinoviev for the Bolsheviks, Martov and
Axelrod for the left-wing Mensheviks; the Social Revolutionaries were
also represented. Three French socialist members of parliament turned
up, but not on behalf of their party which was very much anti-
Zimmerwald. Merrheim and Bourderon, who had signed the joint
Franco-German declaration in Zimmerwald, had not received passports for Kienthal. Another absentee was Trotsky, who was then a
refugee in Paris and had been refused permission by the French
authorities to cross into Switzerland.[2]

The composition and the pronouncements of the Kienthal conference were more to the Left than those of Zimmerwald, but still far
from the extremist Leninist position. Attempts at a more definite
revolutionary line were made some months before Kienthal. In
February 1916 a 'draft manifesto' was published jointly by Trotsky's
Nashe Slovo and *La Vie Ouvrière,* whose editors were the anti-war
trade unionists Rosmer and Merrheim.[3] The document which was
inserted in the *Bulletin* of the International Socialist Commission (the
body elected in Zimmerwald) went further than the Zimmerwald

manifesto. It called for the creation of a new International, from which all those who had collaborated with imperialist governments were to be excluded. The draft manifesto proclaimed:

A remorseless struggle against nationalism, the definite rejection of war credits regardless of the strategic and diplomatic situation of the country concerned, the severe denunciation of the mendacious slogans of national defence and inter-party truce (*L'union sacrée)*, the mobilization of the proletarians for the revolutionary onslaught on bourgeois society – such are the essential conditions for the creation of a truly socialist International.[4]

A set of 'theses', drafted by Lenin and submitted to the ISC by the Bolshevik central committee, was even more outspoken about the need for a complete rupture with the 'social-chauvinists and Kautskyites'.[5] According to this document, the split was already a fact in several sections of the International. As far as revolutionary struggle was concerned, it was not enough to say that the fight must be waged regardless of the country's military situation – the formula used in the *Nashe Slovo-Vie Ouvrière* draft. The Bolshevik 'theses' insisted:

It is necessary to state clearly. . .that revolutionary action during the war is impossible unless 'one's own' government is threatened with defeat; it must be stated clearly that every defeat of the government in a reactionary war facilitates revolution, which alone is capable of bringing about a lasting and democratic peace.[6]

The debates at this second conference were no less controversial or stormy than at the first, but the delegates eventually voted unanimously for a manifesto (drafted chiefly by the French socialist deputy Pierre Brizon) and a resolution. The manifesto consisted largely of anti-war and anti-capitalist generalities. It rejected the 'bourgeois-pacifist illusion' that future wars could be prevented without the overthrow of the world capitalist system. It denounced as deliberate deceit the claim that the destruction of militarism was one of the war aims and declared, 'The militarism of a nation can only be destroyed by the people themselves; and militarism must be destroyed in *all* countries.'[7,8]

The Kienthal resolution was more specific than the manifesto on the questions of the International and of socialist action against the war. It censured the executive committee of the International Socialist

Bureau for its inaction, and especially attacked the Bureau's president, Vandervelde, for combining this post with that of minister in a belligerent government. He had turned the central organ of the Socialist International into 'a subservient instrument, a hostage of one of the imperialist coalitions'. But contrary to Leninist suggestions the resolution failed to call for a decisive break with the 'social-patriots'. It said that the International could re-emerge as a political force only if the world proletariat freed itself from imperialist and chauvinist influence and returned to the class struggle and policies of mass action; but there was no direct or implicit advocacy of the split which Lenin and his friends considered imperative.[9]

The resolution was also more explicit than the manifesto in condemning 'bourgeois pacifism'. It said that while capitalism lasted, all plans for eliminating the danger of future wars by agreed arms limitation or compulsory arbitration were doomed to failure. The workers should dismiss the 'fantastic proposals of bourgeois pacifists and social-nationalists' designed to create new illusions to deflect the masses from the class struggle. The Zimmerwaldians thus officially abandoned the approach of the pre-war congresses of Stuttgart and Basle, which had declared in favour of arbitration and the peaceable settlement of disputes by negotiation and agreement between bourgeois governments, such as a British-German naval treaty.

Dealing with socialist wartime policy, the resolution insisted that 'the attitude of the proletariat regarding the war must not depend upon the military or strategic situation of the belligerent powers.' This was apparently a re-phrasing of the formula in the draft manifesto agreed between *Nashe Slovo* and *La Vie Ouvrière*. There was an element of revolutionary defeatism in that it told the workers to disregard whether their country's military position was jeopardized by their actions. This was insufficiently clear and precise for Lenin, who insisted on 'the threat of defeat' being mentioned; but it went further than some British and French internationalists, who had emphasized their opposition to any revolutionary action which might imperil their country's defence.[10]

The unanimous adoption of the Kienthal resolution indicates that this document, like the Zimmerwald manifesto, resulted from a compromise.[11] Pierre Brizon endorsed the resolution although he had announced that his and his friends' vote on the war credits would depend on France's military situation.[12] On the other hand, Lenin and Zinoviev voted for a resolution which did not propound revolutionary defeatism, civil war or an unqualified rupture with 'social-chauvinists' and 'centrists'.

A few days after the end of the conference the Kienthal manifesto and resolution were published in Swiss socialist papers, in German and in French. [13] A brief inaccurate report appeared in the Parisian paper *Le Temps,* where the conference was said to have ended in failure. *L'Humanité* carried a lengthy report from Grumback, omitting the documents agreed at the conference, and a scornful article by Renaudel. The executive of the French Socialist Party dissociated itself from Kienthal and its decisions (as it had in respect of Zimmerwald) and rebuked the three deputies who attended.

In Italy the Zimmerwald union had a mouthpiece: the Socialist Party's central organ *Avanti,* whose editor was the Zimmerwaldian Serrati. But all the paper could get past the censor was the statement of the conference having been held, a list of affiliated organizations, and photos of Kienthal and the inn where the meetings had taken place. However, in Italy, as in other countries, large numbers of illegal leaflets with the text of the manifesto and the resolution were printed and distributed. [14]

11 Stockholm: The Abortive Peace Conference; the Third Zimmerwald Conference, September 1917

Some time after the Kienthal conference the International Socialist Commission (ISC) transferred its seat from Berne to Stockholm, and the Swedish capital became the venue of the third Zimmerwald conference; it met on 5 September 1917, exactly two years after the first. Two momentous events, which decisively affected the course of the First World War, had taken place between Kienthal and Stockholm: the February revolution in Russia, and the USA's entry into the war.

Bread riots and strikes broke out in Petrograd on 8 March 1917 (23 February according to the old Russian calendar then still in force). Within a few days army units mutinied in the capital. On 12 March the Petrograd garrison joined the rebellion, and when the tsar was informed by the army commanders that he could no longer rely on the military he abdicated. A provisional government, headed by the liberal Prince Lvov, took office on 14 March and proclaimed that a constituent assembly would soon be elected.

Like the revolution of 1905, the February Revolution in Russia was wholly spontaneous; no political party played a guiding rôle. As in 1905, soviets (councils of workers' and soldiers' deputies) were elected in all parts of the country. In 1917 there was no clear delimitation of the competencies of these Soviets as against those of the provisional government. The resultant régime was a kind of 'dual power' (to borrow a phrase coined by Lenin), middle-of-the-road bourgeois side-by-side with a revolutionary proletarian element.

The Petrograd soviet, which was to play a crucial part in the events of that year, met for its first plenary session at the end of March 1917 and appealed to workers of all countries to embark on joint mass action for peace.[1] The Petrograd soviet was socialist in composition but not, at that stage, controlled by the Bolsheviks, whose followers were a small minority among the deputies. But the soviet accepted the Zimmerwald maxim of peace without annexations and indemnities; and under its pressure the Russian provisional government made it known that it had renounced annexations as a war aim.

Independently of the soviet's appeal for international socialist action to end the war, some leading Dutch and Scandinavian socialists were preparing to convene a conference of socialist parties from neutral as well as belligerent countries. These two campaigns for an international conference eventually merged, and on 15 May the Petrograd soviet appealed 'to the socialists of all countries', suggesting a conference in Stockholm on 8 July; a month later the All-Russian Congress of Workers' and Soldiers' Deputies endorsed this appeal.

Developments inside Russia and the international echo of the revolution caused consternation and anxiety in the capitals of Russia's Western allies. The danger of a separate Russian-German peace loomed. To counter the threat, delegations of prominent British, French and Belgian pro-war socialists left for Russia with the blessings of their governments, intending to convince their Russian comrades to fight on for a decisive victory. Arthur Henderson, O'Grady and Will Thorne went on behalf of the Labour Party; the French socialist mission included Cachin, Moutet and Albert Thomas, the Belgian Vandervelde, de Brouckère and de Man.[2]

This Western pro-war mission to Russia was counter-productive.

Far from converting the Russians to their 'see-it-through' policy, some of the visiting socialists were so deeply impressed by the Russian desire for peace, and by the widespread belief that international socialist action might shorten the war, that they began to change their minds about the Stockholm conference and an early negotiated peace. In the words of an American historian, 'the war weariness of the Russian masses and the peace hunger of the Russian socialists infected the Allied socialists and revived their socialist faith.'[3]

The leadership of the French and Belgian Socialist Parties, and of the British Labour Party, at first rejected the Stockholm conference proposal: they refused to meet the pro-war socialists of Germany and Austria-Hungary. The atmosphere changed when the socialist missions to Petrograd returned home; and about that time it became clear that the notion of a socialist world peace conference had caught the imagination of the masses not only in Russia but in all countries at war.

In France the turning point was a meeting of the Socialist Party's national council in Paris on 27 May, with Stockholm on the agenda.[4] The majority led by Guesde, Sembat and Renaudel argued against participation; the 'centrists' around Longuet and Pressemane were in favour. The debate was still in progress when Cachin and Moutet, who had just returned from Russia, entered the hall. Before going to Petrograd they had been ardent protagonists of war to the end, and opponents of any contact with the German majority socialists. Now to general astonishment they told the national council, that the party must accept the invitation to Stockholm. The Paris correspondent of the *Manchester Guardian,* who was present, reported that a crowd of several thousands had gathered in the place de la République, outside party headquarters; the people sang the 'Internationale' and chanted: 'Go to Stockholm, down with the War!'[5] According to the report, three members of the national council went into the street and addressed the crowd. One of them, Jean Longuet, said: 'We are going to Stockholm to make peace.' This was greeted with tremendous cheers. When the national council resumed its meeting Longuet moved that the invitation to Stockholm be accepted, and the motion was carried unanimously. Some members said they were still opposed but would vote in favour for the sake of party unity.

Arthur Henderson, too, had come round to the view that opposition to Stockholm should be abandoned. On his return home he convinced the Labour Party executive, and an extraordinary party conference on

10 August produced a big majority in favour of participation. But in September the Blackpool TUC conference pronounced itself decisively against Stockholm 'at the present moment', while endorsing in principle the idea of an international socialist peace conference.

On 28 and 29 August 1917 an inter-Allied socialist conference met in London to discuss the question. The French, British, Italian, Belgian, Russian, Greek, Portuguese and South African parties were represented. All delegations except those from Belgium, Greece and South Africa voted to go to Stockholm.

There is no doubt that the proposal for a socialist world peace conference was popular with the working masses in the belligerent countries in 1917. It was less popular with some *Entente* governments. The socialists of the Central Powers were allowed to go to Stockholm, but the governments of Britain, France, Italy and the United States refused to issue passports to delegates. The Dutch-Scandinavian organizing committee hoped for a change of heart in the capitals concerned; but after repeated postponements all efforts were abandoned in November. The conference which war-weary people all over the world had looked forward to with eager expectation was never held.

It is a moot point whether the Stockholm conference would have changed the course of history. Some historians have argued that at that stage the rulers of all or nearly all belligerent nations would have found irresistible the pressure emanating from this worldwide socialist demonstration for peace, and that negotiations and a peace settlement would have been the most likely outcome. Julius Braunthal, the historian of the International, maintained that by preventing the Stockholm assembly the statesmen of the Western powers played into the hands of Lenin and his Bolsheviks: the failure of the conference project created the psychological pre-conditions for the October Revolution.[6] This view is shared by the American writer Merle Fainsod who thought that the fiasco of Stockholm meant the foundering of all hope for an early end to the bloodshed: had the Stockholm plan succeeded, Russian workers would not have turned to the extreme Left who gained power by promising immediate peace.[7]

The Zimmerwald commission had invited affiliated organizations to a third Zimmerwald conference, also to be held in Stockholm, before it became clear that a general conference would not meet. The Zimmerwaldians would then decide whether they should take part in the general conference. The refusal of passports by the four *Entente* governments would mean the absence of some of the most important sections: not much more than a 'rump' Zimmerwald could assemble in Stockholm in September. Yet thirty-eight delegates did turn up – the same number as had attended the original meeting two years before. Both Bolsheviks and Mensheviks had come from Russia; Axelrod was again one of the Menshevik delegates. Haase and Ledebour were members of the USPD delegation. The German Spartacus League was represented; so were the socialist parties of Switzerland, Poland, Finland and Rumania, the Socialist Youth organizations of Sweden and Norway, and opposition groups within the Swedish and Austrian Social Democratic Parties.

Soon after Lenin's return to Russia in April 1917 an all-Russian Bolshevik Party conference met in Petrograd and decided not to attend the Stockholm general conference. A resolution by Lenin referred to it as a conference 'of direct or indirect agents of the various imperialist governments'. The Bolsheviks were obviously not aware that some of those 'imperialist governments' were viewing the proposed conference with similar hostility, and that the 'imperialists' would succeed in torpedoing it. The Menshevik organizing committee, incidentally, decided on 18 May to attend the Stockholm general conference.

Lenin objected not only to Bolshevik attendance at the general Stockholm conference, he was totally opposed to participation in the third Zimmerwald conference. In his pamphlet 'The Tasks of the Proletariat in the Present Revolution', published in May 1917, he wrote, 'The Zimmerwald bog can no longer be tolerated. We must not, for the sake of the Zimmerwald "Kautskyites", continue the semi-alliance with the chauvinist International of the Plekhanovs and Scheidemanns, . . . We must remain in Zimmerwald *only* for purposes of information.'[8] But this was one of the rare occasions when Lenin was isolated in his own party. At the All-Russian Party conference Zinoviev argued, against Lenin, that if the break with the Zimmerwald majority was inevitable, it should be made at the conference itself, together with Spartacus and other Left allies. This view prevailed at the Bolshevik conference; Lenin alone voted against.

In a 'Postscript' to the pamphlet, written in June 1917, Lenin said the decision to attend Zimmerwald had been a mistake; but the central committee had later gone 'halfway towards correcting that mistake' by resolving that the Bolsheviks would walk out of Zimmerwald if the majority decided in favour of talks with the pro-war socialists.[9]

The first move of the Bolshevik delegation in Stockholm (which did not include Lenin, then in hiding in Finland) was to protest against the admission of the Mensheviks, who had joined the Kerensky government. A Bolshevik delegate read a statement from his party's central committee, saying that the Mensheviks were violating the decisions taken in Zimmerwald and Kienthal by participating in a belligerent capitalist government.[10] The Bolsheviks were trying to gain acceptance for the Leninist interpretation of events in Russia after the February Revolution, that the provisional government, under Prince Lvov as well as under Kerensky, was waging a predatory imperialist war, in alliance with other imperialist powers and in the interests of Russia's capitalist bourgeoisie.[11] This conflicted with the official views of the Mensheviks and Social Revolutionaries who held that the war was being waged for the defence of Russia's revolutionary democracy. The Bolshevik statement also said that the delegation would not take part in further discussions until the conference had made clear whom it supported in Russia: the 'revolutionary internationalists' or the supporters of a repressive capitalist government.

The conference did not pronounce on the statement. After expressing its sympathy with Friedrich Adler, 'this undaunted champion of freedom and justice', who was in prison in Austria after assassinating the prime minister,[12] the proposal for an immediate international mass strike against the war was debated. Only one delegate opposed it – Hugo Haase.[13] The conference decided to address a manifesto embodying the strike slogan 'to the proletariat of all countries', saying *inter alia,*

> The hour has struck for the beginning of a great common struggle...to bring about a peace settlement and to liberate the peoples by the action of the socialist proletariat. The means to achieve this is the common international mass strike. ...The international mass struggle will at the same time mean the salvation of the Russian Revolution.[14]

As no Zimmerwaldian delegates from France, Britain, Italy and the USA were at Stockholm, the conference decided to postpone publication of the manifesto and the call for mass strikes until the assent of the absent *Entente* sections had been obtained; pending this the text of the manifesto was to be kept secret. This might have meant indefinite delay due to wartime conditions.

At this stage the Bolshevik leadership, and Lenin in particular, pressed for immediate publication of the manifesto and the strike call. [15] They had by then set course for the seizure of power in Russia by an armed rising, and felt that a Zimmerwald appeal for an international strike would work in their favour. The strike appeal in the Stockholm draft manifesto was not as absurd as the strike slogans the anti-militarists had propagated at the pre-war congress of the International: the Zimmerwaldians did not maintain that it would be the panacea against war, they merely claimed that conditions were ripe for such actions in the autumn of 1917. All the same, it was unrealistic to believe that mass strikes could effectively be organized at the beginning of the fourth year of the war, or that they would have prospects of success in every major belligerent country, irrespective of its economic, political and military situation, the stability of the régime and its authoritarian or democratic character.

Ever since his return to Russia Lenin had advocated his party's withdrawal from Zimmerwald (except 'for purposes of information'). In spite of this and regardless of what he had written ten years previously, Lenin insisted on the immediate publication of the strike appeal, issued by a conference he thought his party should have boycotted. The commission decided against immediate publication, but on 10 November, three days after the Bolshevik October Revolution, the manifesto was published in the journal of the Swedish left-wing socialists.

There were no more Zimmerwald conferences after Stockholm. The International Socialist Commission continued to engage in propaganda for a while but the movement soon petered out. The publication in Sweden of the strike appeal went unheeded. No party or groups of the Zimmerwald union called upon the working class of its country to join an international mass strike against the war. [16]

12 American Socialism and the First World War

The United States declared war on Germany on 6 April 1917. The immediate cause was the German resumption of unrestricted submarine warfare early in 1917. The Germans had expected this reaction

but thought the U-boats would starve Britain into surrender within a few months and thus render American intervention ineffective. This was a miscalculation: Britain survived the submarine threat, and United States participation was an important factor in clinching the issue in 1918.

The wartime atmosphere in the USA differed from that in the European Allied countries.[1] The USA was not in danger of being invaded, like France and Russia, or subjected to air raids and a naval blockade, like Britain. Understandably, there was strong opposition to the abandonment of neutrality. Not only socialists and revolutionary syndicalists like the Industrial Workers of the World (IWW), but many radicals and progressives, and above all German-Americans and Irish-Americans, disapproved of the declaration of war.

President Wilson set up a Committee of Public Information under the veteran progressive journalist George Creel to counter this opposition and win support for government policy. The effect of official war propaganda on the one hand and staunch pacifism or isolationism on the other was the polarization of opinion: widespread chauvinism co-existed with stubborn dissent and resistance to the administration's policies. War hysteria and violent Germanophobia were more prevalent than in the European *Entente* countries.[2] That was one aspect of the American scene; another was the comparative popularity of anti-war groups such as the Socialist Party. This fairly small party (its total membership was just over 100,000 at the end of the First World War but then began to dwindle) had joined the Zimmerwald Movement when the country was still neutral; afterwards most leaders and the majority of the rank-and-file opposed the war as a capitalist-imperialist venture, claiming that profit motives were behind it, and in particular the safeguarding of investments in Western Europe. The Socialist Party's anti-war stand certainly enjoyed a measure of popular support. In mayoral elections in 1917, socialist candidates polled 22 per cent of the vote in New York City; nearly 34 per cent in Chicago, 44 per cent in Dayton, Ohio, and 25 per cent in Buffalo.[3]

If war hysteria was worse than in France or Britain, so was governmental repression of dissent and of active opposition. In June 1917 Congress passed the Espionage Act which provided for imprisonment of up to twenty years for making 'false statements with intent to interfere with the operation or success of the military or naval forces'. An even more flagrant violation of the First Amendment to the Constitution, which forbids the curtailment of free speech, was the

Sedition Act of May 1918: it declared disloyal or abusive utterances about the form of government, the flag, or the uniform of the United States, or any language intended to obstruct the war effort, to be punishable offences. It also introduced censorship of postal communications by empowering the postmaster-general to deny the use of the mails to all written or printed matter which, in his opinion, violated the Espionage or Sedition Acts.

This repressive legislation was applied rigorously, above all against left-wing critics of the government's war policy. Over 2000 persons were prosecuted and over 1500 arrested for 'seditious utterances'. Trials continued for several months after the end of the war. In the autumn of 1917, ninety-five leading members of the IWW were sentenced to lengthy terms of imprisonment. Up to June 1918, Federal Courts sentenced at least eleven persons to prison for ten years, six for fifteen years, and twenty-one for twenty years.

The most famous case of a prosecution under the wartime acts was that of the Socialist Party's leader Eugene V. Debs, four times candidate for the United States presidency. After a four-day trial in September 1918 he was sentenced to ten years imprisonment for violating the Espionage Act. The court found that his crime consisted in statements he had made in Canton, Ohio on 16 June 1918, when addressing a socialist convention. His speech was restrained by any standards. He expressed solidarity with the Bolshevik Revolution and its leaders, denounced the secret treaties between tsarist Russia and the other European *Entente* powers, and asserted that throughout history it had always been the ruling classes which declared wars while the subject masses had to fight the battles and cut one another's throats. The most objectionable passage to the authorities in their pursuit of the war concerned this enforced passivity of the working classes:

> They have always taught and trained you to believe it to be your patriotic duty to have yourselves slaughtered at their command. But in all the history of the world you, the people, have never had a voice in declaring war...Let me emphasize the fact...that the working class who fight all the battles,...who make the supreme sacrifices,...who freely shed their blood and furnish the corpses, have never yet had a voice in either declaring war or making peace.[5]

In this speech Debs also mentioned the case of a woman militant who

had been sent to prison for ten years for anti-war utterances, after a 'mock trial' where her conviction was 'a foregone conclusion'. He criticized the Western Allied governments for not responding to Bolshevik Russia's call for an international conference to lay down the terms of a just and lasting peace. But there was no reference to the war being unjust or predatory, no criticism of the United States government's decision to go to war, or of their conduct of the war − nothing that could be construed as apt to 'interfere with the operation or success' of the armed forces.

The court's view that he deserved to go to prison for ten years was upheld by the Supreme Court in March 1919. Debs was released on 25 December 1921, under an amnesty proclaimed by President Harding. In 1920, while still in prison, he was again − for the fifth and last time − the Socialist Party's presidential candidate; he received over 900,000 votes.

13   Russian Defencists and Defeatists

The gulf between the establishment and the socialist movement was greater in Russia than in any other major country at war. In parts of Central and Western Europe, socialist parties had attained a degree of respectability, and co-operation between moderate socialists and bourgeois parties or governments seemed no longer impossible; in France such co-operation materialized in 1899, when Alexandre Millerand joined Waldeck-Rousseau's Cabinet of Republican Defence.

In Russia socialist hostility towards the tsarist régime was still total in 1914, and the refusal by both the Menshevik and the Bolshevik members of the *Duma* to vote for the war credits did not come as a surprise. But Russian socialism was not spared the divisions which the First World War produced in nearly all socialist parties. There were Russian pro-war and anti-war socialists, and more or less the same shades of opinion within each group as in the French, German and British parties.

The veteran Menshevik G.V. Plekhanov and I.A. Rubanovich, one of the leaders of the Social Revolutionary Party, were prominent 'defencists'; and most emigré Russian socialists, especially those living in the *Entente* countries, accepted the watchword of 'national defence', that is, they wanted the victory of Russia and her allies. But unlike some German, French and British supporters of the war, the Russian defencists maintained an unremitting hatred of their country's régime. This is reflected in the wording of a 'manifesto' issued by Russian socialists in exile (mainly Mensheviks and Social Revolutionaries) after a conference in Lausanne from 5 to 9 September 1915.[1]

The manifesto's line was that a German victory would be disastrous for the toiling Russian masses. It argued that to desire the defeat of Russia out of hatred for the tsarist government was to confuse the régime with the fatherland: 'Russia does not belong to the tsar but to the Russian working people. In defending Russia the working people defend themselves and the cause of their liberation.' If the revolutionaries refused to take part in the defence of Russia until the government had fallen, 'they will only delay its fall.' The manifesto exhorted the working people to be active in *ad hoc* organizations created to stimulate the war effort, such as the 'War Industry Committees', and proclaimed:

> Freedom cannot be achieved except in the course of national self-defence. However, we are far from saying: 'First a victory over the external enemy and only then the overthrow of the internal one'. It is quite possible that the overthrow of the latter could become a pre-condition and a guarantee of the salvation of Russia from the German threat.[2]

The dividing line between the pro-war and anti-war Russian Social Democrats was not that which separated Mensheviks from Bolsheviks. Some Bolsheviks — G.A. Alexinsky and N.D. Sokolov for example — backed Plekhanov's defencist policy while the 'Mensheviki-Internationalists', led by Martov and Axelrod, opposed the war and the slogan of 'national defence'. For Lenin, of course, Plekhanov and those who endorsed the manifesto of September 1915 were 'social-patriots' or 'social-chauvinists'. Lenin sometimes applauded the views Martov expressed about the war and about national defence, but in general he classed him with Axelrod as a man of the 'confused and vacillating centre', that is, non-defencists who hesitated to break with the 'opportunists', and who did not wish openly for Russia's defeat.

As for Lenin's brand of 'revolutionary defeatism', both Russian and non-Russian Marxists denounced the concept as illogical and harmful to the socialist cause. Thus on the eve of the Second World War, Fenner Brockway (then an ILP leader, later a labour Peer) rejected revolutionary defeatism as 'both illogical and psychologically disastrous from an international socialist point of view': if, in the event of war between Britain and Germany, the socialists of either country were to work for the defeat of their own government, then 'our propaganda would be mutually destructive'.[3] It is worth remembering that Brockway adopted an anti-war stance both in 1914 and in 1939.

Lenin's ambiguous formula was, not surprisingly, grossly mis-understood by non-socialist writers and historians. For example the British historian Sir John Wheeler-Bennett believed that Lenin's signature under the ignominious peace treaty of Brest-Litovsk, in March 1918, was an application of the defeatist doctrine. An even more glaring misconception is reflected in his assumption that Zinoviev, Kamenev, and the other old Bolshevik defendants in the Moscow purge trials of 1936 and 1937 were really guilty of sabotage and treasonable contacts with Germany and Japan, and that their actions had been consistent with Lenin's concept of revolutionary defeatism.[4]

Lenin's formula is not only ambiguous but also unrealistic. It is contrary to historical experience for war to end in the defeat of *all* belligerents. As Kautsky pointed out, the revolutionary consequences of defeat do not normally spread from the vanquished to the victorious side.[5] The Russian revolution did produce a revolutionary upsurge in Germany, but chiefly because the Kaiser's army had to fight on two fronts and had suffered a crushing defeat in the west, which spelt victory for her remaining enemies. Being victorious, they did not have to fear revolutionary contagion.

Whatever its failings and internal contradictions, revolutionary defeatism was espoused by Lenin and his Bolsheviks, the political party which changed the course of history by seizing power in Russia. In the context of socialist attitudes and actions between 1914 and 1918 the impact of Leninist doctrine and policy on international socialism deserves closer examination.

The first version of the defeatist formula occurs in the 'Theses on the War', drafted by Lenin at the beginning of September 1914 and purporting to be a resolution of a group of 'members of the Russian

Social Democratic Labour Party'.[6] Point six of the 'Theses' declared
that the paramount task of Russian Social Democrats was to wage a
determined struggle 'against Great-Russian and tsarist-monarchist
chauvinism', and added:

> From the viewpoint of the working class and the toiling masses of
> all the peoples of Russia, the defeat of the tsarist monarchy and its
> army, which oppress Poland, the Ukraine, and many other
> peoples of Russia, and foment hatred among the peoples so as to
> increase Great-Russian oppression of the other nationalities, and
> consolidate the reactionary and barbarous government of the
> tsar's monarchy, would be the lesser evil by far.[7]

The 'Theses' also denounced the 'betrayal of socialism' by the German
Social Democrats and other leaders of the Second International who
supported their governments in the war. But the passage concerning
defeatism has a purely Russian connotation: it declared only *Russia's*
defeat to be desirable. It is hardly surprising that this was widely
interpreted as meaning that Lenin and his followers wanted Russia to
lose and her enemies to win the war, just as in 1904 – 5 he had wanted
the mikado to defeat the tsar.

   This was how Leon Trotsky understood the passage.[8] Trotsky was
not then a Bolshevik, but even the Bolshevik leadership inside Russia
construed the passage that way. In November 1914 the five Bolshevik
Duma deputies were arrested, together with Kamenev, member of the
Party's central committee, while holding a clandestine meeting to
discuss the 'Theses on the War'. In the ensuing trial the deputies and
Kamenev stated explicitly that they did not agree with points six and
seven which described Russia's defeat as the 'lesser evil' and called for
civil war.[9] They told the court that the defeatist formula conflicted
with the joint statement by the Bolshevik and Menshevik groups in the
Duma on 8 August, that they could not vote for the war credits, but
would abstain because a 'No' vote might be held to indicate a wish for
German victory. Apparently the six Bolsheviks felt that point six
expressed such a wish. Their statement was certainly not a dishonest
plea in mitigation; it would have been incompatible with Bolshevik
principles to conceal their real views in court.

   The six accused were not the only Bolsheviks to oppose the concept
of defeatism. V.A. Karpinsky, a friend of Lenin's and director of the
Russian library in Geneva, insisted in a long letter (of 27 September
1914) that point six should be re-edited, lest the impression gained

ground that the Bolsheviks wanted Germany to win the war. A.G. Shlyapnikov, another leading Bolshevik, said that while the 'Theses' in general met with the approval of party members, the defeatist slogan was causing bewilderment.[10] In the Bolshevik Party's 'manifesto' of 1 November 1914, the controversial formula was rephrased, perhaps to avoid suspicion of a pro-German bias. Unlike the first version, the manifesto, signed by the central committee, implied that the policy was valid internationally, that it should be pursued not only by Russian but by all socialists in the warring countries. But it still saw in the tsarist monarchy 'the most reactionary and barbarous of governments, which is oppressing the largest number of nations and the greatest mass of the population of Europe and Asia'. In Bolshevik eyes, tsarist Russia was the worst of all imperialist régimes, as it had been for Marx and Engels in the nineteenth century and the one most deserving of defeat.

In spite of the attempt in this manifesto to transfer the defeatist concept into a supra-national imperialistic context, there was still resistance in the Bolshevik Party to the singling out of the tsarist régime as the worst of all. When a resolution of similar tenor was tabled four months later at a conference in Berne of Bolshevik groups outside Russia, Nikolai Bukharin and other delegates criticized its one-sided, anti-Russian defeatist drift. In the end a compromise text drafted by Lenin on 'The Defeat of the Tsarist Monarchy' was unanimously adopted; it read:

> In each country the struggle against a government that is waging an imperialist war should not falter at the possibility of that country's defeat as a result of revolutionary propaganda. The defeat of the government's army weakens the government, promotes the liberation of the nationalities it oppresses, and facilitates civil war against the ruling classes. This holds particularly true in respect of Russia. A victory for Russia will bring in its train a strengthening of reaction, both throughout the world and within the country, and will be accompanied by the complete enslavement of the peoples living in areas already seized. In view of this, we consider the defeat of Russia the lesser evil in all conditions.[11]

Thus, while placating his critics with the first paragraph, Lenin managed to incorporate the substance of his concept of defeatism in the conference resolution. The tsarist monarchy is no longer referred to as the 'most reactionary and most barbarous of governments', but the last paragraph confirms that the 'lesser evil' is Russia's defeat by *the Central Powers.*

In a pamphlet entitled 'Socialism and War', written just before the Zimmerwald conference, Lenin added a new international dimension to his concept. He reiterated that in an imperialist war a revolutionary class must desire its own government's defeat, and went on to say:

> Only a bourgeois who believes that a war started by governments must necessarily end as a war between governments,and wants it to end as such, can regard as 'ridiculous' and 'absurd' the idea that the socialists of *all* the belligerent countries should express their wish that *all* their 'own' governments should be defeated. On the contrary, it is a statement of this kind that would be in keeping with the innermost thoughts of every class-conscious worker, and be in line with our activities for the conversion of the imperialist into a civil war. [12]

What Lenin apparently visualized was a process beginning with Russia's defeat and military collapse, more or less as it happened, followed by a revolution which would rapidly spread to all countries at war, victors and vanquished alike. The process would end with the worldwide struggle between proletariat and bourgeoisie, and the ultimate triumph of socialist revolution. [13]

Whatever compromise formulae the Bolshevik *emigré* groups hammered out in their discussions, party workers inside Russia continued to balk at wishing Russia to be defeated. Lenin's belief that such a wish would be 'in keeping with the innermost thoughts of every class-conscious worker' was not borne out by the behaviour of the class-conscious Bolshevik militants in Russia. He must have been aware of this, because on 29 February 1916 his journal *Sotsial-Demokrat,* published in Switzerland, reported that the Moscow branch of the Bolshevik Party had endorsed the manifesto of 1 November 1914, 'except for the passage referring to the defeat of one's own country'. [14]

The downfall of the tsarist régime and the emergence of workers' soviets in all parts of Russia was bound to work a change in the way Russian socialists viewed the problems of war and peace. Almost overnight, Russia had become a free, progressive country. The release of political prisoners, the return of revolutionary socialists from

Siberia and from abroad, the sudden transition to free speech, a free press, freedom of association, and so on, caused those socialists who had opposed the war from the start (Mensheviks as well as Bolsheviks) to ask themselves whether they could maintain this opposition. The answer of most was to switch from their anti-war stance to revolutionary defencism. All socialists thought this was a 'bourgeois-democratic' revolution, not a socialist one, but it was seen as a great stride towards the ultimate socialist objective. Most also felt that it would change the character of the war waged by Russia; they were determined to force the provisional government to renounce all imperialist and annexationist war aims. National defence would then be justified as revolutionary defence, because its success was a pre-condition for the progress of the revolution and the consummation of its long-term objectives.

Bolshevik Party organizations inside Russia and their organ, *Pravda,* did not keep aloof from this trend towards revolutionary defencism – at least not until Lenin returned from exile about the middle of April.[15] Immediately after the tsar's abdication and the formation of a provisional government under Prince Lvov, which included only one (moderate) socialist, A.F. Kerensky, the bureau of the Bolshevik central committee passed a resolution defining its attitude: it described the provisional government as counter-revolutionary and called for the establishment of the 'democratic dictatorship of the workers and peasants' – the Bolshevik watchword in the revolution of 1905. But the Bolshevik leaders did not proclaim all-out struggle against the government and, above all, they adopted a defencist position regarding the war.

This became more marked when Kamenev and Stalin returned from their Siberian exile at the end of March. Together with the Bolshevik *Duma* deputy, Muranov, they gained control of *Pravda* and under its new editorship the paper declared that the party would support the provisional government insofar as it was 'fighting against reaction and counter-revolution'. As for the war, so long as the German army obeyed the kaiser, the Russian soldier must 'stand firmly at his post and answer bullet with bullet and shell with shell'.[16] The party's slogan would not be a meaningless 'down with the war': they intended to exert pressure upon the provisional government to appeal to all belligerent countries for immediate peace negotiations. As Trotsky remarked, this was exactly the position of the defencists, and of the 'centrists' in other countries – Kautsky, Longuet, and Ramsay MacDonald.[17]

Pravda was outspoken about the party's new line: 'All "defeatism'', or rather what an undiscriminating press...has branded with that name, died at the moment when the first revolutionary regiment appeared on the streets of Petrograd.' Trotsky had rejected Lenin's defeatist formulae when they were accepted, albeit reluctantly at first, by the Bolshevik Party. Over a decade later, when Trotsky wrote his *History of the Revolution,* he seems to have come round to the view that Lenin had been right on this point all along. He then commented on *Pravda's* initial repudiation of defeatism after the February Revolution: 'This was a direct abandonment of Lenin. "Defeatism" was not invented by a hostile press..., it was proclaimed by Lenin in the formula: "The defeat of Russia is the lesser evil.'' The appearance of the first revolutionary regiment, and even the overthrow of the monarchy, did not alter the imperialist character of the war.'[18]

This is logically unassailable. In Lenin's view, which Trotsky then shared, the war had not ceased to be imperialist and predatory in March 1917, so it would have been inconsistent to abandon the policy or the slogan of revolutionary defeatism. But when Trotsky wrote this he must have forgotten (if indeed he had ever been aware) that *Lenin himself never repeated the 'defeatist' formula after the February Revolution.* He went on describing the war waged by the provisional government as reactionary and predatory; and after his return to Russia he persuaded his party, with some difficulty, to shed its newly-acquired defencism and return to its pre-revolutionary anti-war policy. But in none of his published writings between the two revolutions of 1917 did he express a wish for the defeat of Russia or call his government's defeat the 'lesser evil'.

News of the February Revolution reached Lenin on 15 March, when Zurich newspapers reported the tsar's abdication and the formation of a provisional government. Without waiting for communications from Russia and more detailed and reliable information than the Swiss press could have been expected to provide, Lenin denounced the new government as reactionary and imperialistic. On 17 March he drafted his 'Theses on the workers' tasks in the Russian Revolution', for the benefit of Bolshevik Party members about to leave their Scandinavian exile for Russia. He asserted that the new government, which represented the capitalists and landlords, could not give the people peace, bread or full freedom. The predatory treaties which the tsar's government had concluded with Britain, France, Italy, Japan, and so on, were still being kept secret by the new government:

> It wants to conceal from the people...the fact that it stands for continuation of the war, for victory over Germany. It is not in a position to...propose to all belligerent countries an immediate ceasefire, to be followed by peace based on complete liberation of all the colonies and dependent and unequal nations. That requires a workers' government acting in alliance with, first, the poorest section of the rural population, and, second, the revolutionary workers of all countries in the war.[19]

Lenin stuck to this condemnation of the provisional government and its war policy, and to his call for a 'workers' government', throughout the period between the February and the October Revolutions. He did not change his mind when a more left-wing government was formed, including socialist (Menshevik and Social Revolutionary) ministers, and when Kerensky, a moderate socialist, became prime minister, or when the government, under pressure from the Petrograd soviet (the acknowledged temporary spokesman of the Russian working class and peasantry), adopted a formula on Zimmerwald lines for a peace based on self-determination, without annexations and indemnities.

To begin with, there was some substance in the accusations Lenin levelled at the provisional government. Two of its leading members, Foreign Minister Milyukov and War Minister Guchkov, were partisans of 'war until total victory' and of annexations, including Constantinople and part of Galicia. When the government informed Russia's allies of its abandonment of annexationist claims at the end of April 1917, Milyukov added a note confirming the continued validity of the secret treaties. But after mass demonstrations of protest Milyukov and Guchkov had to resign on 15 May, and a coalition government was formed with socialist participation.

Lenin remained implacably hostile. He brushed aside the government's 'no-annexation' statements as dishonest and hypocritical. When the Russian army launched a big offensive in June, Lenin said this was evidence of the unaltered predatory character of Russia's war. In a *Pravda* article on 4 July, he ridiculed the 'high-sounding phrases' about peace, socialism and revolution, bandied about by the Menshevik Tsereteli and the Social Revolutionary Chernov, both ministers in the coalition government:

> The revolutionary armies of Russia have been sent into battle in the name of the imperialist designs of Britain, France, Italy,

Japan and America. No argument from Chernov, once a Zimmerwaldist and now Lloyd George's partner, can conceal the fact that while the Russian army and the Russian proletariat do not really pursue any annexationist aims, this does not in the least change the imperialist, predatory nature of the struggle between the two world trusts. [20]

Lenin's revolutionary strategy was firmly established long before he returned to Russia. His first written reaction to the Revolution (17 March) was penned in ignorance of the emergence of soviets, the 'dual power' element in the revolution. This new factor, based on the precedent of 1905, figured in an article (published only some years later) which he wrote in Zurich on 25 March. He repeated his denunciation of the government 'of capitalists and landlords', adding that it was pointless to exhort them to declare in favour of a truly democratic peace. Only the transfer of political power to the soviets could achieve such a peace. An All-Russian Soviet of Workers', Soldiers' and Peasants' Deputies (or the Petrograd soviet temporarily acting for it) would declare that it was not bound by any treaties signed by the tsarist or the bourgeois governments, and would publish those secret treaties forthwith. It would call publicly for an immediate armistice and a democratic peace, but would stress that nothing good could be expected from the bourgeois governments. The Soviet would 'call upon the workers of all countries to overthrow them and to transfer all political power to Councils of Workers' Deputies'. The notion of the Russian revolution spreading to the advance capitalist countries was already present in Lenin's strategic calculations. [21]

Lenin's views of the provisional government and the war were incompatible with the defencist stance the Bolshevik leadership in Russia had adopted. A showdown was unavoidable, and it occurred as soon as Lenin returned to Russia, after the journey in the famous 'sealed train' across Germany, Sweden and Finland. He arrived in Petrograd on the night of 16 April and expounded his view of the situation on the next day, first at a Bolshevik meeting, and then at a joint meeting of Bolsheviks and Mensheviks. [22] He then stated his case in writing, in ten 'Theses' on 'The tasks of the proletariat in the present revolution'. These became the basis of the policy which carried the party to victory in less than seven months and made Lenin and his followers rulers of Russia.

In the 'Theses' Lenin described the government of 'Lvov and Co.'

as 'capitalist' and the war as 'predatory' and 'imperialist', and declared that 'not the slightest concession to revolutionary defencism is permissible.' The party must expose the government's false promises, and in particular the mendacious denial of annexationist designs. The first stage of the revolution had placed power in the hands of the bourgeoisie, because the proletariat was not yet sufficiently class-conscious and organized. But the country was in the process of passing to the second stage, which would give power to the working class and the poor peasantry. Characteristic features of this transitional phase were, on the one hand, the confidence the masses still had in the capitalist government, and on the other the existence of a maximum of legally recognized rights. Russia was now 'the freest of all the belligerent countries in the world'. As the Bolsheviks were still a minority in most soviets there must be no attempt to seize power by force; it was the party's task to convince the masses of workers, mainly 'honest defencists', by explaining to them patiently the link between the capitalist régime and the war, and that the attainment of a just, democratic peace depended upon the transfer of power to the workers and poor peasants. [23]

The 'April Theses', with their insistence on total opposition to the provisional government and the war, produced incomprehension and bewilderment among Russian socialists, including several prominent members of Lenin's party. The first reaction of some old Bolsheviks was outright rejection. On 21 April *Pravda* carried an article by Kamenev in which he called Lenin's analysis 'unacceptable' because it assumed that the bourgeois-democratic revolution was completed and would immediately grow into socialist revolution − which was not, in fact, what Lenin had argued in his 'Theses'. According to Trotsky who though not yet a Bolshevik, approved the general tenor of the 'Theses' a number of old Bolsheviks were so upset that they resigned from the party, to join either the Mensheviks or the group round Maxim Gorky's paper *Novaya Zhizn (New Life)* which occupied a position halfway between the two main social democratic parties. Lenin was all but isolated among the party's leaders, many of whom felt that his long absence from his native country had made him out of touch with life in Russia and unable to form an objective view of the issues of the day. [24]

It took Lenin less than a month to convert his party to his line. An 'All-Russian Conference' of the Bolshevik Party was held in Petrograd from 7 to 12 May to decide on policy and elect leading party bodies. The 149 delegates (131 voting, eighteen non-voting) represented about 79,000 members. The conference adopted a 'Resolution on the War' which Lenin had drafted and which repeated, with some additions, the essence of the April 'Theses': refusal to support the provisional government, rejection of revolutionary defencism, support for mass fraternization across battle-lines, and democratic peace depending upon the transfer of political power to 'the class of the proletarians and semi-proletarians'.[25]

In a passage of special interest in the light of what happened after the October coup, the conference 'reiterates its protest against the base slander spread by the capitalists against our party to the effect that we are in favour of a separate peace with Germany.' This 'base slander' was repudiated by Lenin and other Bolsheviks on a number of occasions. On 22 June Lenin addressed the first All-Russian Congress of Soviets of Workers' and Soldiers' Deputies, where he said *inter alia:* 'There can be no separate peace treaty for us,...we reject it as we reject all agreement with the capitalists. To us, a separate peace treaty would mean coming to terms with the German plunderers...'[26]

As already mentioned, the concept of revolutionary defeatism was not repeated by the Bolsheviks after the February Revolution. Neither the April 'Theses' nor any Bolshevik conference resolution or any of Lenin's articles or speeches of that period contain the assertion that the defeat of Russia would be the 'lesser evil', or that defeat was desirable as a factor facilitating revolution. This omission is not consistent with the way Lenin argued the defeatist case. He had declared it 'axiomatic' that revolutionaries must wish for their government's defeat in a reactionary war; and after the February Revolution he kept repeating that the provisional government was waging a reactionary, 'imperialist, predatory war'.

Though the (unavowed) abandonment of the defeatist slogan cannot be squared with Lenin's views, it is understandable from the viewpoint of political expediency. Previous statements and resolutions about the defeat of Russia being the 'lesser evil' were linked with references to the nature of the tsarist régime.[27] But according to Lenin's 'April Theses' Russia had emerged from the uprising a free country. To describe the defeat of the Russian republic in the war against Hohenzollern Germany and Habsburg Austria as a 'lesser evil' would have disastrously impaired the Bolshevik Party's prospects of gaining mass allegiance. The working people, as Lenin acknowledged, were mostly 'honest defencists': they would have turned away from a party which declared the country's defeat to be desirable. After three years the people had had enough of bloodshed and exhaustion and were yearning for peace, so Bolshevik agitation for an early peace met with increasingly strong mass response, but Lenin realized that a defeatist slogan would antagonize the masses and frustrate efforts to gain the influence the party needed in its bid for power.[28]

By not reviving the defeatist formula after the February Revolution Lenin demonstrated the fundamental ambiguity of his concept. He talked about 'patiently explaining' to the masses the party's views and policies, but how to explain to workers and poor peasants that a wish for the defeat of republican Russia did not mean a wish for the victory of imperial Germany? Lenin's failure to resume the defeatist slogan also demonstrated implicitly how unthinkable it would have been for some foreign socialist parties to profess and practise defeatism. If it was impossible for the Bolsheviks, under Lvov or Kerensky, to express hopes for the country's defeat, it was equally impossible for the socialists of, say, France or Belgium, however strongly they criticized their governments, to say publicly that they wanted their country's defeat in a defensive war against a more aggressive and less democratic enemy.

Another incongruity of the defeatist doctrine became apparent during the final phase of the Kerensky interlude. In October 1917, when he was in hiding in Finland, Lenin kept urging a hesitant Bolshevik leadership to seize power by an armed rising. He emphasized that the matter brooked no delay because the Kerensky government and the Russian bourgeoisie had decided to surrender Petrograd to the Germans, and leave the enemy to strangle the incipient revolution. In a 'Letter to Comrades', written about a week before the coup, Lenin dealt with the 'weak, timid, confused' arguments of those leading Bolsheviks (like Zinoviev and Kamenev) who were opposed to an uprising. One of these weak counter-arguments, Lenin alleged, had been that the bourgeois leaders would be unable to hand Petrograd over to the Germans, because it was not the bourgeoisie which did the fighting but 'our heroic sailors'. Lenin replied that although the sailors did the fighting it would be easy for the government and high-ranking officers to surrender Petrograd by opening the northern front, by giving freedom of action to the German navy, or by sabotaging food deliveries to the armed forces, thereby 'bringing our troops to *complete* desperation and impotence'.[29]

This paradoxical scenario formed part of the background to the dispute between Bolshevik advocates and opponents of an immediate rising. There was this capitalist-imperialist government, resolved upon sustaining a major defeat by surrendering the country's capital to the imperialist enemy. There were the 'heroic sailors', apparently revolutionary and therefore anti-war to a man, but defending the capital to prevent the defeat the government was planning. Lenin was in effect accusing the Kerensky government of 'counter-revolutionary defeatism', but it might not have occurred to him or the Bolsheviks who advised against the uprising that the soldiers and sailors would practise revolutionary defencism — something Lenin and his party had declared impermissible in a warring country still in the hands of the imperialist bourgeoisie.

14   Revolutionary Defeatism: International and Historical Aspects

As a political slogan in the First World War, revolutionary defeatism was strictly limited in time and space. It was a purely Russian phenomenon, confined to Lenin and the bulk of the Bolshevik leadership, and was official party policy for only two and a half years, between September 1914 and March 1917.

None of the prominent internationalists in any belligerent country other than Russia ever used the slogan; none of the groups or individuals concerned ever expressed their preference for their government's defeat in the war as 'the lesser evil'. Karl Liebknecht declared that the proletarian revolutionaries' main enemy was 'in their own country' (*Der Hauptfeind steht im eigenen Land*). His position was consistent with the Leninist watchword of turning imperialist war into civil war, but he did not express a wish for the defeat of the kaiser's government. No defeatist statements from French, British or Italian internationalists are on record.

An unequivocal rejection of defeatist argumentation can be found in Rosa Luxemburg's 'Junius' pamphlet, *The Crisis of Social Democracy,* written in prison in 1915, published by the Berne 'International Socialist Commission' in 1916 and illegally distributed in Germany.[1]

In her pamphlet (German title, *Die Krise der Sozialdemokratie)* Rosa Luxemburg castigated the German Social Democratic Party's policy of supporting the war and accepting the party-political truce; she accused the party's Reichstag group of betraying the principles of international socialism by voting for the war credits on 4 August 1914. She demolished the official claim that Germany was waging a defensive war by quoting passages from the 'White Book' published by the German foreign office in August 1914. The White Book said explicitly that Germany, though aware of the danger of war because of Austria's attitude towards Serbia, had assured her ally of German help in whatever action the Vienna government might take against Serbia.

Luxemburg concluded that it had been obvious to the SPD that Germany was not waging a war of defence. Germany had declared war on France whose people *and* government wanted peace; the war with Britain had been made inevitable by the intensified building of German 'dreadnoughts': 'The naval programme of December 1899 was a German declaration of war which England acknowledged on 4 August 1914.'[2] The political truce, which the party had accepted and was adhering to, went much further than in the Western *Entente* countries: 'In Britain there is complete freedom of the press, while in France the press is not gagged nearly as excessively as in Germany.'[3]

Her analysis of the background of the war was not directed exclusively against Germany. No country, she argued, could invoke the right of national defence — the era of wars of national defence was over. France and Britain were not defending their national but their world-political positions, 'their imperialist possessions which are threatened by the designs of the German upstart'. 'Imperialist policy is not the creation of any particular state or number of states' it is the product of a certain degree of maturity in the world development of capital, an intrinsically international phenomenon. . .which no single state can evade.[4]

Luxemburg's arguments thus far would have been largely non-controversial among internationalists during the First World War. Lenin could endorse nearly all of them. But her position differed fundamentally from that of Lenin about the policy German Social Democracy should have adopted at the beginning of the war: she did not advocate revolutionary defeatism.

It is the duty of Social Democrats to defend their country in a great historic crisis. And this is precisely the grave fault the Social

Democrats in the Reichstag committed. They solemnly declared on 4 August: 'We do not desert the fatherland in the hour of its peril'; yet at the same moment they denied their own words. They did desert the fatherland in the hour of its greatest peril. For in that hour it was their foremost duty to the fatherland to expose the real background of this imperialist war, to tear to shreds the tissue of patriotic and diplomatic lies which served to conceal this plot against the fatherland; to state clearly and emphatically that *in this war victory and defeat would be equally disastrous for the German people;*...to proclaim the need for arming the people forthwith and for entrusting the people with the decision on war and peace; to demand that parliament meet in permanent session for the duration of the war...; to demand the immediate abolition of all political disfranchisement, since only a free people can effectively defend its country. (Emphasis added.)[5]

The party should also, in Luxemburg's view, have adopted 'the truly national programme of the patriots and democrats of 1848, the programme of Marx, Engels and Lassalle: the rallying cry of the united, great German republic'.

Plekhanov and other 'social-patriots' interpreted the wartime programme outlined in the 'Junius' pamphlet as basically defencist, especially in view of a passage where the author declared that it was shameful for a nation to capitulate before the external enemy, 'just as it is shameful for a political party to capitulate before the internal enemy'.[6] There is indeed some confusion and inconsistency in her statements on this issue, as Lenin was not slow to point out;[7] but she made it clear that in her opinion German workers and their party should never support 'national defence' under the auspices of the bourgeoisie and the imperial government.

The Junius pamphlet recalls the defencist argument Engels advanced in 1892, when he expressed certainty that, in the event of war against a Franco-Russian coalition the German working class would resolutely repel any French invasion of Germany.[8] But Luxemburg's pamphlet goes on to say, Engels had in mind the old tsarist Russia, before the revolution of 1905:

Besides, Engels was thinking of a truly national war of defence, waged by Germany against simultaneous aggression from the East and the West...It is quite plain that Engels, when speaking of national defence from the point of view of Social Democratic policy, did not mean support for the Prussian-Junker militarist government and its general staff, but revolutionary action on the model of the French Jacobins.[9]

While Luxemburg's formulations about the right attitude of a proletarian party in a war sometimes lack precision and consistency, there is no doubt about her rejection of support for the kaiser's war. The best solution from her point of view would have been the overthrow of the imperialist warlords by revolutionary proletarian action, followed by a war of revolutionary defence, if necessary. Failing that, she would have preferred an early compromise peace, without victors or vanquished, to a long-drawn-out struggle ending in decisive victory or mutual exhaustion.

Rosa Luxemburg was not a defencist, but it is wrong to attribute to her indirect or sub-conscious defeatism. This is what her biographer J.P. Nettl was trying to do. His thesis was that she and her radical friends in Germany were hoping (without admitting it) for their country's defeat.[10] According to Nettl, Rosa Luxemburg did not voice such hopes because of 'her immense and often repeated concern with the human loss involved'; her desire for the defeat of German imperialism conflicted with her wish for an early end to the war and the bloodshed. It is true that she was deeply concerned with the loss of life and wanted the slaughter to stop as soon as possible. But this was not why she refused to embrace the Leninist concept of revolutionary defeatism, which is not mentioned in the pamphlet but which she must have known about. The real reason appears to be that she did not share Lenin's belief in a necessary connection between military defeat and the prospects of socialist revolution.

Germany's defeat, Luxemburg proclaimed, would be as disastrous for the nation as a German victory. She described the consequences, as she saw them, of an *Entente* victory − correctly, by and large. She challenged the assumption of French socialist leaders that a German defeat would mean the demise of militarism and imperialism in that country; on the contrary, militarism and imperialism would thrive, after defeat as well as after victory. For Germany, an *Entente* victory would spell the loss of some territory and of her colonies; it would lead to the disintegration of the Habsburg monarchy and of the Ottoman empire. But new antagonisms would inevitably arise; there would be frantic rearmament, above all in defeated Germany, with a new world war as the end result.[11]

The 'Junius' pamphlet does not follow Lenin in calling for 'the transformation of the imperialist war into civil war', but the closing paragraph implicitly points to international proletarian revolution as a means of ending the slaughter: 'This madness, this hellish nightmare will only cease when the workers of France, Germany, Britain and Russia wake up at least from their intoxication, fraternally clasp hands and drown the bestial chorus of the imperialist warmongers and the shrieks of capitalist hyenas with the labour movement's great battle-cry: "Proletarians of all countries, unite!"'[12]

In a fifteen page article written in the summer of 1916, Lenin hailed the 'Junius' pamphlet as 'on the whole...a splendid Marxist work' and extended 'hearty greetings' to its author (whose identity he did not know at the time), but he had a number of earnest criticisms to make. Junius had failed to see and explain the connection between the treachery of the 'social-chauvinists' and opportunism as a trend pervading the whole history of the Second International. This failure to link social-chauvinism with long-standing opportunism accounted for the reluctance of 'Junius' and other German Leftists to break with the pro-war and the centrist Social Democrats – to split the SPD and create a new, revolutionary socialist party.

Lenin's main criticism focused on the issue of national defence; he attacked Junius's thesis that the German Social Democrats should have opposed the imperialist war by putting forward a national programme – arming the people and so on – modelled on the revolutionary policy of the French Jacobins of 1793. It was strange and indeed almost incredible, he commented, that after proving that this was an imperialist and not a national war Junius should 'drag a national programme into this war', instead of proclaiming the need for civil war against the bourgeoisie.[13]

Lenin was right in noting some inconsistency in Luxemburg's advocacy of a national programme in an imperialist war. Curiously enough, he paid little attention to her rejection of defeatism, to her statement that the country's defeat would be just as disastrous as victory. This rates merely a footnote in his article, saying that the thesis of defeat and victory being equally disastrous was 'the point of view not of the revolutionary proletariat but of the pacifist petty bourgeoisie', and briefly restating his argument that revolutionary proletarian action during a war is impossible without the risk of defeat, and that defeats 'help the cause of the revolutionary class'.[14]

Lenin's claim to unwavering fidelity to Marxist teachings was frequently challenged during the war, usually by opponents, but in one instance by a close friend and supporter – Innessa Armand, with whom he kept up a regular correspondence. Her letters to Lenin have not been published, but from his replies it appears that she contended that his wartime position differed essentially from his pre-war stance and from what Engels had said in 1891 and 1892 about socialists defending Germany against aggression.[15] Engels's insistence that German workers would fight to ensure German victory in such a war was surely incompatible with the defeat of one's government being the 'lesser evil'. Armand must have suggested that Lenin was right in prescribing revolutionary defeatism for socialists of all countries at war, and that Engels had been wrong to counsel national defence in a hypothetical war with France and Russia.

Lenin would have none of this. He maintained that Engels had been right in 1891 and that, in view of subsequent changes in the world political situation, he, Lenin, was also right regarding the war which had then lasted just over two years. In elaborating this proposition he got hopelessly bogged down in self-contradiction and inconsistency.

What, according to Lenin, were the differences between 1891 and 1914 – 16? The war in progress was imperialist on all sides: Inessa Armand, who like Lenin was an internationalist and anti-war, would not dispute that. The war of the early 1890s (which failed to break out) could not have been imperialist on Germany's part because imperialism came into existence only in 1898 – 1900.[16] Hence, France and Russia could not have been waging an imperialist war either, but their war would have been reactionary, designed 'to turn back the development of Germany, to return her from national unity to dismemberment'. When Armand pointed out that dismemberment of Germany was also a possiblity in the war of 1914 – 17, Lenin objected that she was 'simply sliding away from the assessment of what exists to what is *possible*. That is not historical. It is not political. . . All kinds of things are "possible".[17]

Inessa Armand could have retorted (and quite possibly did) that the threat of dismemberment in the 1890s was no more than a possibility either, if Germany had then had to fight a war on two fronts.[18] But Lenin's argument about imperialism not existing in 1891 is just as much of a quibble. It is true that according to his theory 'imperialism' was a fairly recent development – the last stage of capitalism; but that was no reason to deny the possibility of 'imperialist wars' before the turn of the century. He had used the terms in a less restrictive sense.

In his critique of the 'Junius' pamphlet, some five months before that letter to Armand, he had tried to prove that the wars of the French Revolution ceased to be national in character under the first Empire and 'became imperialist wars and in turn led to wars of national liberation *against* Napoleonic imperialism'. In the same article he wrote that the Seven Years' War between Britain and France in the eighteenth century was fought for the possession of colonies: 'In other words, they waged an imperialist war (which is possible on the basis of slavery and primitive capitalism as well as on the basis of modern highly developed capitalism).'[19] Lenin said that in July 1916; in December he discovered that the German empire, a highly developed capitalist country and possessor of colonies in Africa and the Pacific, could not have waged an imperialist war in 1891 because what he chose to call imperialism would not emerge for another seven or eight years.

Lenin would never have admitted any discrepancy between his position and the orthodox Marx-Engels position. As the controversy with Armand demonstrated, he would not want to be told that he was right *against* Marx or Engels. In a letter to Armand, he agreed in theory that Marx and Engels were 'not infallible';[20] in practice his fundamentalist approach made him try to establish his case by proving it compatible with the teachings and policies of Marx and Engels.

Some of the short-term consequences of the First World War bore out Lenin's defeatist conception. There were revolutionary upheavals in all defeated countries, but also in Italy which had been on the winning side. In Russia, Germany, Austria and Turkey (but not in Bulgaria) republican régimes replaced the monarchy. But only in Russia did the revolution − the October coup and ensuing civil war − produce fundamental changes in the political and socio-economic fields; only in Russia did a régime emerge which claimed to be proletarian socialism. Socialists played a prominent part in the German, Austria and Hungarian revolutions, but soon lost all or nearly all of their influence. The paradoxical outcome was that capitalism survived where socialist revolution had been overdue, according to general Marxist consensus. 'Socialism' triumphed in the one country which Marxists agreed had not been ripe for it.

An Authoritarian system of nationalized production and centralized economic planning was eventually established in Russia. Its socialist character is acknowledged by some Marxist tendencies but denied by others. Non-communist Marxist theoreticians also maintained that Soviet direction within the new Communist International exerted a debilitating or even paralysing influence upon the world socialist movement – that a socialist régime in Russia actually worked against the interests of socialist world revolution.

In Germany, the long-term effect of defeat was a colossal reverse for socialism. The treaty of Versailles, imposed by the victors, aroused strong feelings of resentment and national hatred in the German people. The National Socialists successfully exploited these feelings to create an ultra-nationalist, bellicose mass movement. The Nazis also had a measure of success in saddling the Social Democrats with the blame both for defeat and for signing a humiliating peace treaty. The outcome was the emergence, in the heart of Europe, of an anti-socialist totalitarian dictatorship, with a racialist and militarist ideology, bent on wiping out the results of the lost war in a renewed bid for world domination. This vindicated Rosa Luxemburg's prediction of the consequences of a German defeat – recrudescence of militarism and imperialism, and frantic re-armament leading to another world war – and refuted, in the long term, the Leninist expectation that defeat would produce proletarian revolution and socialism.

Germany's defeat in the Second World War did not bear out Lenin's anticipations either. It did not lead to intensified nationalism and re-armament; the collapse of the Nazi bid for world dominion had demonstrated the futility of all such ventures. Nor was defeat followed by socialist revolution. In East Germany a régime emerged modelled on Soviet communism, resulting from Russian occupation rather than German working-class action. The long-term outcome in West Germany was a stable capitalist economy with a Western-style bourgeois-democratic superstructure.

Conclusion

Less than half this volume deals with what Marx and Engels said and wrote about wars occurring in their lifetimes. The larger part describes the thoughts and actions of their disciples and followers, and of some non-Marxist socialists, between 1895 (the year of Engels's death) and 1918. Marxist politicians and writers, and especially those active during the First World War, claimed that their analyses and policies were in harmony with the criteria and strategies recommended by Marx and Engels. With which claimants would Marx and Engels have agreed? What policy would they have suggested and pursued if they had survived until the end of the First World War?

As I said in the preface, Marx and Engels never formulated guidelines for a 'correct' socialist attitude to war. The only constant feature in their choice between opposing camps was that they were invariably hostile to tsarist Russia. Most of the time they were hoping that Russia's defeat in such a war would spark off revolution. That apart, they favoured the 'more progressive' side, the camp whose victory they believed would further the revolutionary cause. They sympathized with the Italians and Hungarians against the Habsburgs in and after 1848, but had no use in their younger days for 'reactionary' small nations like the Croats, the Danes, the Dutch or the Swiss. Sometimes they 'played it by ear' in giving their support, and occasionally they advanced very odd reasons for their choice. For example, one of Marx's reasons for wanting the Germans to beat the French in 1870 was that this outcome would establish the superiority of his theory over that of Proudhon and other French writers. In 1878 they sided with Turkey against Russia, not only because they hated tsarist autocracy but because they admired the efficiency and 'high moral standards' of the Turkish peasants.

Lenin considered it an 'axiom' that a socialist would want the defeat of his own government in a reactionary war but this was definitely not a Marxist axiom. Had Marx and Engels been 'defeatist' in a Leninist

252

sense they would have told the British and French workers during the Crimean War — a reactionary war by any standards — that it was in their interest to see their governments defeated; instead, Marx and Engels hoped for the victory of the Anglo-French alliance. When war between Britain and Russia seemed possible in the 1870s, Engels told the General Council of the First International that Britain should arm herself to win such a war. Engels rejected revolutionary defeatism outright in 1885, in a letter to Laura Lafargue. He criticized William Morris and other British socialists for hoping that war with Russia over Afghanistan (which did not break out) would end in British defeat, rebellion in India and revolution in Britain itself. It could be right, Engels said, for a socialist to be unpatriotic, but quite wrong to be defeatist in a war against the Russian tsar.

There was no trace of what Lenin called 'social-patriotism' in the attitude of Marx and Engels to contemporary wars. They would have backed Germany against Russia, and supported Germany's cause when they felt it was just or progressive, but they often denounced the war policies of their native Prussia and of their adopted British homeland. Engels wanted Prussian defeat by Austria in 1866, and in the Franco-German war of 1870 – 1 he and Marx supported the French Republic after the downfall of Napoleon III; they even hoped for intervention by Britain and other countries in France's favour. In Britain's wars with Persia and China in the 1850s they sympathized with the Asian countries and condemned Britain's aggressions and atrocious actions, such as the bombardment of Canton.

They understood the reasons for the Indian Mutiny, but did not think, or even wish, that it would mean the end of colonial rule and independence for India. Decolonization (as it is now called) did not seem a practical proposition then. Twenty-five years later, in 1882, Engels declared a gradual progress towards independence to be possible; he thought it would be the consequence of proletarian revolution in the metropolitan country. In the last war on which Engels expressed his views, he welcomed China's defeat by Japan in 1895 on the grounds that it would make for social progress in Asia and hasten the triumph of socialism in Europe.

Marx and Engels would probably have been 'pro-Boer', in the South African War of 1899 – 1902, and would have denounced Britain's aggressive bid to grab the goldmines of the Transvaal. They would have disagreed violently with leading Fabians like the Webbs and Bernard Shaw, who felt that socialism was not concerned with international conflicts but solely with changing the economic system. But Marx and Engels might have agreed with H.M. Hyndman that South Africa belonged 'neither to Boer nor to Briton' but to the black native tribes.

They would perhaps have sympathized with the USA's war against Spain in 1898, without necessarily disagreeing with Kautsky about the American economic motivation to end Spanish rule in Cuba. Both would have welcomed the Cubans independence which resulted, but would not have approved the annexation of Puerto Rico. The war of conquest in the Philippines would have met with their condemnation, and they would have been critical of those American socialists who attached little importance to fighting against their government's reactionary colonial war.

In 1904 – 5 Marx and Engels would probably have sided with Japan against tsarist Russia, as did Lenin, Hyndman, Jules Guesde and many other socialists. The Russian Revolution, which the two friends had hoped for and frequently predicted, broke out in 1905 as a result of this war. Marx and Engels would have greeted it with enthusiasm, and have regarded it as vindication of their consistent hostility to tsarist Russia.

Like nearly all socialists all over the world, Marx and Engels would have denounced Italy's predatory war of 1911 – 12 against Turkey. They might have endorsed the position of the Socialist International in the Balkan Wars, as expressed in the Basle Manifesto of November 1912, which denounced the designs of the Habsburg Dual Monarchy against Serbia and the tsar's intrigues against Turkey, but did not take sides in the showdown threatening between St Petersburg and Vienna. The main concern of the International was to prevent the war from spreading and assuming European dimensions. This was in line with what Engels felt towards the end of his life, when horror at the devastation and inevitable holocaust in such a war had replaced the bellicosity of his (and Marx's) youthful years. Had they been alive in 1912, they would probably have approved the International's call for a peaceful solution of the Balkan crisis and for general European *détente*. Something like an independent Balkan federation had been advocated by Engels as early as 1853; he regarded the creation of 'a free and independent Christian state on the ruins of the Moslem empire in Europe' as a means of depriving the tsar of the role as the 'national liberator and protector' of the Christian peoples of the Balkan peninsula.

Although they invariably took Turkey's side in conflicts with Russia, Marx and Engels were clearly in favour of ending Turkish rule in Europe, and they would have been likely to share Lenin's satisfaction at Turkey's defeats in the First Balkan War. But like most leaders of the Second International they would have refused to share Lenin's hopes − soon to be fulfilled − for war between Austria-Hungary and Russia.

It is impossible to say with any degree of certainty what their attitude would have been during most of the First World War, when régimes of various political shades and stages of economic and social development were involved on both sides. The Russian February Revolution would have simplified the situation: tsarism was overthrown, and a liberal republican government disavowed the annexationist plans of the fallen autocracy. From March 1917 onwards, Marx and Engels would undoubtedly have hoped for the victory of the *Entente,* whose principal members were all democracies − with Russia, in Lenin's words, the freest of them all. The Central Powers, on the other hand were all monarchies, not fully or not at all democratic, and more reactionary than Britain, France, the United States and the Russian Republic under Prince Lvov or Kerensky. Marx and Engels would have regarded the victory of Russia and her allies as more likely to benefit socialist revolution, and they would have backed the Russian 'defencists' against Lenin and his followers.

Marx and Engels would have had no use for the misleading and logically unsound Leninist concept of revolutionary defeatism in countries fighting a 'reactionary' war. But, before March 1917, they would also have rejected Plekhanov's line of support for the *Entente* powers. Tsarist Russia, to be sure, was then a little less oppressive and autocratic than in the nineteenth century; yet Marx and Engels would not have wanted the victory of an alliance while the tsar was still there and still determined on territorial expansion. They might have criticized the German Social Democrats' support for the kaiser's war (especially after the violation of Belgium's neutrality) and the vote for the war credits; but since the tsar was one of the enemies they would not have been as savage in their castigation as Rosa Luxemburg. On the other hand, they would have been outraged by the SPD's insistence that Alsace-Lorraine should remain part of Germany, and would certainly have reminded Scheidemann and his friends that during and after the Franco-German war of 1870−1 the German socialists, including August Bebel and Wilhelm Liebknecht, had opposed the annexation of Alsace-Lorraine or any other French territory. Engels was sure that the German Social Democrats, in or out of office, would respect the principle of self-determination for Alsace-Lorraine.

Marx and Engels would have welcomed the Russian October Revolution and agreed with Rosa Luxemburg that it was the most momentous event of the war. Like Luxemburg they would have regarded the Bolshevik régime as the dictatorship of the proletariat, but might have changed their minds in after-years. They would probably have endorsed Rosa Luxemburg's attacks on the suppression of civil liberties in Bolshevik Russia, and might well have subscribed to her dictum: 'Freedom only for the supporters of the government...is no freedom at all. Freedom is always and exclusively freedom for those who dissent.'

Their approach to the question of a separate peace with Germany would have been pragmatic. They would have felt, like Lenin, that no socialist principle was involved and that the signing of the treaty of Brest-Litovsk was unavoidable in view of the disastrous military situation. There is no doubt that they would have denounced passionately all anti-Bolshevik interventions by foreign powers.

The views Marx and Engels might have held about events after 1918, and especially about the Second World War, will be the subject of the Epilogue at the end of the second volume of this study.

Notes

PART 1 − Marx and Engels and the Wars of the Nineteenth Century

Chapter 1: The 'Revolutionary Wars' of 1848−9

1   *Neue Rheinische Zeitung,* 10 September 1848; K. Marx and F. Engels, *Werke* (henceforward *MEW),* V, 396
2. *Neue Rheinische Zeitung* (henceforward NRZ), June 1848; K. Marx and F. Engels, *Collected Works* (henceforward *CW),* VII, 34. Most articles on Schleswig-Holstein and the war against Denmark were written by Engels.
3. 'Letter from Germany', first published in English in G.J. Harney's *Democratic Review,* July 1850; *CW,* X, 393 − 4
4. See below, 63 − 4
5. 'Germany's Foreign Policy' in *NRZ,* 3 July 1848; *MEW,* V, 155
6. *CW,* XI, 49
7. 'The Italian Liberation Struggle and the Cause of its Present Failure' in *NRZ,* 12 August 1848; *CW,* VII, 385*ff; MEW,* V, 366*ff*
8. A reference to the successful resistance of the French First Republic to foreign armed intervention
9. *NRZ,* 31 March 1849; *CW,* VII, 170*ff; MEW,* VI, 386*ff*
10. Trotsky voiced his criticisms not as a journalist observer but as a prominent member of the central committee of the Soviet Communist Party. In 1927, during the showdown in the USSR between Stalin's ruling faction and the inner-party opposition (Trotsky, Zinoviev, Kamenev and so on), which led to Trotsky's expulsion, Trotsky reiterated his loyalty to the Soviet state and its defence. To illustrate that this did not conflict with his criticisms of the Stalinist leadership, he evoked the precedent of Clemenceau's policy in 1914, when the German army was about

fifty miles from Paris: Clemenceau waged a determined struggle against the incompetence of the Viviani government and its conduct of the war; he gained power and secured victory. Trotsky said the opposition within the CSPU would likewise seek to wrest power if war should come, so as to wage it with revolutionary firmness. Stalin and his followers exploited Trotsky's statement by persuading the party rank-and-file (largely ignorant of France in the First World War) that Trotsky would take advantage of military reverses to seize power by force (which Clemenceau had not done) – in other words, that Trotsky was prepared to pursue a policy of (counter-revolutionary) defeatism in case of war. The detailed account of this controversy is in I. Deutscher, *The Prophet Unarmed,* 349 – 56

11. *NRZ,* 19 May 1849
12. *ibid., CW,* IX, 463
13. 'The Revolutionary Movement' in *NRZ,* 1 January 1849; *MEW,* VII, 148 – 50
14. *NRZ,* 19 May 1849; *MEW,* VI, 506
15. *NRZ,* 18 and 25 June 1848; *MEW,* V, 80 – 2 and 108 – 9
16. 'The Magyar Struggle' in *NRZ,* 13 January 1849; *MEW,* VI, 173
17. 'The Revolutionary Movement', *op. cit.*
18. 'The Magyar Struggle', *op. cit.*
19. 'Democratic Pan-Slavism' in *NRZ,* 15 February 1849; *MEW,* VI, 275
20. 'The Magyar Struggle', *CW,* VIII, 238; *MEW,* VI, 176
21. K. Kautsky, *Sozialisten und Krieg,* 107 – 8
22. Kautsky letter to Engels, 11 May 1882, in F. Engels, *Briefwechsel mit Karl Kautsky,* 56
23. Preface, *CW,* VIII, xxv
24. Cf. above, 4 – 5

Chapter 2: The 'Eastern Question' and the Crimean War

1. *CW,* XII, 13 – 17
2. *ibid.,* 17
3. *New York Daily Tribune* (henceforward *NYDT); CW,* XII, 32 – 6
4. *NYDT,* 5 August 1853; *ibid.,* 212
5. *NYDT, ibid.,* 163
6. Marx thought the earl of Aberdeen, prime minister at the time, vacillating and soft

7. *NYDT,* 25 July 1853; *CW,* XII, 196
8. *NYDT,* 5 August 1853; *ibid.,* 212 – 13
9. *NYDT,* 18 November 1853; *ibid.,* 476
10. *CW,* XXXIX, 423 – 6
11. *NYDT,* 2 February 1854; *CW,* XII, 555, 557 – 8
12. *ibid.,* 553 – 4
13. *ibid.,* 33
14. *NYDT,* 10 July 1854; *CW,* XIII, 256
15. Published in *Neue Oder-Zeitung,* 2 January 1855; *ibid.,* 555
16. *NYDT,* 27 April 1855; *CW,* XIV, 142 – 5
17. *ibid.,* 144
18. *NYDT,* 31 October 1854; *CW,* XIII, 504
19. *CW,* XIV, 614 and 623*ff.*

Chapter 3: Britain's Wars against Persia and China 1856 – 60

1. Cf. V.G. Kiernan, *Marxism and Imperialism,* 176
2. *NYDT,* 30 July 1853; *CW,* XII, 201
3. *NYDT,* 7 January 1857; quoted in K. Marx and F. Engels, *On Colonialism,* 83 – 5
4. *NYDT,* 10 April 1857; *ibid.,* 86 and 105
5. *ibid.,* 91
6. *ibid.,* 105 – 6
7. *NYDT,* 5 June 1857; *ibid,* 111 – 16
8. *On Colonialism,* 205
9. *ibid.,* 204
10. *ibid.,* 220
11. *ibid.,* 204

Chapter 4: The Indian Mutiny

1. *On Colonialism,* 118
2. K. Marx & F. Engels, *The First Indian War of Independence, 1857 – 59,* 174 – 5
3. *ibid.,* 97
4. *ibid.,* 85
5. *ibid.,* 126
6. *MEW,* XXIX, 259

7. K. Marx, *Capital* (8th edition), I, 350 – 2
8. *The First Indian War,* 19 – 20
9. Unwillingness to regard India as ripe for independence was also implicit in what Engels wrote in a letter to Kautsky in September 1882, which dealt with colonial policy *after* the proletarian revolution. Engels thought that the colonies with a European population (Canada, the Cape, Australia) would become independent: 'on the other hand, the countries inhabited by a native population, which are simply subjugated – India, Algeria, the Dutch, Portuguese and Spanish possessions – must be taken over for the time being by the proletariat and led as rapidly as possible towards independence.' *(On Colonialism)*. Engels apparently saw colonial emancipation as a gradual and laborious process. As for Ireland – 'England's first colony' in Engels's phrase – the solution Marx and Engels envisaged was not complete and separate independence, but repeal of the Union and its replacement by 'a free and equal federation with Great Britain' (cf. Marx's letter to S. Meyer and A. Vogt 9 April 1870; *ibid.,* 299). While sympathizing with the Irish struggle and defending the Fenians, Marx and Engels roundly condemned terrorist outrages like the Phoenix Park murder, which Engels denounced as a 'boastful and senseless' act and as 'crass stupidity'. (Letter to E. Bernstein 26 June 1882; *MEW,* XXXV, 339)

Chapter 5: The Italian War of 1859 and its Aftermath

1. *MEW,* XIII, 282; the article was in fact written in London
2. *ibid.,* 161 – 7
3. The New York paper carried this as its leading article on 24 January 1859, thereby accepting Marx's views as its own
4. *MEW,* XIII, 365 – 71
5. *ibid.,* 391 – 3
6. See above, 12 – 13
7. *MEW,* XIII, 404
8. *ibid.*
9. *NYDT,* 12 February 1861; *MEW,* XV, 241
10. *ibid.,* 250
11. *ibid.,*251
12. *ibid.,* 252 – 3; *CW,* XVI, 240
13. *MEW,* XIII, 573

14. *ibid.,* 611
15. *ibid.,* 612
16. F. Lassalle, *Gesammelte Reden und Schriften,* I, 29
17. *ibid.,* 102
18. *ibid.,* 107
19. *MEW,* XXIX, 432
20. *ibid.,* 'Boustrapa' was Marx's and Engels's nickname for Napoleon III
21. Cf. 42 above

Chapter 6: Conflicts in the Western Hemisphere in the 1860s

1. K. Marx and F. Engels, *Surveys from Exile*
2. *MEW,* XV, 329 – 38
3. *ibid.,* 338
4. *Die Presse,* 25 November 1861; *ibid.,* 339 – 47
5. *ibid.,* 346
6. K. Marx and F. Engels, *The Civil War in the United States,* 351 – 2
7. *Die Presse,* 25 November 1861; *MEW,* XV, 346
8. *The Civil War,* 34 – 41
9. *ibid.,* 41
10. *ibid.,* 47 – 8
11. *MEW,* XXX, 254 – 6
12. *ibid.,* 270 – 1
13. *MEW,* XV, 525 – 6
14. *ibid.,* 552-3
15. This was written over a year before Lincoln's Gettysburg address
16. *MEW,* XXX, 294
17. Abraham Lincoln was the son of a poor pioneer farmer and an illiterate mother
18. K. Marx and F. Engels, *Letters to Americans,* 65 – 6
19. *ibid.,* 71 – 2
20. *The Civil War,* 276 – 7
21. *MEW,* XV, 361 – 5
22. *ibid.,* 366 – 73
23. The Marx-Engels-Lenin Institute in Moscow has a different explanation in its editorial notes (cf. *MEW,* XV, 665). The aim of the intervention, Note 170 says, was to topple the Juarez government, turn Mexico into a colony of the European powers and use its

territory for pro-Southern assistance in the United States. This is not Marx's interpretation. While he apparently thought it possible that Napoleon III wanted to make Mexico a French colony, he did not suggest that intervention on the side of the Confederacy was one of the objectives of the European expedition. The view of the Marx-Engels-Lenin Institute is not consistent with the facts: in 1863 – 4, when the American Civil War was still undecided, French forces controlled nearly all of Mexico but did not cross into US territory or give any military aid to the Confederacy

24. *MEW*, XV, 366
25. *MEW*, XXXI, 155
26. *ibid.*, 157
27. *ibid.*, 159

Chapter 7: Rising in Poland 1863

1. *MEW*, XXX, 324
2. *ibid.*, 327
3. *ibid.*
4. *ibid.*,333
5. 'Deutscher Bildungsverein für Arbeiter'; *MEW*, XV, 576 – 7
6. *MEW*, XXX, 377
7. Another erroneous Engels prophecy: the following summer joint Austrian-Prussian action wrested the duchies from Denmark. Russia was in no way involved.
8. *MEW*, XVI, 153 – 63
9. Lassalle, *op, cit.*, IV, 305 – 6
10. *ibid.*, 306
11. See above, 44; as early as 1859 Lassalle had urged Prussia to fight Denmark for the duchies.

Chapter 8: The Wars of German Unification 1864 – 71

1. Letter to his uncle in Holland, March 1864; *MEW*, XXX, 650
2. *MEW*, V, 395
3. *MEW*, XXX, 377; he also concluded that the duke of Augustenburg had just title to Holstein, but that his claim to Schleswig was doubtful
4. Letter 4 December 1863; *ibid.*, 379
5. Letter 2 November 1864; *MEW*, XXXI, 7
6. *MEW*, XXX, 384

7. Resolution drafted for General Association of German workers; Lassalle, *op. cit.,* IV., 307

8. A reference to the suggestion that the duchies should cease to be part of Denmark but that the Danish king should be duke of Schleswig-Holstein through a personal union, along the lines of the British-Hanoverian links between 1714 and 1837

9. Letter 6 December 1863; Lassalle, *op, cit.,* IV, 309

10. *ibid.,* 312

11. *MEW,* XXXI, 200

12. *ibid.,* 204

13. *MEW,* XVI, 169 – 89

14. *MEW,* XXXI, 200 – 1

15. *ibid.,* 226 – 7

16. *ibid.,* 233

17. *ibid.,* 240 – 1

18. *ibid.,* 241

19. Letter to Engels 20 July 1870; *MEW,* XXXIII, 5

20. K. Marx and F. Engels, *Writings on the Commune,* 216

21. Letter to Marx 31 July 1870; *MEW,* XXXIII, 16

22. Letter to xxxxxxxxx 15 August 1870; *ibid.,* 39 – 42

23. *ibid.,* 40

24. *ibid.,* 41 – 2

25. *Writings on the Commune, op. cit.,* 38

26. Quoted in Marx and Engels, *Selected Correspondence,* 300-1

27. *MEW,* XXXIII, 127

28. Letter to Marx 31 July 1870; *ibid.,* 16

29. They were eventually annexed, but not to any single German state; they became *Reichslände,* imperial territory directly under the emperor's sovereignty. As the German emperor was also king of Prussia, Alsace and Lorraine were really under Prussian administration

30. *MEW,* XXXIII, 43

31. *Writings on the Commune,* 46

32. Letter to Marx 4 September 1870; *MEW,* XXXIII, 51

33. Letter to Marx 7 September 1870, *ibid.,* 57

34. 17 December 1870; *MEW,* XVII, 111 – 12

35. Letter to de Paepe, a leading member of the Belgian section of the International, 14 September 1870; *MEW,* XXXIII, 147

36. Letter to Marx 12 September 1870; *ibid.,* 61 – 2

37. *Pall Mall Gazette,* 17 September 1870; *MEW,* XVII, 105 – 8

38. They were released on 30 March 1871, but the charges were not withdrawn. The German supreme court subsequently quashed their sentences. Bebel and Liebknecht were also arrested and tried; they both served two years
39. Letter to de Paepe 14 September 1870
40. King William had declared that he was fighting to repel the French emperor's aggression, but was not making war on the French people
41. *Pall Mall Gazette,* (henceforward *PMG), 29 October 1870; *MEW,* XVII, 154 – 6
42. *PMG,* 21 November 1870; *ibid.,* 178 – 9
43. *PMG,* 26 November 1870; *ibid.,* 184 – 8
44. *PMG,* 8 December 1870; *ibid.,* 201 – 2
45. *PMG,* 17 December 1870; *ibid.,* 212
46. *MEW,* XXXIII, 162 – 4
47. *ibid.,* 176 – 8
48. *ibid.,* 180 – 3
49. Eventually reduced to half that sum
50. *PMG,* 8 February 1871; *MEW,* XXXIII, 257
51. *Writings on the Commune,* 34
52. *ibid.,* 51 – 97
53. *ibid.,* 52
54. *ibid.,* 51 – 2
55. A similar accusation was made by the Russian Bolsheviks in 1917, that Kerensky and his 'provisional government' planned to abandon Petrograd and leave it to the Germans to stamp out the spark of revolution in the Russian capital. Cf. L. Trotsky, *History of the Russian Revolution,* 914 – 16
56. *Writings on the Commune,* 95

Chapter 9: The 'Russian Menace' in the 1870s and 1880s

1. *PMG,* 21 November 1870
2. *MEW,* XVII, 286
3. G. Mayer, *Engels,* II, 204 – 7
4. *MEW,* XXXIV, 48
5. *ibid.,* 74
6. *ibid.,* 296
7. Cf. B.D. Wolfe, *Marxism, One Hundred Years in the Life of a Doctrine,* 57 – 8

9. Salisbury had represented Britain at the abortive Constantinople conference prior to the Russo-Turkish war. He became foreign secretary in March 1878
10. *MEW,* XXXIV, 320 – 4
11. *ibid.,* 324
12. *ibid.,* 597 – 8, *n* 429; as the manuscripts of Marx's letters are not extant, Liebknecht's pamphlet is the only source
13. Letter to Marx 9 September 1879; *ibid.,* 105
14. Letter to N.F. Danielson 12 September 1880; *ibid.,* 464; Wolfe, *op. cit.,* 64 and *n* 25. Danielson, Russian economist and 'Narodnik', was the translator of Marx's *Das Kapital;* he was later attacked by Lenin as a 'utopian'
15. This organ of the (illegal) German Party was edited and printed in Zurich while Bismarck's Anti-Socialist Law was in force (1878 – 90)
16. Letter to Eduard Bernstein 22 February 1882; *MEW,* XXXV, 278 – 84
17. *ibid.,* 283 – 4
18. Letter to August Bebel 22 December 1882; *ibid.,* 416

Chapter 10: Colonial Conflicts and Problems 1882

1. Letters to Marx and Karl Kautsky 12 September 1882; *MEW,* XXXV, 92 and 356
2. Letter to Eduard Bernstein 9 August 1882; *ibid.,* 349
3. *ibid.,* 422
4. *ibid.,* 357 – 8; *Selected Correspondence,* 399
5. Here follows the strange passage about the 'savage tribes' which might have to 'disappear from the face of the earth', mentioned above, 16
6. Letter 11 May 1882; *Briefwechsel,* 56
7. Kautsky, *op. cit.,* 660 – 2
8. *ibid.,* 662

Part II – Socialism after Marx – The Approach of Armageddon

Chapter 1: The Danger of European War in the 1880s and 1890s

1 A group led by William Morris and Belfort Bax, which had seceded from H.M. Hyndman's Democratic Federation

2. Letter to Laura Lafargue, daughter of Karl Marx, 16 April 1885; *MEW,* XXXVI, 298 – 9

3. *Le Cri du peuple,* 31 March 1885

4. This war was the setting for Bernard Shaw's *Arms and the Man*

5. Letter to August Bebel 17 November 1885, *MEW,* XXXVI, 390 – 1

6. *ibid.,* 526

7. *ibid.,* 316 – 17

8. 'Introduction' in December 1887 to a pamphlet by his late friend, Sigismund Borkheim, on events in Prussia 1806 – 7; *MEW,* XXI, 350 – 1

9. Two years earlier, in his letter to Bebel, he had spoken of six million; in 1889 – 90, the figure was ten to fifteen million, and in 1891 – 2 'fifteen to twenty million'. Ninety million armed men confronted one another during the First World War

10 *MEW,* XXII, 44 – 8; cf. Mayer, *op.cit.,* II, 504 – 6

11. Mayer, *op.cit.,* II, 285

12. *ibid.,* 507

13. Letter to Bebel 29 September 1891; *MEW,* XXXVIII, 159 – 63

14. Austria's Polish province – her share of the partition booty

15. 13 October 1891; *MEW,* XXXVIII, 174 – 6

16. Letter dated 24 – 6 October 1891; *ibid,* 187 – 9

17. When an analogous situation arose during the Second World War, certain 'orthodox Marxist' groups clung to 'revolutionary defeatism' in the democratic countries at war with Hitler's Germany. Even after the Nazis had done to the socialist and labour movement in German-occupied Europe exactly what Engels said a victorious Russia would do to German socialism, these groups still claimed that an abandonment of 'defeatism' would betray 'Marxist-Leninist' principles.

18. *MEW,* XXII, 252 – 6, in Engels's translation for *Neue Zeit*

19. After Germany's defeat in two world wars, France and Denmark annexed far less, Russia and her Polish satellite far more German territory than Engels anticipated

20. Quoted in Wolfe, *op. cit.,* 73. Bebel made a number of similar statements in the following years. The last occasion was in 1907, when he was 67; like Engels, he declared himself ready to 'shoulder a rifle' to defeat Russian aggression

21. October 1892; *MEW,* XXXVIII, 498

22. 24 October 1892; *ibid.,* 503

23. cf. Mayer, *op. cit.,* II, 514
24. Kautsky, *op. cit.,* 308
25. *ibid.,* 305
26. *MEW,* XXXIX, 90 – 1; as an illustration of Engels's point, the Weimar Republic retained the style of *'Deutsches Reich',* an empire without an emperor

Chapter 2: The Sino-Japanese War 1894 – 5 and its Aftermath

1. Letter to Karl Kautsky 24 September 1894; *MEW,* XXXIX, 301
2. *ibid.,* 298 – 9
3. V.I. Lenin, *Collected Works* (henceforward *CW),* VIII, 48
4. *ibid.,* 88
5. Published in Germany; Lenin was also the author of the paper's editorial, cf. A.B. Ulam, *The Bolsheviks,* 159
6. *CW,* IV, 372 – 7

Chapter 3: Colonial Wars of the United States 1898 – 1901: Cuba and the Philippines

1. Kautsky, *op. cit.,* 312 – 16; cf. also V.I.Lenin, *Imperialism, the Highest Stage of Capitalism* (Moscow 1920)
2. See below, 119-25
3. Kautsky, *op. cit.,* 316 *ff*
4. For the following, cf. D.B. Schirmer, *Republic or Empire: American Resistance to the Philippine War*
5. *See below, 121*

Chapter 4: The South African (Boer) War 1899 – 1902

1. G.B. Shaw, *Fabianism and the Empire,* 3
2. cf. below, 122
3. E.R. Pease, *History of the Fabian Society,* 129 – 32
4. Shaw, *op. cit.,* 23 – 4
5. M. Cole, *The Story of Fabian Socialism,* 102
6. Review of *History of the Fabian Society,* in *The Socialist Review* 1916, 249
7. *ibid.*
8. B. Webb, *Our Partnership* (written in the 1920s and 1930s, but not published until 1948, five years after the author's death), 193 – 4
9. Shaw, *op. cit.,* 22
10. *ibid.,* 35

11. Webb, *op.cit.*, 192
12. F.J. Gould, *Hyndman, Prophet of Socialism,* 129
13. *Justice,* 27 July 1901
14. *ibid.,* 3 August 1901
15. Bax died in 1926; had he lived to see his 'United Africander Republic', he might not have cared for what he saw
16. Pease, *op. cit.,* 129

Chapter 5: The Russo-Japanese War 1904 – 5 and the Russian Revolution of 1905

1. Cf. above, 113
2. Father of the British politician of the same name
3. J. Martov and F. Dan, *Geschichte der Russischen Sozialdemokratie,* 94
4. *CW,* VIII, 52 – 3
5. In *Proletary,* 9 June 1905; *ibid.,* 482 – 5
6. Martov and Dan, *op. cit.,* 92; cf. also I. Deutscher, *The Prophet Armed,* 86 – 7
7. See above, 111
8. Kautsky, *op. cit.,* 319 – 20
9. Ulam, *op. cit.,* 227
10. *ibid.,* 255 *ff.* The first *Duma* in which the bourgeois-liberal 'Constitutional Democrats' (the 'Cadets') were the strongest party was dissolved after just two months, but the second *Duma* was even more radical in composition. The third *Duma,* elected under a restrictive new law at the end of 1907, had a strong reactionary right wing. Count Witte had been dismissed in 1906 and replaced by the conservative Stolypin

Chapter 6: Socialists Debate the Threat of War 1906 – 13

1. As Karl Kautsky remarked in 1937 (*op. cit.,* 398 – 9), Germany thus acquired a new potential enemy quite pointlessly; the 'great German navy' saw no full-scale action in the First World War
2. A. Rosmer, *Le Mouvement ouvrier pendant la guerre* (henceforward *MOPG),* 79 – 83
3. C. Tsuzuki, *Hyndman and British Socialism,* 210
4. *ibid.*
5. Kautsky, *op. cit.,* 398
6. For the following see Tsuzuki, *op. cit.,* 205 – 14

7. In 1911 it was to merge with other groups to form the British Socialist Party (BSP)

8. *Morning Post,* 6 July 1910, quoted by Tsuzuki, *op. cit.,* 210; it was in this letter that Hyndman advocated 'an aerial fleet'

9. See below, 144 – 5

10 'The Conference of the British Social Democratic Party', in *Zvezda,* 16 April 1911; *CW,* XVII, 173 – 6. When Quelch died in September 1913, Lenin wrote a laudatory obituary, devoid of any criticism; *CW,* XIX, 369 – 71

11. In 1919 the BSP took part in the foundation of the Communist Party of Great Britain

12. Article in *Pravda,* 14 May 1913; *CW,* XIII, 93 – 5

13. Cf. below 136 – 7 and 144 – 4

14. Kautsky, *op. cit.,* 397

15. M. Beer, *Social Struggles and Modern Socialism,* 154 – 8; Kautsky *op. cit.,* 336

16. Kautsky, *op. cit.,* 340

17. *ibid.,* 338 – 9

18 *CW,* XIII, 80 – 93

19. Kautsky, *op. cit.,* 344

20. *CW,* XIII, 91

21. Kautsky, *op. cit.,* 343

22. In the Weimar Republic he was one of the leading lights of the Deutsche Volkspartei (German People's Party), the right-of-centre party of Stresemann, Hugo Stinnes and the Ruhr tycoons

23. Kautsky, *op. cit.,* 343

24. *ibid.,* 341

25. *ibid.,* 347

26. Ledebour, unlike Lensch, did not forsake the cause. He voted against the war credits, played an active part in the *Spartakus* rising of January 1919, and remained a left-wing socialist until his death in 1947 at the age of 97

27. Kautsky, *op. cit.,* 348; W. Stewart, J. Keir Hardie, 301

Chapter 7: Curtain-raisers to World War: The Italo-Turkish and Balkan Wars

1. For the following see Kautsky, *op.cit.,* 354

2. The twenty-four-hour strike was largely a failure in Venice, where a large part of the work-force was engaged in the manufacture of arms and ammunition

3. Kautsky, *op. cit.,* 362

4. For the following see Kautsky, *op. cit.*, 363 – 5; J. Braunthal, *Geschichte der Internationale,* I, 345

5. Kautsky, *op. cit.*, 365

6. L. Trotsky, *The Balkan Wars, 1912 – 13. The War Correspondence of Leon Trotsky,* 152

7. *Neue Zeit,* 30 September 1911

8. Kautsky, *op. cit.*, 354

9. *Pravda,* September 1912; *CW,* XVIII, 337 – 8

10. *Pravda,* 16 October 1912 (all *Pravda* dates in this chapter are old style); *ibid.*, 349

1 1 . 'A democratic federation of the Balkan peoples' was recommended by the Basle manifesto. It is remarkable that no federal solution was found for the communist Balkan states after the Second World War

12. *Pravda,* 21 October 1912; *CW,* XVIII, 368 – 9

13. *Pravda,* 7 November 1912; *ibid.*, 397 – 9

14. *Pravda,* 18 October 1912

15. *CW,* XVIII, 353 – 4

16. *Pravda,* 28 October 1912; *ibid.*, 372 – 3

17. *Pravda,* 29 March 1913; *CW,* XIX, 39

18. *CW,* XXXV, 76

19. Trotsky, *The Balkan Wars, op. cit.*, 152 – 3

20. *ibid.*, 153

21. *ibid.*, 157; not in *Kievskaya Mysl* but in the Odessa paper *Odesskie Novosti*

22. *ibid.*, 262 *(Kievskaya Mysl)*

23. In *Luch; ibid.*, 316

24. *ibid.*, 366 – 7

25. *ibid.*, 281 – 3

26. L. Trotsky, *Terrorism and Communism* (pamphlet), 96

27. *ibid.*, 58 – 9

28. *ibid.*, 61

29. The Nazis had a similiar provision, called *Sippenhaftung* (collective family liability), during the Second World War

30. L. Trotsky, *Their Morals and Ours,* 26

31. Similar arguments were put forward in defence of the Hiroshima bomb in 1945

Part III — The First World War

Chapter 1: International Socialism at the Outbreak of the First
World War

1. After the war Bosnia became — and still is — part of Yugoslavia
2. Quoted in Kautsky, *op. cit.,* 371 – 2
3. *ibid.,* 441
4. Sembat and Jaurès favoured a general strike *before* the outbreak
   of war, since it would not be possible once war had started. Jaurès
   suggested that the strike should be called off in a country which
   offered to submit the dispute to arbitration. Jules Guesde argued
   that a general strike would harm advanced socialism; the country
   where the labour movement was strongest would be smashed in
   the war; cf. Kautsky, *op. cit.,* 370
5. *ibid.,* 371 – 4
6. War hysteria was worse in Austria, except in the Slav regions. A
   similar mood could be seen in Russia; where there had been mass
   riots in St Petersburg a few weeks earlier, there were huge
   patriotic demonstrations
7. Kautsky, *op. cit.,* 373 – 4
8. *ibid.,* 445
9. German chancellor from 1928 to 1930
10. Cf. for the following Kautsky, *op. cit.,* 445 – 6; Rosmer, *MOPG,*
    312 – 27
11. Huysmans, apparently the interpreter, quoted the German phrase
    used by Müller: *'Ein Ja-stimmen ist ausgeschlossen'* (a yes-vote is
    out of the question)
12. Cf. above, 131
13. This remark is reported by Müller but not by the other three
14. Rosmer, *MOPG,* 97 – 119
15. Jouhaux became, and remained, an ardent supporter of the
    French war effort
16. Rosmer, *MOPG,* 118 – 19
17. *ibid.,* 490 – 2
18. *ibid.,* 271 – 4
19. *ibid.,* 280 – 2
20. Never published, but quoted by Rosmer, *MOPG,* 276
21. An ambiguous term, as Engels explained in 1893, cf. above, 112;
    Guesde's objection was presumably to the imperial monarchy,
    not to the national-political unity of Germany

Chapter 2: Socialist Reaction to the War in 1914

1. Cf. Kautsky, *op. cit.,* 430
2. See above, 109
3. Kautsky, *op. cit.,* 494
4. *ibid.,* 443
5. See above, 139
6. Kautsky, *op. cit.,* 449 – 60
7. *ibid.,* 452; see below, 215 – 18
8. *ibid.,* 448 – 9
9. He was one of the German delegates who signed the armistice at Compiègne in November 1918, and was assassinated by right-wing extremists in 1921
10. P. Scheidemann, *Der Zusammenbruch (The Collapse),* 10; see also Scheidemann, *Memoirs of a Social Democrat,* 196 – 7
11. One left-wing member, Kuhnert, left the chamber before the vote was taken
12. Kautsky, *op. cit.,* 459
13. *ibid.*
14. Subsequently many Social Democrat deputies, including Haase and Eduard Bernstein, joined the opposition to the government and the war. This led to a split in the SPD and the formation of the Independent Social Democratic Party (USPD)
15. Cf. for the following Kautsky, *op. cit.,* 458 – 9; Scheidemann, *Memoirs,* 201 – 2
16. Scheidemann, *Memoirs,* 203; fourteen years after the event, Scheidemann still thought the 'Yes' vote on the credits had been correct; that is, that the Social Democrats would or should have supported the war even if they had known they had been misled
17. Martov-Dan, *op cit.,* 275
18. Kautsky, *op. cit.,* 493
19. *ibid.,* 500 – 1
20. Camille Huysmans, International secretary, eventually transferred the bureau to Amsterdam in neutral Holland. His attempts to organize conferences from there were foiled by the refusal of *Entente* socialists to meet German Social Democrats
21. Cf. C.A. Macartney, *The Habsburg Empire, 1790 – 1918,* 811
22. G.D.H. Cole, *A History of the Labour Party from 1914,* 20 – 1
23. *The Socialist Review,* November – December 1916, 351 – 3
24. Blanc, Brizon and Raffin-Dugens

25. G.D.H. Cole, *op. cit.,* 3 – 15
26. *ibid.,* 18
27. *The Socialist Review,* October – December 1914, 316 – 17
2 8 . Edward R. Pease, the society's secretary for twenty-five years and its historian, wrote (in January 1916) that 'in accordance with the rule that forbids it to speak, unless it has something of value to say, it has made no pronouncement and adopted no policy' : *History of the Fabian Society,* 234. As Pease mentioned, the membership was divided on the war: Clifford Allen, a member of the executive, was organizing opposition to conscription and government policy, while other leading Fabians had joined the army; the poet Rupert Brooke was one of several who did not survive. Cf. also G. Lichtheim, *A Short History of Socialism,* 234, and M. Cole, *Beatrice Webb,* 128 – 31. The Webbs, like many Fabians at the time of the Boer War, seem to have felt that war was of no concern to socialists
29. *The Socialist Review,* October – December 1914, 398 – 400
30. H.H. Tiltman, *James Ramsay MacDonald, Labour's Man of Destiny,* 96
31. *ibid.,* 112
32. *The Socialist Review,* August – September 1916, 287
33. G.D.H. Cole, *op. cit.,* 21

Chapter 3: Discord over Issues of War and Peace – the Austrian Socialists

1. Cf. for the following Braunthal, *History of the International,* II, 61 – 3; Kautsky, *op. cit.,* 481 – 7
2. When Austria's parliament met in May 1917, the split in the German SPD had occurred; the anti-war Independent Social Democratic Party *(Unabhängige Sozialdemokratische Partei Deutschlands – USPD)* had been founded the previous month
3. Quoted in Kautsky, *op. cit.,* 481
4. See below, 215 – 18
5. Austria's Social Democrats supported the movement for *Anschluss,* the return of German Austria to the motherland, until the Nazi takeover in Germany in 1933
6. Braunthal, *Hist. Int., op. cit.,* I, 62
7. *ibid.*
8. Adler was released when the monarchy fell at the end of the war. Between the wars he was general secretary of the Labour and Socialist International; he died in 1960
9. Kautsky, *op. cit.,* 483

10. T.G. Masaryk, *The Making of a State (*English title of 'World Revolution')
11. Quoted in Kautsky, *op. cit.,* 485

Chapter 4: The French Socialists and the War

1. Cf. below, 218 – 22
2. Braunthal, *Hist. Int.,* II, 56; Rosmer, *Le Mouvement ouvrier pendant la Première Guerre Mondiale* (henceforward *MOPPGM),* 188
3. Kautsky, *op. cit.,* 494
4. See below, 195 – 6
5. For the following see Rosmer, *MOPG,* 172 – 81
6. Braunthal., *Hist. Int.,* II, 54
7. *ibid,* 54; Kautsky, *op. cit.,* 500
8. See below, 216
9. The roles of the papers were reversed after the war and the party schism: *L'Humanite* became, and still is, the Communist Party daily, while *Le Populaire* was the official daily of the SFIO between the wars
10. Braunthal, *Hist. Int.,* II, 54 – 5

Chapter 5: Socialist War Aims: the Alsace-Lorraine Question

1. Cf. above, 112
2. See below, 188-9; Scheidemann's Reichstag speech, December 1915; for the following account, see also E.R. Bevan, *German Social Democracy During the War*
3. Bevan, *op. cit,* 57 – 8
4. See below, 225
5. Scheidemann, *Memoirs,* II, 10
6. *ibid.,* 11 – 18
7. Prime minister and minister of education respectively between the wars
8. Scheidemann, *Memoirs,* II, 20 – 1
9. *ibid.,* 21
10. *ibid.,* 24
11. 'Marinismus', a word Scheidemann coined
12. Quoted in Kautsky, *op. cit.,* 534
13. *ibid.,* 498 – 9
14. *ibid.,* 516 – 19

15. *Manchester Guardian,* 31 May and 2 June 1917
16. *Manchester Guardian,* 2 June 1917. The Austrian delegates were not arrested on their return through Germany

Chapter 6: The German 'Peace Resolution'; Social Democracy Splits

1. Scheidemann, *Memoirs,* II, 48 – 9; K.S. Pinson, *Modern Germany, Its History and Civilization,* 334; Bevan, *op. cit.,* 184 – 5
2. Pinson, *op. cit.*
3. Bevan, *op. cit.,* 187
4. For the following, see Bevan, *op. cit.,* 40 – 62; Pinson, *op. cit.,* 33
5. Rosmer, *MOPG,* facsimile opposite 176
6. Bevan, *op. cit.,* 45 – 7
7. *ibid.,* 60 – 1; Pinson, *op. cit.,* 331
8. Bevan, *op. cit.,* 95
9. *ibid.,* 152. Chairman at the Gotha congress was veteran socialist Wilhelm Bock, who had presided over an earlier Gotha congress, in 1875, when a united Social Democratic Party resulted from the merger of the Lassallean General German Workers' Association and the (Marxist) Social Democratic Labour party led by August Bebel and Wilhelm Liebknecht
10. The 'Junius' pamphlet is discussed on 244*ff* in connection with Lenin's critique
11. Cf. for the following Bevan, *op. cit.,* 32 – 3 and 47
12. *ibid.,* 51 – 2
13. English translation in R.H. Lutz, *The Fall of the German Empire, 1914 – 18,* II, 14 – 15
14. Kautsky, *op. cit.,* 472
15. Lutz, *op. cit.,* 18 – 23
16. Scheidemann, *Memoirs,* 372 – 4

Chapter 7: British Marxism and the War

1. Published in *Justice* on 13 August 1914; cf. Tsuzuki, *op. cit.,* 220
2. *ibid.,* 219
3. Gould, *op. cit.,* 206
4. W. Kendall, *The Revolutionary Movement in Britain, 1900 – 21,* 88
5. Cf. for the following, Kendall, *op. cit.,* 88 – 90; Tsuzuki, *op. cit.,* 224 – 6
6. H.M. Hyndman, *The Future of Democracy,* 70

7. *English Review,* XVIII, 443 – 55
8. *ibid.,* 456 – 66
9. In his reply (XIX, 219) Harrison claimed he had been misunder-stood on this point, but did not make clear what he did mean
10. *English Review,* XIX, 52 – 69
11. *ibid.,* 54
12. 'The Coming Triumph of Marxist Socialism' in *English Review,* XIX, 292
13. *ibid.,* 298
14. See above, 131 – 2
15. *English Review,* XIX, 217
16. *ibid.,* 298
17. Gould, *op. cit.,* 202 – 3
18. *Justice,* 6 May 1915; quoted in Tsuzuki, *op. cit.,* 221
19. *English Review,* XIX, 69
20. Cf. for the following, Tsuzuki, *op. cit.,* 225 – 6; Kendall, *op. cit.,* 91 – 2
21. Kendall, *op. cit.,* 94 – 100
22. In 1920 it was taken over by the Communist Party of Great Britain and renamed *The Communist*
23. Following account from Gould, *op. cit.,* 210 – 11; Kendall, *op. cit.,* 101 – 4 Tsuzuki, *op. cit.,* 233 – 5
24. *Justice,* 28 October 1915
25. Kendall, *op. cit.,* 102
26. *ibid.*
27. Cf. Lenin, *CW,* XXI 99 – 100
28. The bulk of BSP members joined the Communist Party of Great Britain (CPGB) on its foundation. Hyndman's NSP resumed the name Social Democratic Federation in 1919. It was a small sect without influence during the inter-war period. Hyndman died in 1921
29. Cf. Tsuzuki, *op. cit.,* 222 – 3; Gould, *op. cit.,* 216 – 18
30. Kendall, *op. cit.,* 170 – 82
31. He later had reservations about Soviet and Comintern interference in the communist movement outside Soviet Russia, and he never joined the British Community Party; cf. Kendall, *op. cit.,* 284 – 91
32. See below, 212*ff*
33. For example, 'Lessons of the Russian Revolution'

Chapter 8: International Conferences before Zimmerwald

1. Kautsky, *op. cit.,* 533 – 53; Braunthal, *Hist. Int.,* II, 40 – 64, *Gesch. Int.,* II, 50 – 69; Rosmer, *MOPG,* 368 – 418
2. E. Belfort Bax, *Reminiscences and Reflections of a Mid and Late Victorian,* 251
3. This actually happened in December 1914, before the Copenhagen meeting, following a suggestion by the Dutch socialist, P.J. Troelstra, during the preparatory discussions
4. Rosmer, *MOPG,* 191 – 208; Braunthal, *Gesch. Int.,* II, Kendall, op. cit., 92 – 3
5. Implied in a report in *L'Humanité,* 16 February 1915; Rosmer *MOPG,* 197
6. Bataille Syndicaliste, 19 February 1915, quoted in *MOPG,* 200 – 1, *n* 1
7. Soviet foreign minister in the 1930s
8. Scheidemann, *Memoirs,* I, 370 – 1
9. *ibid.,* 370
10. For the following, see Rosmer, *MOPG, op.cit.,* 306 – 10
11. *Sotsial-Demokrat,* 1 June 1915; *CW,* XXI, 199 – 203
12. A typical example of Lenin's habit of lumping together opponents of completely different hues, in this case pro-war and anti-war ('centrist') socialists
13. Later, in October 1915, Lenin called it 'a miserable pacifist resolution'; *CW,* XXI, 388
14. See above, 195 – 6
15. Kautsky, *op. cit.,* 539 – 40

Chapter 9: Zimmerwald, September 1915

1. Cf. Kautsky, *op. cit.,* 541 – 2
2. Rosmer, *MOPG, op. cit.,* 377 – 8
3. L.D. Trotsky, *My Life,* 257
4. For the Zimmerwald story and its problems, see Rosmer, *MOPG,* 373 – 88; Kautsky, *op. cit.,* 543 – 50; Braunthal, *Gesch. Int.,* II, 61 – 3; A Balabanoff, *Errinerungen und Erlebnisse,* 114 – 15
5. *CW,* XXI, 345 – 8
6. Rosmer, *MOPG,* 379 – 82, for the full text
7. *CW,* XXI, 383 – 8

Chapter 10: Kienthal: The Second Zimmerwald Conference, April 1916

1   Balabanoff, *op. cit.*, 126 – 7; the Independent Social Democratic Party of Germany (USPD), the Serbian Party and organizations in other countries declared their adherence after Kienthal
2. For the following, cf. Balabanoff, *op. cit.*, 126 – 33; Rosmer, *MOPPGM,* 87 – 97 and 233 – 5; Kautsky, *op. cit.*, 551 – 3; Braunthal, *Gesch. Int.*, II, 63 – 6
3. Rosmer, *MOPPGM,* 82 – 6
4. *ibid.*, 85
5. *CW,* XXII, 173 – 9
6. *ibid.*, 177
7. Rosmer, *MOPPGM* 95 – 7
8. Echoing Karl Liebknecht's message to the ILP *Labour Leader,* published on 31 December 1914: 'Each socialist party has its enemy...in its own country. There it has to fight it. The liberation of each nation must be its own work.'
9. Text in Rosmer, *MOPPGM* 233 – 6
10. Monatte, Merrheim, Fairchild
11. When the vote was taken, most delegates said that they had specific reservations, but would support the resolution; cf. Balabanoff, *op, cit.*, 131
12. Soon afterwards the three French socialist deputies who had attended the conference – Blanc, Brizon and Raffin-Dugens – cast their votes in parliament *against* the war budget
13. Rosmer, *MOPPGM,* 97 – 9
14. British Zimmerwaldians did not display much interest in the Kienthal documents. In 1916 the ILP's *Socialist Review* mentioned the conference but not the manifesto or the resolution

Chapter 11: Stockholm: The Abortive Socialist Peace Conference; the Third Zimmerwald Conference, September 1917

1. For the following, see Braunthal, *Gesch. Int., op. cit.*, II, 79 – 88
2. See M. Fainsod, *International Socialism and the World War,* 128 – 32
3. *ibid.*, 131 – 2
4. Braunthal, *Gesch. Int.*, II, 85 – 6; Fainsod, *op. cit.*, 134 – 5
5. *Manchester Guardian,* 2 June 1917
6. Braunthal, *Gesch, Int.*, II, 107
7. Fainsod, *op. cit.*, 145 – 6

8. *CW,* XXIV, 82
9. *ibid.,* 90
10. Braunthal, *Gesch. Int., op.cit.,* II, 107
11. Cf. below, 237
12. See above, 179
13. Balabanoff, *op. cit.,* 169
14. Braunthal, *Hist. Int.,* II, 93 – 4
15. *ibid.,* 94; Balabanoff, *op. cit.,* 172
16. The fact that two international socialist conferences – the third Zimmerwald and the (abortive) general peace conference – were scheduled for the same town at about the same time has caused some confusion among writers dealing with the events of 1917. Trotsky, for all his close association with Zimmerwald, managed to mix up the two events. In his *History of the Russian Revolution* (341 – 2) he mentions that Lenin was isolated in his party with his proposal to boycott Zimmerwald in 1917, and then goes on to say: 'The Stockholm conference. . . was never held – a result of those same inner diseases of Zimmerwald which had led Lenin to break with it.' Trotsky wrote these lines more than a decade after the events; by then he had apparently forgotten that the Zimmerwald conference did meet in Stockholm in September 1917, while the failure of the general conference to materialize had nothing to do with the 'inner diseases' of the Zimmerwald movement.

Chapter 12: American Socialism and the First World War

1. For the following, see L.M. Hacker and B.B. Kendrick, *The United States Since 1865,* 440 – 1; E. W. Hawley, *The Great War and the Search for a Modern Order. A History of the American People and their Insitutions,* 21 – 4; A.S. Link, *American Epoch. A History of the United States since the 1890s,* 213 – 16
2. Some states prohibited church services in German and its teaching in schools. Hysteria expurgated the vocabulary: 'Sauerkraut' became 'liberty cabbage', 'German measles' were 'liberty measles'
3. Link, *op. cit.,* 213 *n* 3
4. E.V. Debs, *Eugene V. Debs Speaks,* 260 – 2

Chapter 13: Russian Defencists and Defcatists

1. See G. Katkov, *Russia 1917. The February Revolution,* 59 – 62; Martov-Dan, *op. cit.,* 275

2. Katkov, *op. cit.,* 61
3. *Inside the Left,* London 1942, 330
4. J. Wheeler-Bennett, *Brest-Litovsk. The Forgotten Peace,* XIII
5. *Inside the Left,* 466
6. *CW,* XXI, 15 – 19
7. *ibid.,* 18
8. In 1915 Trotsky described the wish for Russia's defeat as 'absolutely unjustifiable'. Later he recanted and endorsed Lenin's formula.
9. Martov-Dan, *op. cit.,* 282
10. Cf. for the following, Rosmer, *MOPPGM,* 104
11. *CW,* XXI, 163
12. *ibid.,* 315
13. Cf. Lenin's letter to Shlyapnikov of 31 October 1914; *CW,* XXXV, 171 – 2, in which he speaks of appeals to workers of the warring countries to wage 'joint civil war against the bourgeoisie'
14. Rosmer, *MOPPGM,* 104
15. For the following, see Trotsky, *Russian Rev.,* 300 – 44; Martov-Dan, *op. cit.,* 292 – 302
16. *Pravda,* 28 March 1917 (new style, as all dates in this chapter); cf. Trotsky, *Russian Rev.,* 305
17. ibid.
18. ibid.
19. *CW,* XXXIII, 288
20. *CW,* XXV, 113 – 15
21. *CW,* XXIII, 333 – 9
22. Such meetings reflected a *rapprochement* between the two parties, whose leaders held similar views of the war. There was a tendency towards unification, and mergers between branch organizations took place in the provinces. The reversal of the Bolshevik Party's course under Lenin put paid to this tendency
23. *CW,* XXIV, 19 – 23
24. Trotsky, *Russian Rev.,* 326
25. *CW,* XXIV, 270 – 3
26. *CW,* XXV, 33 – 4
27. For example, *CW,* XXI, 18, and see above, 234
28. In his last (unfinished) article Trotsky acknowledged the ineffectiveness of the defeatist slogan in the First World War
29. *CW,* XXVI, 195 – 215

Chapter 14: Revolutionary Defeatism: International and Historical Aspects

1 For the following, see R. Luxemburg, *Politische Schriften,* II, 19 – 152; 'Junius' was her pen-name
2. *ibid.,* 53
3. *ibid.,* 107
4. *ibid.,* 119
5. *ibid.,* 130 – 1
6. *ibid.,* 113
7. See below, 248
8. See above, 103 – 4
9. 'Junius', 130
10. *Rosa Luxemburg,* abridged version, OUP 1963, 375 – 6
11. *ibid.,* 143 – 4
12. *ibid.,* 152
13. *CW,* XXII, 305 – 19
14. *ibid.,* 318 – 19
15. See above, 103 – 4; for the following cf. Wolfe, *op. cit.,* 92 – 5
16. Letter of 25 December 1916; *CW,* XXXV, 268
17. *ibid.*
18. The danger of dismemberment is a dubious criterion for the justice of a war. During the final phase of the Second World War, facing total defeat in the east and the west, Hitler's Germany claimed to be fighting to prevent dismemberment. She was, and still is, dismembered, but neither Marx nor Engels, nor indeed Lenin, would have said that Germany was fighting a just war in 1944 – 5
19. *CW.* XXII, 310
20. *CW,* XXXV, 269

Bibliography

Balabanoff, Angelica, *Erinnerungen und Erlebnisse*. Berlin, 1927.

Bax, Ernest Belfort, *Reminiscences and Reflections of a Mid and Late Victorian*. London, 1918.

Beer, Max, *Social Struggles and Modern Socialism*. London, 1925.

Bevan, E.R., *German Social Democracy During the War*. London, 1918.

Braunthal, Julius, *Geschichte der Internationale*. Hanover, 1916.

——, *History of the International*. London, 1966.

Cole, G.D.H., *A History of the Labour Party from 1914*. London, 1951.

Cole, Margaret, *Beatrice Webb*. London, 1946.

——, *The Story of Fabian Socialism*. London, 1961.

Debs, Eugene V., *Eugene V. Debs Speaks* (ed. G.Y. Tussey). New York, 1972.

Deutscher, Isaac, *The Prophet Armed*. London, 1954.

——, *The Prophet Unarmed*. London, 1959.

Engels, Friedrich, *Briefwechsel mit Karl Kautsky* (ed. Benedikt Kautsky). Vienna, 1955.

Fainsod, Merle, *International Socialism and the World War*. Cambridge (Mass.), 1935.

Gould, F.J., *Hyndman, Prophet of Socialism*. London, 1928.

Hacker, L.M. and Kendrick, B.B., *The United States since 1865*. New York, 1956.

Hawley, E.W., *The Great War and the Search for a Modern Order. A History of the American People and their Institutions*. New York, 1979.

Hyndman, Henry M., *The Future of Democracy*. London, 1915.

——, 'The Coming Triumph of Marxist Socialism' in *English Review*, February 1915.

Hyndman, H.M., and Bax, B.B., 'Socialism, Materialism and the War' in *English Review*, December 1914.

Katkov, George, *Russia 1917. The February Revolution*. London, 1969.

Kautsky, Karl, *Sozialisten und Krieg*. Prague, 1937.

Kendall, Walter, *The Revolutionary Movement in Britain, 1900 – 21*. London, 1969.

Kiernan, V.G., *Marxism and Imperialism*. London, 1974.

Lassalle, Ferdinand, *Gesammelte Reden und Schriften* (ed. E. Bernstein). Berlin, 1919.

Lenin, V.I., *Collected Works*. Moscow, 1963 – 70.

Lichtheim, George, *A Short History of Socialism*. London, 1970.

Link, Arthur S., *American Epoch. A History of the United States since the 1890s*. New York, 1956.

Lutz, R.H., *The Fall of the German Empire, 1914 – 1918*. Stanford University, 1932.

Luxemburg, Rosa ('Junius'), *Die Krise der Sozialdemokratie*. In *Politische Schriften* Vol. II (ed. O. Flechtheim). Frankfurt, 1966.

Macartney, C.A., *The Habsburg Empire, 1790 – 1918*. London, 1968

Martov, J. and Dan, F., *Geschichte der Russischen Sozialdemokratie*. Berlin, 1926.

Marx, Karl, *Capital,* London, 1902 (8th Edition), vol. I

Marx, Karl and Engels, Friedrich, *Werke*. (East) Berlin, 1964 – 83.

——,*Collected Works*. Moscow, 1974 –

——,*On Colonialism*. Moscow, 1960.

——,*The First Indian War of Independence, 1857 – 9*. Moscow, 1960.

——,*Surveys from Exile (*ed. David Fernbach). Harmondsworth, 1975.

——, *The Civil War in the United States*. New York, 1961.

——, *Letters to Americans* (ed. Alexander Trachtenberg). New York, 1965.

——, *Writings on the Commune*. New York and London, 1971

——, *Selected Correspondence* (ed. Dona Torr). London, 1943.

Masaryk, T.G., *The Making of a State*. London, 1927.

Mayer, Gustav, *Engels* (2 vols). Frankfurt, 1975.

Pease, Edward R., *History of the Fabian Society*. London, 1916.

Pinson, K.S., *Modern Germany. Its History and Civilization*. New York and London, 1969.

Rosmer, Alfred, *Le Mouvement ouvrier pendant la guerre. De l'union sacrée à Zimmerwald*. Paris, 1936.

——, *Le Mouvement ouvrier pendant la Première Guerre Mondiale*. Paris, 1959.

Scheidemann, Philipp, *Der Zusammenbruch*. Berlin, 1927.

——, *Memoirs of a Social Democrat*. London, 1929.

Schirmer, Daniel B., *Republic or Empire: American Resistance to the Philippine War*. Cambridge (Mass.), 1972.

Shaw, George Bernard, *Fabianism and the Empire*. London, 1900.

Stewart, William, *J. Keir Hardie*. London, 1921.

Tiltman, H. Hessell, *James Ramsay MacDonald, Labour's Man of Destiny*. London, 1929.

Trotsky, Leon D., *The Balkan Wars, 1912 – 13. The War Correspondence of Leon Trotsky* (ed. George Weissman and Duncan Williams). New York, 1980.

——, *Terrorism and Communism*. Petrograd, 1920.

——, *My Life. An Attempt at an Autobiography*. Harmondsworth, 1975.

——, *Their Morals and Ours*. New York, 1942.

——, History of the Russian Revolution. London, 1977.

Tsuzuki, C., *Hyndman and British Socialism*. London, 1961.

Ulam, Adam B., *The Bolsheviks*. New York, 1965.

Webb, Beatrice, *Our Partnership*. London, 1948.

Wolfe, Bertram D., *Marxism, One Hundred Years in the Life of a Doctrine*. London, 1967.

Index